M000287713

PEARSON

COMMON CORE

Literature

Common Core
Companion Workbook

GRADE 6

PEARSON

HOBOKEN, NEW JERSEY • BOSTON, MASSACHUSETTS
CHANDLER, ARIZONA • GLENVIEW, ILLINOIS

Copyright © Pearson Education, Inc., or its affiliates. All Rights Reserved. Printed in the United States of America. This publication is protected by copyright, and permission should be obtained from the publisher prior to any prohibited reproduction, storage in a retrieval system, or transmission in any form or by any means, electronic, mechanical, photocopying, recording, or likewise. The publisher hereby grants permission to reproduce these pages, in part or in whole, for classroom use only, the number not to exceed the number of students in each class. For information regarding permissions, write to Rights Management & Contracts, Pearson Education, Inc., 221 River Street, Hoboken, New Jersey 07030.

Common Core State Standards: © Copyright 2010. National Governors Association Center for Best Practices and Council of Chief State School Officers. All rights reserved.

ISBN-13: 978-0-13-327106-5
ISBN-10:   0-13-327106-4
5 6 7 8 9 10 11 12 13 V039 18 17 16 15 14

Table of Contents

The instruction and activities in this book are organized around the Common Core State Standards for English and Language Arts.

Reading Standards for Literature   1

© Pearson Education, Inc., or its affiliates. All rights reserved.

Reading Standards for Informational Text   89

© Pearson Education, Inc., or its affiliates. All rights reserved.

© Pearson Education, Inc., or its affiliates. All rights reserved.

Writing Standards   172

Writing 1: Write arguments to support claims with clear reasons and relevant evidence.

a. Introduce claim(s) and organize the reasons and evidence clearly.

b. Support claim(s) with clear reasons and relevant evidence, using credible sources and demonstrating an understanding of the topic or text.

c. Use words, phrases, and clauses to clarify the relationships among claim(s) and reasons.

d. Establish and maintain a formal style.

e. Provide a concluding statement or section that follows from the argument presented.

Writing 2: Write informative/explanatory texts to examine a topic and convey ideas, concepts, and information through the selection, organization, and analysis of relevant content.

a. Introduce a topic; organize ideas, concepts, and information, using strategies such as definition, classification, comparison/contrast, and cause/effect; include formatting (e.g., headings), graphics (e.g., charts, tables), and multimedia when useful to aiding comprehension.

b. Develop the topic with relevant facts, definitions, concrete details, quotations, or other information and examples.

c. Use appropriate transitions to clarify the relationships among ideas and concepts.

d. Use precise language and domain-specific vocabulary to inform about or explain the topic.

e. Establish and maintain a formal style.

f. Provide a concluding statement or section that follows from the information or explanation presented.

© Pearson Education, Inc., or its affiliates. All rights reserved.

Writing 3: Write narratives to develop real or imagined experiences or events using effective technique, relevant descriptive details, and well-structured event sequences.

   a. Engage and orient the reader by establishing a context and introducing a narrator and/or characters; organize an event sequence that unfolds naturally and logically.

   b. Use narrative techniques, such as dialogue, pacing, and description, to develop experiences, events, and/or characters.

   c. Use a variety of transition words, phrases, and clauses to convey sequence and signal shifts from one time frame or setting to another.

   d. Use precise words and phrases, relevant descriptive details, and sensory language to convey experiences and events.

   e. Provide a conclusion that follows from the narrated experiences or events.

Writing 4: Produce clear and coherent writing in which the development, organization, and style are appropriate to task, purpose, and audience.

Writing 5: With some guidance and support from peers and adults, develop and strengthen writing as needed by planning, revising, editing, rewriting, or trying a new approach.

© Pearson Education, Inc., or its affiliates. All rights reserved.

Writing 6: Use technology, including the Internet, to produce and publish writing as well as to interact and collaborate with others; demonstrate sufficient command of keyboarding skills to type a minimum of three pages in a single sitting.

Writing 7: Conduct short research projects to answer a question, drawing on several sources and refocusing the inquiry when appropriate.

Writing 8: Gather relevant information from multiple print and digital sources; assess the credibility of each source; and quote or paraphrase the data and conclusions of others while avoiding plagiarism and providing basic bibliographic information for sources.

Writing 9: Draw evidence from literary or informational texts to support analysis, reflection, and research.

a. Apply grade 6 Reading standards to literature (e.g., "Compare and contrast texts in different forms or genres [e.g., stories and poems; historical novels and fantasy stories] in terms of their approaches to similar themes and topics").

b. Apply grade 6 Reading standards to literary nonfiction (e.g., "Trace and evaluate the argument and specific claims in a text, distinguishing claims that are supported by reasons and evidence from claims that are not").

© Pearson Education, Inc., or its affiliates. All rights reserved.

Writing 10: Write routinely over extended time frames (time for research, reflection, and revision) and shorter time frames (a single sitting or a day or two) for a range of discipline-specific tasks, purposes, and audiences.

Speaking and Listening Standards   285

Speaking and Listening 1: Engage effectively in a range of collaborative discussions (one-on-one, in groups, and teacher-led) with diverse partners on grade 6 topics, texts, and issues, building on others' ideas and expressing their own clearly.

a. Come to discussions prepared, having read or studied required material; explicitly draw on that preparation by referring to evidence on the topic, text, or issue to probe and reflect on ideas under discussion.

b. Follow rules for collegial discussions, set specific goals and deadlines, and define individual roles as needed.

c. Pose and respond to specific questions with elaboration and detail by making comments that contribute to the topic, text, or issue under discussion.

d. Review the key ideas expressed and demonstrate understanding of multiple perspectives through reflection and paraphrasing.

Speaking and Listening 2: Interpret information presented in diverse media and formats (e.g., visually, quantitatively, orally) and explain how it contributes to a topic, text, or issue under study.

© Pearson Education, Inc., or its affiliates. All rights reserved.

Speaking and Listening 3: Delineate a speaker's argument and specific claims, distinguishing claims that are supported by reasons and evidence from claims that are not.

Speaking and Listening 4: Present claims and findings, sequencing ideas logically and using pertinent descriptions, facts, and details to accentuate main ideas or themes; use appropriate eye contact, adequate volume, and clear pronunciation.

Speaking and Listening 5: Include multimedia components (e.g., graphics, images, music, sound) and visual displays in presentations to clarify information.

Speaking and Listening 6: Adapt speech to a variety of contexts and tasks, demonstrating command of formal English when indicated or appropriate.

Language Standards   320

Language 1: Demonstrate command of the conventions of standard English grammar and usage when writing or speaking.

a. Ensure that pronouns are in the proper case (subjective, objective, possessive).

b. Use intensive pronouns (e.g., *myself*, *ourselves*).

c. Recognize and correct inappropriate shifts in pronoun number and person.

d. Recognize and correct vague pronouns (i.e., ones with unclear or ambiguous antecedents).

e. Recognize variations from standard English in their own and others' writing and speaking, and identify and use strategies to improve expression in conventional language.

© Pearson Education, Inc., or its affiliates. All rights reserved.

Language 2: Demonstrate command of the conventions of standard English capitalization, punctuation, and spelling when writing.

a. Use punctuation (commas, parentheses, dashes) to set off nonrestrictive/ parenthetical elements.

b. Spell correctly.

Language 3: Use knowledge of language and its conventions when writing, speaking, reading, or listening.

a. Vary sentence patterns for meaning, reader/listener interest, and style.

b. Maintain consistency in style and tone.

Language 4: Determine or clarify the meaning of unknown and multiple-meaning words and phrases based on grade 6 reading and content, choosing flexibly from a range of strategies.

a. Use context (e.g., the overall meaning of a sentence or paragraph; a word's position or function in a sentence) as a clue to the meaning of a word or phrase.

b. Use common, grade-appropriate Greek or Latin affixes and roots as clues to the meaning of a word (e.g., *audience, auditory, audible*).

c. Consult reference materials (e.g., dictionaries, glossaries, thesauruses), both print and digital, to find the pronunciation of a word or determine or clarify its precise meaning or its part of speech.

d. Verify the preliminary determination of the meaning of a word or phrase (e.g., by checking the inferred meaning in context or in a dictionary).

© Pearson Education, Inc., or its affiliates. All rights reserved.

Language 5: Demonstrate understanding of figurative language, word relationships, and nuances in word meanings.

a. Interpret figures of speech (e.g., personification) in context.

b. Use the relationship between particular words (e.g., cause/effect, part/whole, item/category) to better understand each of the words.

c. Distinguish among the connotations (associations) of words with similar denotations (definitions) (e.g., *stingy, scrimping, economical, unwasteful, thrifty*).

Language 6: Acquire and use accurately grade-appropriate general academic and domain-specific words and phrases; gather vocabulary knowledge when considering a word or phrase important to comprehension or expression.

Performance Tasks   355

© Pearson Education, Inc., or its affiliates. All rights reserved.

© Pearson Education, Inc., or its affiliates. All rights reserved.

About the *Common Core Companion*

The *Common Core Companion* student workbook provides instruction for and practice with the Common Core State Standards. The standards are designed to help all students become college and career ready by the end of grade 12. Here is a closer look at this workbook:

Reading Standards

Reading Standards for Literature and Informational Texts are supported with instruction, examples, and multiple copies of worksheets that you can use over the course of the year. These key standards are revisited in the Performance Tasks section of your workbook.

Writing Standards

Full writing workshops are provided for Writing standards 1, 2, 3, and 7. Writing standards 4, 5, 6, 8, 9, and 10 are supported with direct instruction and worksheets that provide targeted practice. In addition, writing standards are revisited in Speaking and Listening activities and in Performance Tasks.

Speaking and Listening Standards

Detailed instruction and practice are provided for each Speaking and Listening standard. Additional opportunities to master these standards are provided in the Performance Tasks.

Language Standards

Explicit instruction and detailed examples support each Language standard. In addition, practice worksheets and graphic organizers provide additional opportunities for students to master these standards.

Performance Tasks

Using the examples in the Common Core framework as a guide, this workbook provides opportunities for you to test your ability to master each reading standard, along with tips for success and rubrics to help you evaluate your work.

Reading Standards for Literature

Literature 1

> 1. **Cite textual evidence to support analysis of what the text says explicitly, as well as inferences drawn from the text.**

Explanation

When you analyze a text, you think about different parts of it and how they relate to each other. Your analysis leads you to ideas about what the text means. However, you must support your ideas with evidence from the text. Even when you analyze **explicit** details, or direct statements, in a text, you must support what you are saying. You may also **make inferences**, or reach conclusions, about what a text hints at but does not say directly. It is important to support an inference with evidence from the text that will convince others that your inference is correct.

Successful readers take note of and analyze important explicit details in a text. They also make inferences to comprehend more fully the meaning of a story.

Examples

- Explicit details provide basic information for readers and are directly stated. The following statements all contain explicit details: "Rain had made the track slippery"; "Sally was jealous of Tricia's running ability"; and "Sally realized she had to work at being a friend."

- Inferences are logical guesses that readers make based on details in the text, and on their own experience and knowledge. For example, in a story about two people baking a cake, the author may offer this description: "Laticia and Joe took the cake out of the oven and started laughing. Laticia pointed at the cake pan, and they both laughed harder. Laticia said, 'Wait until Mom sees this. What a way to celebrate a birthday!'"

  The textual evidence of the laughter, Laticia's pointing at the cake pan, and her reference to her mom support these inferences: The cake did not turn out well, Laticia and Joe are siblings, and it might be their mother's birthday.

Academic Vocabulary

explicit details information stated directly in a text

inference a logical guess based on details in the text and on personal experience

textual evidence words or phrases in a text that support an analysis of the text

Apply the Standard

Use the worksheets that follow to help you apply the standard as you read. Several copies of each worksheet have been provided for you to use with a number of different selections.

- Citing Textual Evidence: Supporting an Analysis of Explicit Statements

- Citing Textual Evidence: Supporting an Inference

Name _____ Date _____ Selection _____

Citing Textual Evidence: Supporting an Analysis of Explicit Statements

Analyze a literary work to identify four important things it says explicitly. Enter those statements in the left column of the chart, below. Then, in the right column, cite textual evidence to support and explain your choices.

Explicit Statement from the Text	Textual Evidence: Why the Statement Is Important
1.	
2.	
3.	
4.	

A

Name _____ Date _____ Selection _____

Citing Textual Evidence: Supporting an Analysis of Explicit Statements

Analyze a literary work to identify four important things it says explicitly. Enter those statements in the left column of the chart, below. Then, in the right column, cite textual evidence to support and explain your choices.

Explicit Statement from the Text	Textual Evidence: Why the Statement Is Important
1.	
2.	
3.	
4.	

Name _____ Date _____ Selection _____

Citing Textual Evidence: Supporting an Analysis of Explicit Statements

Analyze a literary work to identify four important things it says explicitly. Enter those statements in the left column of the chart, below. Then, in the right column, cite textual evidence to support and explain your choices.

Explicit Statement from the Text	Textual Evidence: Why the Statement Is Important
1.	
2.	
3.	
4.	

For use with Literature 1

Name _____ Date _____ Selection _____

Citing Textual Evidence: Supporting an Analysis of Explicit Statements

Analyze a literary work to identify four important things it says explicitly. Enter those statements in the left column of the chart, below. Then, in the right column, cite textual evidence to support and explain your choices.

Explicit Statement from the Text	Textual Evidence: Why the Statement Is Important
1.	
2.	
3.	
4.	

D

Name _____ Date _____ Selection _____

Citing Textual Evidence: Supporting an Analysis of Explicit Statements

Analyze a literary work to identify four important things it says explicitly. Enter those statements in the left column of the chart, below. Then, in the right column, cite textual evidence to support and explain your choices.

Explicit Statement from the Text	Textual Evidence: Why the Statement Is Important
1.	
2.	
3.	
4.	

E

Name _____ Date _____ Selection _____

Citing Textual Evidence: Supporting an Analysis of Explicit Statements

Analyze a literary work to identify four important things it says explicitly. Enter those statements in the left column of the chart, below. Then, in the right column, cite textual evidence to support and explain your choices.

Explicit Statement from the Text	Textual Evidence: Why the Statement Is Important
1.	
2.	
3.	
4.	

F

Name _____ Date _____ Selection _____

Citing Textual Evidence: Supporting an Inference

Use the left column of the following chart to make three inferences from the text. Then, in the right column, support each inference with textual evidence.

Inference from the Text	Textual Evidence Supporting the Inference
1.	
2.	
3.	

A

Name _____ Date _____ Selection _____

Citing Textual Evidence: Supporting an Inference

Use the left column of the following chart to make three inferences from the text. Then, in the right column, support each inference with textual evidence.

Inference from the Text	Textual Evidence Supporting the Inference
1.	
2.	
3.	

B

Name _____ Date _____ Selection _____

Citing Textual Evidence: Supporting an Inference

Use the left column of the following chart to make three inferences from the text. Then, in the right column, support each inference with textual evidence.

Inference from the Text	Textual Evidence Supporting the Inference
1.	
2.	
3.	

Name _____ Date _____ Selection _____

Citing Textual Evidence: Supporting an Inference

Use the left column of the following chart to make three inferences from the text. Then, in the right column, support each inference with textual evidence.

Inference from the Text	Textual Evidence Supporting the Inference
1.	
2.	
3.	

D

For use with Literature 1

Name _____ Date _____ Selection _____

Citing Textual Evidence: Supporting an Inference

Use the left column of the following chart to make three inferences from the text. Then, in the right column, support each inference with textual evidence.

Inference from the Text	Textual Evidence Supporting the Inference
1.	
2.	
3.	

For use with Literature 1

Name _____ Date _____ Selection _____

Citing Textual Evidence: Supporting an Inference

Use the left column of the following chart to make three inferences from the text. Then, in the right column, support each inference with textual evidence.

Inference from the Text	Textual Evidence Supporting the Inference
1.	
2.	
3.	

F

Literature 2

> **2. Determine a theme or central idea of a text and how it is conveyed through particular details; provide a summary of the text distinct from personal opinions or judgments.**

Explanation

A theme is an idea about life that an author explores in a literary work.

A work's theme and its subject are not the same. The subject of a work is what the work is about and can often be stated in a word or two, such as *love, sports,* or *growing up*. The **theme,** or central idea, is an idea or a comment about the subject that the story explores, such as *growing up in a big family is a rewarding experience*. An author does not necessarily state the theme of a story directly. Often, the reader has to figure it out by studying the story details that develop the theme.

A good first step when thinking about theme is to **summarize** the text by briefly restating, in your own words, the most important things it says or describes. A summary does not express your personal opinions or judgments.

Examples

- **Summary** The following summary of Francisco Jiménez's story "The Circuit" briefly identifies the main characters, key events, and important details.

  In this story, a young migrant worker named Panchito must move with his family to find work after the strawberry picking season ends. He is not looking forward to moving to Fresno, where there is more work. In Fresno, Panchito works very hard picking grapes. When the season ends, he goes to school while his father and older brother continue to work, this time picking cotton. A teacher named Mr. Lema befriends Panchito and offers to teach him to play the trumpet. When Panchito rushes home to share his happy news, he discovers that his family's belongings are packed and ready for another move.

- **Theme** One of the main themes Jiménez explores in his story is the effect of the cycle of poverty on a young man who wants to connect with others, learn, and find meaning in his life. Details in the story, such as having to move often in search of work, help develop this theme.

Academic Vocabulary

theme the central idea or insight into life that a story explores

summary a brief restatement of the important details in a work

Apply the Standard

Use the worksheets that follow to help you apply the standard as you read. Several copies of each worksheet have been provided for you to use with a number of different selections.

- Summarizing a Literary Work
- Determining the Theme or Central Idea of a Work

Name _____ Date _____ Selection _____

Summarizing a Literary Work

Use the following organizer to list the most important details in the text. Then, use that information to write a summary. Remember to keep your opinions out of the summary.

Main Characters

Key Events, Descriptions, or Details
1.
2.
3.
4.
5.

Summary ....

A

Name _____ Date _____ Selection _____

Summarizing a Literary Work

Use the following organizer to list the most important details in the text. Then, use that information to write a summary. Remember to keep your opinions out of the summary.

Main Characters

Key Events, Descriptions, or Details
1.
2.
3.
4.
5.

Summary ....

Name _____ Date _____ Selection _____

Summarizing a Literary Work

Use the following organizer to list the most important details in the text. Then, use that information to write a summary. Remember to keep your opinions out of the summary.

Main Characters

Key Events, Descriptions, or Details

1.

2.

3.

4.

5.

Summary ....

Name _____ Date _____ Selection _____

Summarizing a Literary Work

Use the following organizer to list the most important details in the text. Then, use that information to write a summary. Remember to keep your opinions out of the summary.

Main Characters

Key Events, Descriptions, or Details
1.
2.
3.
4.
5.

Summary ....

Name _____ Date _____ Selection _____

Summarizing a Literary Work

Use the following organizer to list the most important details in the text. Then, use that information to write a summary. Remember to keep your opinions out of the summary.

Main Characters

Key Events, Descriptions, or Details
1.
2.
3.
4.
5.

Summary ....

E

Name _____ Date _____ Selection _____

Summarizing a Literary Work

Use the following organizer to list the most important details in the text. Then, use that information to write a summary. Remember to keep your opinions out of the summary.

Main Characters

Key Events, Descriptions, or Details
1.
2.
3.
4.
5.

Summary ....

Name _____ Date _____ Selection _____

Determining the Theme or Central Idea of a Work

Use the following organizer to state the subject and theme and to list details from the text that convey the theme. Explain how each detail you list helps develop the theme.

Subject ....

Theme (the central idea about life that the author explores) ....

....

....

Details that Convey Theme

1. Detail: ....

   How it Develops theme: ....

2. Detail: ....

   How it Develops theme: ....

3. Detail: ....

   How it Develops theme: ....

For use with Literature 2

Name _____ Date _____ Selection _____

Determining the Theme or Central Idea of a Work

Use the following organizer to state the subject and theme and to list details from the text that convey the theme. Explain how each detail you list helps develop the theme.

Subject ....

Theme (the central idea about life that the author explores) ....

....

....

Details that Convey Theme

1. Detail: ....

    How it Develops theme: ....

2. Detail: ....

    How it Develops theme: ....

3. Detail: ....

    How it Develops theme: ....

Name _____ Date _____ Selection _____

Determining the Theme or Central Idea of a Work

Use the following organizer to state the subject and theme and to list details from the text that convey the theme. Explain how each detail you list helps develop the theme.

Subject ....

Theme (the central idea about life that the author explores) ....

....

....

Details that Convey Theme

1. **Detail:** ....

   How it Develops theme: ....

2. **Detail:** ....

   How it Develops theme: ....

3. **Detail:** ....

   How it Develops theme: ....

C

Name _____ Date _____ Selection _____

Determining the Theme or Central Idea of a Work

Use the following organizer to state the subject and theme and to list details from the text that convey the theme. Explain how each detail you list helps develop the theme.

Subject ....

Theme (the central idea about life that the author explores) ....

....

....

Details that Convey Theme

1. Detail: ....

    How it Develops theme: ....

2. Detail: ....

    How it Develops theme: ....

3. Detail: ....

    How it Develops theme: ....

Name _____ Date _____ Selection _____

Determining the Theme or Central Idea of a Work

Use the following organizer to state the subject and theme and to list details from the text that convey the theme. Explain how each detail you list helps develop the theme.

Subject ....

Theme (the central idea about life that the author explores) ....

....

....

Details that Convey Theme

1. Detail: ....

   How it Develops theme: ....

2. Detail: ....

   How it Develops theme: ....

3. Detail: ....

   How it Develops theme: ....

E

Name _____ Date _____ Selection _____

Determining the Theme or Central Idea of a Work

Use the following organizer to state the subject and theme and to list details from the text that convey the theme. Explain how each detail you list helps develop the theme.

Subject ....

Theme (the central idea about life that the author explores) ....

....

....

Details that Convey Theme

1. Detail: ....

   How it Develops theme: ....

2. Detail: ....

   How it Develops theme: ....

3. Detail: ....

   How it Develops theme: ....

Literature 3

> **3.** Describe how a particular story's or drama's plot unfolds in a series of episodes, as well as how the characters respond or change as the plot moves toward a resolution.

Explanation

The **plot** of a literary work is the related series of episodes or events that move the action forward. The episodes center on a **conflict,** or struggle, in which the main character is engaged. The conflict increases as the story or drama develops, until it finally reaches a **climax,** or high point. Eventually, the episodes lead to the **resolution**, the final outcome of the story or drama, and the conflict is resolved. Often, the **main character** changes or grows in response to the conflict. Other characters may also face conflicts, but the main character faces the most important conflicts.

Examples

- The **plot** consists of episodes or events that move the story forward. One story's plot begins by introducing a girl who would like to become a veterinarian. She joins 4-H to learn how to raise a large animal on her parents' farm. Next, she takes a difficult science course in school but almost fails the class. The story comes to a **climax** when the animal she is raising, a calf, becomes seriously ill. These episodes create conflicts for the girl.

- The central **conflict** involves the struggles of a girl, the **main character,** to become a veterinarian and to help the calf. For example, she realizes that she needs the science course to become an animal doctor, so she finds an older student to tutor her. When her calf gets sick, she calls in a veterinarian to treat it. She also gets a job after school to pay for the medicine that saves her calf. The girl, then, overcomes the obstacles she faces, and her struggle helps her develop as a character.

- The story comes to a **resolution** when the girl passes her science course and her calf regains its health. The conflict in the story has been resolved.

Academic Vocabulary

plot series of episodes or events that move a story or drama forward

conflict struggle to which the main character must respond

climax high point in the action of the plot

resolution outcome of the story

Apply the Standard

Use the worksheets that follow to help you apply the standard as you read. Several copies of each worksheet have been provided for you to use with a number of different selections.

- Analyzing How a Plot Develops
- Analyzing How a Character Develops

Name _____ Date _____ Selection _____

Analyzing How a Plot Develops

Use the organizer below to analyze how the plot develops in a story or drama. Describe the main conflict the character faces. Then, list two or three key events that occur during the course of the story. Next, tell how the conflict comes to a climax. Finally, explain how the story reaches a resolution.

Plot Diagram

Name of story or drama: ....

Conflict: ....

....

....

| Event 3: | Climax: |

| Event 2: |

| Event 1: | Resolution: |

PLOT

For use with Literature 3

Name _____ Date _____ Selection _____

Analyzing How a Plot Develops

Use the organizer below to analyze how the plot develops in a story or drama. Describe the main conflict the character faces. Then, list two or three key events that occur during the course of the story. Next, tell how the conflict comes to a climax. Finally, explain how the story reaches a resolution.

Plot Diagram

Name of story or drama: ....

Conflict: ....

....

....

Event 3:

Climax:

Event 2:

Event 1:

Resolution:

PLOT

For use with Literature 3

Name _____ Date _____ Selection _____

Analyzing How a Plot Develops

Use the organizer below to analyze how the plot develops in a story or drama. Describe the main conflict the character faces. Then, list two or three key events that occur during the course of the story. Next, tell how the conflict comes to a climax. Finally, explain how the story reaches a resolution.

Plot Diagram

Name of story or drama: ....

Conflict: ....

....

....

Event 3:

Climax:

Event 2:

Event 1:

Resolution:

PLOT

Name _____ Date _____ Selection _____

Analyzing How a Plot Develops

Use the organizer below to analyze how the plot develops in a story or drama. Describe the main conflict the character faces. Then, list two or three key events that occur during the course of the story. Next, tell how the conflict comes to a climax. Finally, explain how the story reaches a resolution.

Plot Diagram

Name of story or drama: ....

Conflict: ....

....

....

Event 3:

Climax:

Event 2:

Event 1:

Resolution:

PLOT

D

Analyzing How a Plot Develops

Use the organizer below to analyze how the plot develops in a story or drama. Describe the main conflict the character faces. Then, list two or three key events that occur during the course of the story. Next, tell how the conflict comes to a climax. Finally, explain how the story reaches a resolution.

Plot Diagram

Name of story or drama: ....

Conflict: ....

....

....

Event 3:

Climax:

Event 2:

Event 1:

Resolution:

PLOT

Name _____ Date _____ Selection _____

Analyzing How a Plot Develops

Use the organizer below to analyze how the plot develops in a story or drama. Describe the main conflict the character faces. Then, list two or three key events that occur during the course of the story. Next, tell how the conflict comes to a climax. Finally, explain how the story reaches a resolution.

Plot Diagram

Name of story or drama: ....

Conflict: ....

....

....

Event 3:

Climax:

Event 2:

Event 1:

Resolution:

PLOT

Name _____ Date _____ Selection _____

Analyzing How a Character Develops

Use the following organizer to analyze how a character develops in response to conflict in a story or drama.

Title: _____	Character: _____

Conflict the Character Faces

↓

How the Character Changes

↓

Meaning of the Change

For use with Literature 3

Name _____ Date _____ Selection _____

Analyzing How a Character Develops

Use the following organizer to analyze how a character develops in response to conflict in a story or drama.

Title: _____ **Character:** _____

Conflict the Character Faces

↓

How the Character Changes

↓

Meaning of the Change

B

Name _____ Date _____ Selection _____

Analyzing How a Character Develops

Use the following organizer to analyze how a character develops in response to conflict in a story or drama.

Title: _____ Character: _____

Conflict the Character Faces

↓

How the Character Changes

↓

Meaning of the Change

C

Name _____ Date _____ Selection _____

Analyzing How a Character Develops

Use the following organizer to analyze how a character develops in response to conflict in a story or drama.

Title: _____ **Character:** _____

Conflict the Character Faces

↓

How the Character Changes

↓

Meaning of the Change

D

Name _____ Date _____ Selection _____

Analyzing How a Character Develops

Use the following organizer to analyze how a character develops in response to conflict in a story or drama.

Title: _____ **Character:** _____

Conflict the Character Faces

↓

How the Character Changes

↓

Meaning of the Change

E

Name _____ Date _____ Selection _____

Analyzing How a Character Develops

Use the following organizer to analyze how a character develops in response to conflict in a story or drama.

Title: _____ **Character:** _____

Conflict the Character Faces

↓

How the Character Changes

↓

Meaning of the Change

F

Literature 4

> **4. Determine the meaning of words and phrases as they are used in a text, including figurative and connotative meanings; analyze the impact of a specific word choice on meaning and tone.**

Explanation

Good writers choose their words carefully. They choose language that expresses exactly what they want to say and conveys to the reader how they feel about their subject. The overall attitude, or feeling, that a writer expresses about a subject is called **tone**. To determine the meaning and tone of a literary text, you need to analyze the words and phrases the author uses, paying special attention to connotations and figurative language. **Figurative language** is language that is used imaginatively, rather than literally. **Connotations** are the negative or positive ideas associated with a word. Writers use figurative language to state ideas in vivid and imaginative ways.

As you read, think about how the author's use of figurative language and connotations influences your understanding of a text.

Examples

- **Figurative language** goes beyond the literal, word-for-word meaning. For example, "She was as sharp as a tack" is a simile that describes someone's intelligence. She isn't literally sharp, but the expression conveys how smart she is.

- **Connotative meaning** refers to the feelings and emotions associated with a word. For example, the words *skinny* and *slender* both describe someone who is thin, but *slender* has a more positive connotation. A writer's use of either *skinny* or *slender* will affect the reader's image of a character.

- **Tone** refers to the author's attitude toward a subject. For example, these two responses to a party convey different tones. "Sorry, I can't make it" is an impersonal response. "I can't believe I am missing your party! I'm so upset!" conveys a more dramatic, personal tone.

Academic Vocabulary

figurative language words or phrases that go beyond the literal meaning

connotative meaning feelings and emotions associated with a word or phrase

tone author's attitude toward a subject or character

Apply the Standard

Use the worksheets that follow to help you apply the standard as you read. Several copies of each worksheet have been provided for you to use with different literature selections.

- Understanding Connotations and Figurative Language

- Interpreting Meaning and Tone

Name _____ Date _____ Assignment _____

Understanding Connotations and Figurative Language

Use the organizer to help you identify the figurative or connotative meaning of words and phrases you encounter in your reading. In the first column, record each word or phrase. Then write its figurative or connotative meaning in the second column.

Word or Phrase	Figurative or Connotative Meaning

A

For use with Literature 4

Name _____ Date _____ Assignment _____

Understanding Connotations and Figurative Language

Use the organizer to help you identify the figurative or connotative meaning of words and phrases you encounter in your reading. In the first column, record each word or phrase. Then write its figurative or connotative meaning in the second column.

Word or Phrase	Figurative or Connotative Meaning

B

Name _____ Date _____ Assignment _____

Understanding Connotations and Figurative Language

Use the organizer to help you identify the figurative or connotative meaning of words and phrases you encounter in your reading. In the first column, record each word or phrase. Then write its figurative or connotative meaning in the second column.

Word or Phrase	Figurative or Connotative Meaning

Name _____ Date _____ Assignment _____

Understanding Connotations and Figurative Language

Use the organizer to help you identify the figurative or connotative meaning of words and phrases you encounter in your reading. In the first column, record each word or phrase. Then write its figurative or connotative meaning in the second column.

Word or Phrase	Figurative or Connotative Meaning

Name _____ Date _____ Assignment _____

Understanding Connotations and Figurative Language

Use the organizer to help you identify the figurative or connotative meaning of words and phrases you encounter in your reading. In the first column, record each word or phrase. Then write its figurative or connotative meaning in the second column.

Word or Phrase	Figurative or Connotative Meaning

E

Name _____ Date _____ Assignment _____

Understanding Connotations and Figurative Language

Use the organizer to help you identify the figurative or connotative meaning of words and phrases you encounter in your reading. In the first column, record each word or phrase. Then write its figurative or connotative meaning in the second column.

Word or Phrase	Figurative or Connotative Meaning

For use with Literature 4

Name _____ Date _____ Assignment _____

Interpreting Meaning and Tone

Use the organizer to help you interpret the effect of words and phrases on tone or meaning. Write 3 or 4 striking words or phrases from your reading on the left. On the right, interpret both their meaning and tone.

Word or Phrase	Effect on Tone or Meaning

A

Name _____ Date _____ Assignment _____

Interpreting Meaning and Tone

Use the organizer to help you interpret the effect of words and phrases on tone or meaning. Write 3 or 4 striking words or phrases from your reading on the left. On the right, interpret both their meaning and tone.

Word or Phrase	Effect on Tone or Meaning

For use with Literature 4

Name _____ Date _____ Assignment _____

Interpreting Meaning and Tone

Use the organizer to help you interpret the effect of words and phrases on tone or meaning. Write 3 or 4 striking words or phrases from your reading on the left. On the right, interpret both their meaning and tone.

Word or Phrase	Effect on Tone or Meaning

C

Name _____ Date _____ Assignment _____

Interpreting Meaning and Tone

Use the organizer to help you interpret the effect of words and phrases on tone or meaning. Write 3 or 4 striking words or phrases from your reading on the left. On the right, interpret both their meaning and tone.

Word or Phrase	Effect on Tone or Meaning

D

Name _____ Date _____ Assignment _____

Interpreting Meaning and Tone

Use the organizer to help you interpret the effect of words and phrases on tone or meaning. Write 3 or 4 striking words or phrases from your reading on the left. On the right, interpret both their meaning and tone.

Word or Phrase	Effect on Tone or Meaning

E

Name _____ Date _____ Assignment _____

Interpreting Meaning and Tone

Use the organizer to help you interpret the effect of words and phrases on tone or meaning. Write 3 or 4 striking words or phrases from your reading on the left. On the right, interpret both their meaning and tone.

Word or Phrase	Effect on Tone or Meaning

F

For use with Literature 4

COMMON CORE COMPANION • COMMON CORE COMPANION • COMMON CORE COMPANION

Literature 5

> **5. Analyze how a particular sentence, chapter, scene, or stanza fits into the overall structure of a text and contributes to the development of the theme, setting, or plot.**

Explanation

Elements such as sentences, chapters, scenes, and stanzas make up the structure of a literary text and develop the theme, setting, and plot. **Theme** is an idea about life that an author explores in a literary work, such as a comment about society or human nature. This idea is not usually stated directly; the reader infers the theme by studying the characters and events in the text that develop the theme.

Authors build the **setting,** the time and place of a literary work, by inserting sentences and scenes with details. The setting may be real or imaginary; it can be in the past, the present, or the future.

Each event in a literary work should develop the **plot.** The major parts of a plot are the *exposition* (introduction of characters, setting, and conflict), *rising action* (events that increase tension), *climax* (high point of the story), *falling action* (events after the climax), and *resolution* (final outcome).

Examples

- Each stanza of a poem about New York might cover a different quality of the city. The first stanza might describe the hurried pace, the second might describe the imposing architecture, and the third might focus on high fashion. Each stanza contributes to the theme of New York as an exciting city.

- A story that opens with a young woman walking past the Eiffel Tower is obviously set in Paris. If she is wearing a wool coat and gloves, the story probably takes place in winter. If she is talking on a cell phone, the story is set in the present.

Academic Vocabulary

theme theme is an idea about life that an author explores in a literary work

setting time and place of the action in a story

plot the related series of events that move the action forward

Apply the Standard

Use the worksheet that follows to help you apply the standard as you read. Several copies of the worksheet have been provided for you to use with different literature selections.

- Analyzing Text Structure

Name _____ Date _____ Selection _____

Analyzing Text Structure

Use the organizer to list elements of the story and how they contribute to the development of theme, setting, or plot.

Sentence Chapter Scene Stanza	What It Contributes to: Theme Setting Plot

Name _____ Date _____ Selection _____

Analyzing Text Structure

Use the organizer to list elements of the story and how they contribute to the development of theme, setting, or plot.

Sentence Chapter Scene Stanza	What It Contributes to: Theme Setting Plot

For use with Literature 5

Name _____ Date _____ Selection _____

Analyzing Text Structure

Use the organizer to list elements of the story and how they contribute to the development of theme, setting, or plot.

Sentence Chapter Scene Stanza	What It Contributes to: Theme Setting Plot

C

For use with Literature 5

Name _____ Date _____ Selection _____

Analyzing Text Structure

Use the organizer to list elements of the story and how they contribute to the development of theme, setting, or plot.

Sentence Chapter Scene Stanza	What It Contributes to: Theme Setting Plot

For use with Literature 5

Name _____ Date _____ Selection _____

Analyzing Text Structure

Use the organizer to list elements of the story and how they contribute to the development of theme, setting, or plot.

Sentence Chapter Scene Stanza	What It Contributes to: Theme Setting Plot

E

Name _____ Date _____ Selection _____

Analyzing Text Structure

Use the organizer to list elements of the story and how they contribute to the development of theme, setting, or plot.

Sentence Chapter Scene Stanza	What It Contributes to: Theme Setting Plot

Literature 6

> **6. Explain how an author develops the point of view of the narrator or speaker in a text.**

Explanation

To help readers connect to their story, good writers recognize the importance of developing a strong narrator. The **narrator** is the voice that tells a story. The **point of view** is the perspective from which the story is told. **First-person** point of view occurs when the story is told from the point of view of the narrator. The narrator takes part in the action and refers to himself or herself as "I." Readers know only what the narrator sees, thinks, and feels. Some authors tell their stories in **omniscient third-person** point of view, in which the narrator tells what each person thinks and feels. In **limited third-person** point of view, the narrator relates the thoughts and feelings of one character, and everything is viewed from this character's perspective.

The **speaker** is the imaginary voice a poet uses when writing a poem. The speaker is the character who tells the poem. This character, or voice, often is not identified. There can be important differences between the poet and the poem's speaker.

Examples

- A story that starts out with the statement "I turned twelve on the last day of January" is told from the first-person point of view. The pronoun *I* helps you identify the point of view. The narrator in this story takes part in the action and tells what he or she sees, thinks, and feels.

- When a story is told from the third-person point of view, the narrator will use the pronouns *he, she, it, they,* and *them* to talk about characters in the story. The narrator does not refer to himself or herself, but acts as an observer of the characters. This type of narrator might make statements such as "The radio show host had a smooth style," "Erica wrote a prize-winning essay," and "A cloud of bees descended upon the beekeeper, but he kept his cool."

- The speaker in the following poem is not the poet, but a fictional character who is flying:

    From above, I view my home
    So small
    Why did it mean so much?

Academic Vocabulary

point of view the perspective from which a story is told

narrator the voice that tells the story

speaker the voice of a poem

Apply the Standard

Use the worksheet that follows to help you apply the standard as you read. Several copies have been provided for you to use with different literature selections.

- Determining Point of View

Name _____ Date _____ Assignment _____

Determining Point of View

Use the following organizer to analyze the point of view of a story or poem you have read. First, identify the point of view. Then, list several examples to show how the author develops the point of view. Finally, answer the question.

Name of Literature Selection: ....

Point of View: ❏ first-person ❏ third-person
Statements that develop the point of view: **Example 1:**   **Example 2:**   **Example 3:**

If you are analyzing a poem, is the speaker the poet or a fictional character? How do you know?

....

If you are analyzing a story, how can you tell if the point of view is the first-person or third-person?

....

A

Name _____ Date _____ Assignment _____

Determining Point of View

Use the following organizer to analyze the point of view of a story or poem you have read. First, identify the point of view. Then, list several examples to show how the author develops the point of view. Finally, answer the question.

Name of Literature Selection: ....

Point of View: ❏ first-person ❏ third-person
Statements that develop the point of view: **Example 1:**   **Example 2:**   **Example 3:**

If you are analyzing a poem, is the speaker the poet or a fictional character? How do you know?

....

If you are analyzing a story, how can you tell if the point of view is the first-person or third-person?

....

B

Name _____ Date _____ Assignment _____

Determining Point of View

Use the following organizer to analyze the point of view of a story or poem you have read. First, identify the point of view. Then, list several examples to show how the author develops the point of view. Finally, answer the question.

Name of Literature Selection: ....

Point of View: ❑ first-person ❑ third-person
Statements that develop the point of view: **Example 1:**   **Example 2:**   **Example 3:**

If you are analyzing a poem, is the speaker the poet or a fictional character? How do you know?

....

If you are analyzing a story, how can you tell if the point of view is the first-person or third-person?

....

C

Name _____ Date _____ Assignment _____

Determining Point of View

Use the following organizer to analyze the point of view of a story or poem you have read. First, identify the point of view. Then, list several examples to show how the author develops the point of view. Finally, answer the question.

Name of Literature Selection: ....

Point of View: ❑ first-person ❑ third-person
Statements that develop the point of view: **Example 1:**   **Example 2:**   **Example 3:**

If you are analyzing a poem, is the speaker the poet or a fictional character? How do you know?

....

If you are analyzing a story, how can you tell if the point of view is the first-person or third-person?

....

Name _____ Date _____ Assignment _____

Determining Point of View

Use the following organizer to analyze the point of view of a story or poem you have read. First, identify the point of view. Then, list several examples to show how the author develops the point of view. Finally, answer the question.

Name of Literature Selection: ....

| **Point of View:** |
| ❑ first-person |
| ❑ third-person |

| **Statements that develop the point of view:** |
| |
| **Example 1:** |
| |
| |
| |
| **Example 2:** |
| |
| |
| |
| **Example 3:** |
| |
| |
| |

If you are analyzing a poem, is the speaker the poet or a fictional character? How do you know?

....

If you are analyzing a story, how can you tell if the point of view is the first-person or third-person?

....

E

Name _____ Date _____ Assignment _____

Determining Point of View

Use the following organizer to analyze the point of view of a story or poem you have read. First, identify the point of view. Then, list several examples to show how the author develops the point of view. Finally, answer the question.

Name of Literature Selection: ....

| **Point of View:** |
| ❏ first-person |
| ❏ third-person |
| **Statements that develop the point of view:** |
| **Example 1:** |
| **Example 2:** |
| **Example 3:** |

If you are analyzing a poem, is the speaker the poet or a fictional character? How do you know?

....

If you are analyzing a story, how can you tell if the point of view is the first-person or third-person?

....

F

Literature 7

> 7. Compare and contrast the experience of reading a story, drama, or poem to listening to or viewing an audio, video, or live version of the text, including contrasting what they "see" and "hear" when reading the text to what they perceive when they listen or watch.

Explanation

Reading a text is different from experiencing an audio, video, or live performance of it. An **audio** version of a text conveys the reader's voice or the voices of actors playing the characters. Some audio versions also include sound effects that suggest the action. In a **video** version, you view the characters, action, and setting through the "eye" of the camera. You hear dialogue and sound effects through the "ear" of the microphone. Some texts, especially dramas, are also performed live on a stage.

When you read a text, you create a performance of it in your mind. You use your imagination to "hear" the characters speaking and to "see" the setting and how the characters look and behave. Sometimes, the way you picture a work may differ from the interpretations of it by actors or directors. When that occurs, you can learn a great deal by comparing and contrasting the performance in your mind with the audio, video, or live performance of the text.

Examples

- Many popular novels are also available as audio books. When listening to an audio version of a text you have read, ask yourself questions like these: In what ways do the characters' voices differ from the voices you imagined when reading? How does listening to someone else reading the material add to your understanding of the text?

- You may also see a video or live performance of a text you have read. When viewing such a performance, ask yourself questions like these: Are the appearance and behavior of the characters as you imagined them? If not, what explains the differences? Does the video or performance add to your understanding of the text? Why or why not?

Academic Vocabulary

audio recorded sound

video way of presenting moving pictures

Apply the Standard

Use the worksheet that follows to help you apply the standard as you read literature selections. Several copies of the worksheet have been provided for you.

- Comparing and Contrasting Reading a Text with Experiencing a Performance of It

Name _____ Date _____ Selection _____

Comparing and Contrasting Reading a Text with Experiencing a Performance of It

Use the organizer, below, to make your comparison and contrast. Where the ellipses overlap, write the similarities both experiences share. In the outer portions of each ellipse, note elements that differ for each experience. Finally, answer the question at the bottom of the page.

I am comparing _____ with the

❏ audio version.

❏ video version.

❏ live version.

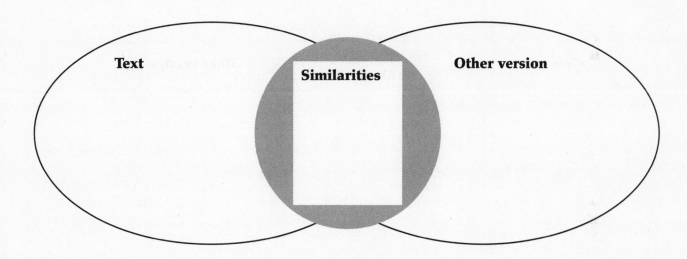

Which version do you prefer? Why? ....

....

....

....

....

....

....

For use with Literature 7

Name _____ Date _____ Selection _____

Comparing and Contrasting Reading a Text with Experiencing a Performance of It

Use the organizer, below, to make your comparison and contrast. Where the ellipses overlap, write the similarities both experiences share. In the outer portions of each ellipse, note elements that differ for each experience. Finally, answer the question at the bottom of the page.

I am comparing _____ with the

❑ audio version.

❑ video version.

❑ live version.

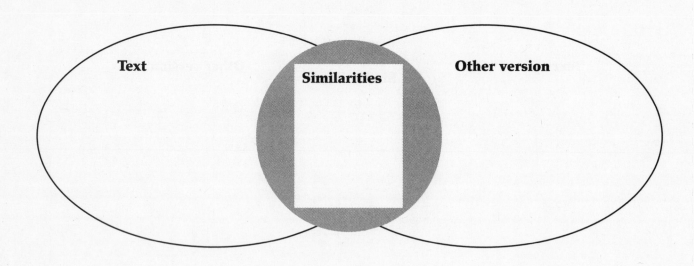

Text

Similarities

Other version

Which version do you prefer? Why? ....

....

....

....

....

....

....

B

Name _____ Date _____ Selection _____

Comparing and Contrasting Reading a Text with Experiencing a Performance of It

Use the organizer, below, to make your comparison and contrast. Where the ellipses overlap, write the similarities both experiences share. In the outer portions of each ellipse, note elements that differ for each experience. Finally, answer the question at the bottom of the page.

I am comparing _____ with the

❏ audio version.
❏ video version.
❏ live version.

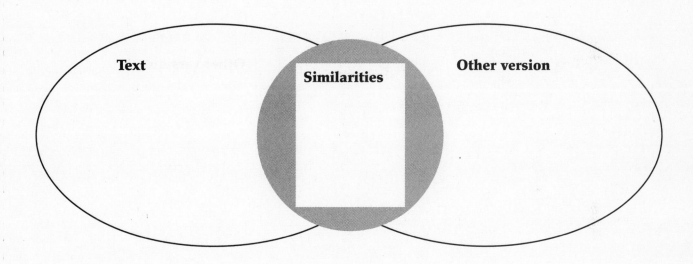

Which version do you prefer? Why? ....

....

....

....

....

....

....

For use with Literature 7

Name _____ Date _____ Selection _____

Comparing and Contrasting Reading a Text with Experiencing a Performance of It

Use the organizer, below, to make your comparison and contrast. Where the ellipses overlap, write the similarities both experiences share. In the outer portions of each ellipse, note elements that differ for each experience. Finally, answer the question at the bottom of the page.

I am comparing _____ with the

❑ audio version.

❑ video version.

❑ live version.

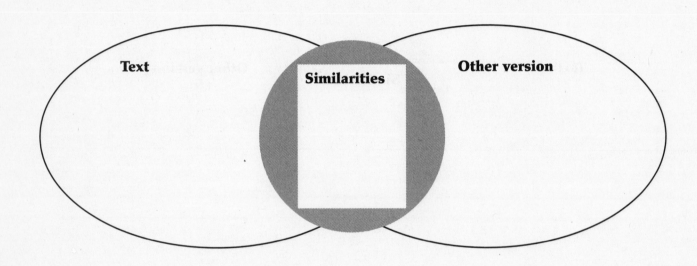

Which version do you prefer? Why? ....

....

....

....

....

....

....

For use with Literature 7

Name _____ Date _____ Selection _____

Comparing and Contrasting Reading a Text with Experiencing a Performance of It

Use the organizer, below, to make your comparison and contrast. Where the ellipses overlap, write the similarities both experiences share. In the outer portions of each ellipse, note elements that differ for each experience. Finally, answer the question at the bottom of the page.

I am comparing _____ with the

❏ audio version.
❏ video version.
❏ live version.

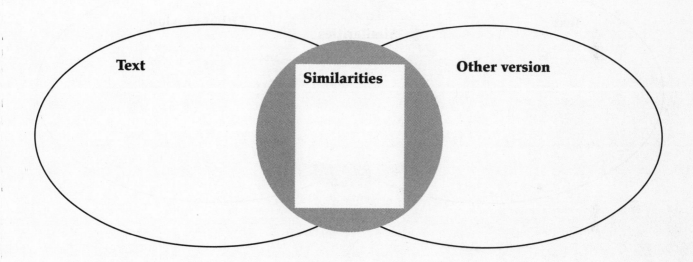

Text   **Similarities**   **Other version**

Which version do you prefer? Why? ....

....

....

....

....

....

....

E

Name _____ Date _____ Selection _____

Comparing and Contrasting Reading a Text with Experiencing a Performance of It

Use the organizer, below, to make your comparison and contrast. Where the ellipses overlap, write the similarities both experiences share. In the outer portions of each ellipse, note elements that differ for each experience. Finally, answer the question at the bottom of the page.

I am comparing _____ with the

❑ audio version.

❑ video version.

❑ live version.

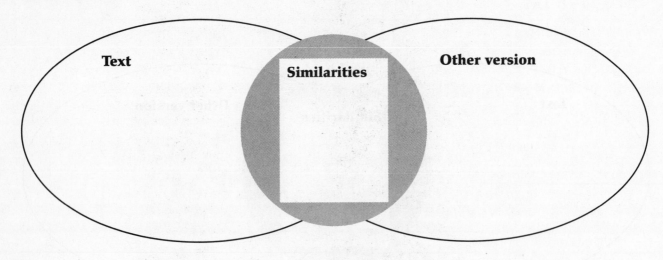

Text   **Similarities**   **Other version**

Which version do you prefer? Why? ....

....

....

....

....

....

....

For use with Literature 7

Literature 9

> 9. **Compare and contrast texts in different forms or genres (e.g., stories and poems; historical novels and fantasy stories) in terms of their approaches to similar themes and topics.**

Explanation

The main types of literature, such as fiction, nonfiction, poetry, and drama, are called **genres.** Each genre can be defined by its use of certain literary structures and elements. In fiction, for example, a narrator tells a story in prose using description and dialogue. Drama relies on dialogue spoken by characters to tell a story. Poetry may or may not tell a story, but it uses such elements as lines, stanzas, sound devices, imagery, rhythm, and figurative language.

Genres can be further broken down into smaller categories called subgenres. Fiction, for example, includes a subgenre called **historical fiction.** Narratives in this category are set in the past and often combine made-up characters and events with real historical figures and events. **Fantasy,** another subgenre, is highly imaginative writing that contains elements not found in real life.

Sometimes works in different genres deal with similar subjects or themes. You can learn a great deal by comparing and contrasting the ways these works approach the theme or topic.

Examples

- You might, for example, compare and contrast a historical novel and a fantasy story that both explore the theme of rebellion. The historical novel is set in colonial America during the Revolution. The heroine, a teenage girl, is a made-up character who witnesses real events from the 1700s. A fantasy story that also explores the theme of rebellion is set in an unreal place called Island Home. The hero, a young man studying to be a magician, joins a group called the Brook Dwellers. These creatures, whose skin is composed of water, are rebelling against a large, stubborn people, Bold-ers.

- A poem about the pleasures of summer consists of a single stanza focusing on a vivid image of the season: the smell of chlorine mixed with the scent of suntan lotion. A short story on the same subject is based on a central conflict: a brother and sister spending the summer in Wyoming overcome feelings of homesickness and learn to enjoy the outdoors.

Academic Vocabulary

genre type or category of literature, such as poetry, drama, or fiction
historical fiction type of story that is set in the past and that combines made-up elements with real ones
fantasy story highly imaginative tale containing elements not found in real life

Apply the Standard

Use the worksheet that follows to help you apply the standard as you read literature selections. Several copies of the worksheet have been provided for you.

- Comparing and Contrasting Texts in Different Forms

Name _____ Date _____ Selection _____

Comparing and Contrasting Texts in Different Forms

Use the organizer, below, to compare and contrast texts in different genres that explore similar themes.

Text 1:	Text 2:
Title and theme:	**Title and theme:**
Genre:	**Genre:**
Structure:	**Structure:**
Similarities to Text 2:	**Similarities to Text 1:**
Differences from Text 2:	**Differences from Text 1:**

A

Name _____ Date _____ Selection _____

Comparing and Contrasting Texts in Different Forms

Use the organizer, below, to compare and contrast texts in different genres that explore similar themes.

Text 1:	**Text 2:**
Title and theme:	**Title and theme:**
Genre:	**Genre:**
Structure:	**Structure:**
Similarities to Text 2:	**Similarities to Text 1:**
Differences from Text 2:	**Differences from Text 1:**

B

Name _____ Date _____ Selection _____

Comparing and Contrasting Texts in Different Forms

Use the organizer, below, to compare and contrast texts in different genres that explore similar themes.

Text 1:	Text 2:
Title and theme:	**Title and theme:**
Genre:	Genre:
Structure:	Structure:
Similarities to Text 2:	**Similarities to Text 1:**
Differences from Text 2:	**Differences from Text 1:**

C

Name _____ Date _____ Selection _____

Comparing and Contrasting Texts in Different Forms

Use the organizer, below, to compare and contrast texts in different genres that explore similar themes.

Text 1:	Text 2:
Title and theme:	**Title and theme:**
Genre:	**Genre:**
Structure:	**Structure:**
Similarities to Text 2:	**Similarities to Text 1:**
Differences from Text 2:	**Differences from Text 1:**

D

Name _____ Date _____ Selection _____

Comparing and Contrasting Texts in Different Forms

Use the organizer, below, to compare and contrast texts in different genres that explore similar themes.

Text 1:	Text 2:
Title and theme:	**Title and theme:**
Genre:	**Genre:**
Structure:	**Structure:**
Similarities to Text 2:	**Similarities to Text 1:**
Differences from Text 2:	**Differences from Text 1:**

E

Name _____ Date _____ Selection _____

Comparing and Contrasting Texts in Different Forms

Use the organizer, below, to compare and contrast texts in different genres that explore similar themes.

Text 1:	Text 2:
Title and theme:	**Title and theme:**
Genre:	**Genre:**
Structure:	**Structure:**
Similarities to Text 2:	**Similarities to Text 1:**
Differences from Text 2:	**Differences from Text 1:**

F

Literature 10

> **10. By the end of the year, read and comprehend literature, including stories, dramas, and poems, in the grades 6–8 text complexity band proficiently, with scaffolding as needed at the high end of the range.**

Explanation

Complexity refers to how difficult a work of literature is to understand. Some stories, dramas, and poems have familiar subjects, include directly stated ideas and themes, and have a simple style, featuring conversational vocabulary and short sentences. Other literary works, however, discuss unfamiliar concepts, contain implied ideas and themes, and include advanced vocabulary, figurative language, and long sentences.

You will be reading literary works in different genres (types or categories of literature), including stories, dramas, and poems. You will also be expected to **comprehend,** or understand the meaning and importance of, texts of greater complexity than you have read before. To comprehend complex texts, use the reading strategies described below.

Examples

- **Monitor** your comprehension by stopping occasionally and asking yourself questions about what you have just read. Do this whenever something happens that you might not have understood completely. For example, in Isaac Bashevis Singer's story "Zlateh the Goat," stop to ask yourself what is going to happen to Zlateh when Aaron gets her to the town butcher. Ask yourself why Reuven, the father of the family, has to sell Zlateh.

- In the same story, you can also use **context** to understand what is going on. When Leah, the mother of the family, wipes away tears upon learning that Zlateh the goat is going to be sold to the town butcher, you can figure out that something bad will probably happen to Zlateh. Leah's tears show that she cares deeply about Zlateh and feels sad about what is probably going to happen.

- Aaron tunnels into a warm haystack with Zlateh. To better understand the scene, **visualize** what it might have felt like to be surrounded by warmth and hay on all sides. Contrast that feeling with being out in the brutal cold and whiteness of the snowstorm. **Connect** those feelings with your own experience in snowstorms or in cold weather.

Academic Vocabulary

complexity the degree to which a story, poem, drama, or other work is difficult to understand
comprehend understand the meaning and importance of something

Apply the Standard

Use the worksheet that follows to help you apply the standard as you read. Several copies of the worksheet have been provided for you to use with different literature selections.

- Comprehending Complex Texts

Name _____ Date _____ Selection _____

Comprehending Complex Texts

Explain what makes the story, poem, drama, or other selection you are reading complex. Then explain how the strategy on the left in the chart helps you comprehend the selection.

What makes this selection complex?

....

....

Strategy	How the Strategy Helped Me Comprehend the Selection
monitoring comprehension	
using context	
visualizing	
connecting	

Name _____ Date _____ Selection _____

Comprehending Complex Texts

Explain what makes the story, poem, drama, or other selection you are reading complex. Then explain how the strategy on the left in the chart helps you comprehend the selection.

What makes this selection complex?

....

....

Strategy	How the Strategy Helped Me Comprehend the Selection
monitoring comprehension	
using context	
visualizing	
connecting	

Comprehending Complex Texts

Explain what makes the story, poem, drama, or other selection you are reading complex. Then explain how the strategy on the left in the chart helps you comprehend the selection.

What makes this selection complex?

....

....

Strategy	How the Strategy Helped Me Comprehend the Selection
monitoring comprehension	
using context	
visualizing	
connecting	

For use with Literature 10

Name _____ Date _____ Selection _____

Comprehending Complex Texts

Explain what makes the story, poem, drama, or other selection you are reading complex. Then explain how the strategy on the left in the chart helps you comprehend the selection.

What makes this selection complex?

....

....

Strategy	How the Strategy Helped Me Comprehend the Selection
monitoring comprehension	
using context	
visualizing	
connecting	

D

Name _____ Date _____ Selection _____

Comprehending Complex Texts

Explain what makes the story, poem, drama, or other selection you are reading complex. Then explain how the strategy on the left in the chart helps you comprehend the selection.

What makes this selection complex?

....

....

Strategy	How the Strategy Helped Me Comprehend the Selection
monitoring comprehension	
using context	
visualizing	
connecting	

E

Name _____ Date _____ Selection _____

Comprehending Complex Texts

Explain what makes the story, poem, drama, or other selection you are reading complex. Then explain how the strategy on the left in the chart helps you comprehend the selection.

What makes this selection complex?

....

....

Strategy	How the Strategy Helped Me Comprehend the Selection
monitoring comprehension	
using context	
visualizing	
connecting	

F

Reading Standards for Informational Text

Informational Text 1

> 1. **Cite textual evidence to support an analysis of what the text says explicitly as well as inferences drawn from the text.**

Explanation

When you read an informational text, think about the different parts of it and how they relate to each other. Your analysis leads you to ideas about what the text means. However, you must support your ideas with evidence from the text. When you analyze **explicit** details, or direct statements, in a text, you must determine if they are important and how they work together to contribute to the overall meaning of a work.

Sometimes, an author will hint at the meaning of his or her text rather than state it directly. In such cases, you should **make inferences,** or reach conclusions, about what a text hints at but does not say directly. It is important to support an inference with evidence from the text that will convince others your inference is correct.

Successful readers take note of and analyze important explicit details in a text. They also make inferences to comprehend more fully the meaning of a story.

Examples

- **Explicit details** provide basic information for readers and are directly stated. For example, "During the Middle Ages, serfs lived and worked in small communities called manors" and "The manor was ruled by a nobleman" are explicit details.

- **Inferences** are logical guesses readers make based on details in the text and their own personal experience and knowledge. Inferences are what you figure out on your own. For example, an author writing about the Middle Ages might also provide these details about the life of a serf: "Serfs were responsible for doing all of the work on the manor farm. They could not leave the manor or marry without permission. Men, women, and children worked together. Serfs tried to save money to buy their freedom." Although the text doesn't explicitly say it, you can infer that serfs had little freedom and had very difficult lives. When you make an inference, be prepared to cite textual evidence as support.

Academic Vocabulary

explicit details information that is directly stated in the text

inference logical guess based on details in the text and personal experience

textual evidence words or phrases that support an analysis

Apply the Standard

Use the worksheets that follow to help you apply the standard as you read. Several copies of each worksheet have been provided for you to use with different informational texts.

- Citing Textual Evidence: Supporting an Analysis of Explicit Statements

- Citing Textual Evidence: Supporting an Inference

Name _____   Date _____   Selection _____

Citing Textual Evidence: Supporting an Analysis of Explicit Statements

Analyze an informational text to identify three important things it says explicitly. Enter those statements in the left column of the following chart. Then, in the right column explain why the explicit statement is important and how it contributes to your overall understanding of the text.

Explicit Statement from the Text	Textual Evidence: Why the Statement Is Important and What It Adds to Your Understanding of the Text
1.	
2.	
3.	

Name _____ Date _____ Selection _____

Citing Textual Evidence: Supporting an Analysis of Explicit Statements

Analyze an informational text to identify three important things it says explicitly. Enter those statements in the left column of the following chart. Then, in the right column explain why the explicit statement is important and how it contributes to your overall understanding of the text.

Explicit Statement from the Text	Textual Evidence: Why the Statement Is Important and What It Adds to Your Understanding of the Text
1.	
2.	
3.	

B

Name _____ Date _____ Selection _____

Citing Textual Evidence: Supporting an Analysis of Explicit Statements

Analyze an informational text to identify three important things it says explicitly. Enter those statements in the left column of the following chart. Then, in the right column explain why the explicit statement is important and how it contributes to your overall understanding of the text.

Explicit Statement from the Text	Textual Evidence: Why the Statement Is Important and What It Adds to Your Understanding of the Text
1.	
2.	
3.	

C

Name _____ Date _____ Selection _____

Citing Textual Evidence: Supporting an Analysis of Explicit Statements

Analyze an informational text to identify three important things it says explicitly. Enter those statements in the left column of the following chart. Then, in the right column explain why the explicit statement is important and how it contributes to your overall understanding of the text.

Explicit Statement from the Text	Textual Evidence: Why the Statement Is Important and What It Adds to Your Understanding of the Text
1.	
2.	
3.	

D

Name _____ Date _____ Selection _____

Citing Textual Evidence: Supporting an Analysis of Explicit Statements

Analyze an informational text to identify three important things it says explicitly. Enter those statements in the left column of the following chart. Then, in the right column explain why the explicit statement is important and how it contributes to your overall understanding of the text.

Explicit Statement from the Text	Textual Evidence: Why the Statement Is Important and What It Adds to Your Understanding of the Text
1.	
2.	
3.	

Name _____ Date _____ Selection _____

Citing Textual Evidence: Supporting an Analysis of Explicit Statements

Analyze an informational text to identify three important things it says explicitly. Enter those statements in the left column of the following chart. Then, in the right column explain why the explicit statement is important and how it contributes to your overall understanding of the text.

Explicit Statement from the Text	Textual Evidence: Why the Statement Is Important and What It Adds to Your Understanding of the Text
1.	
2.	
3.	

F

Name _____ Date _____ Selection _____

Citing Textual Evidence: Supporting an Inference

Use the left column of the following chart to make four inferences from the text. Then, in the right column, support each inference with textual evidence.

Inferences from the Text	Textual Evidence Supporting the Inference
1.	
2.	
3.	
4.	

A

Name _____ Date _____ Selection _____

Citing Textual Evidence: Supporting an Inference

Use the left column of the following chart to make four inferences from the text. Then, in the right column, support each inference with textual evidence.

Inferences from the Text	Textual Evidence Supporting the Inference
1.	
2.	
3.	
4.	

B

Name _____ Date _____ Selection _____

Citing Textual Evidence: Supporting an Inference

Use the left column of the following chart to make four inferences from the text. Then, in the right column, support each inference with textual evidence.

Inferences from the Text	Textual Evidence Supporting the Inference
1.	
2.	
3.	
4.	

C

Name _____ Date _____ Selection _____

Citing Textual Evidence: Supporting an Inference

Use the left column of the following chart to make four inferences from the text. Then, in the right column, support each inference with textual evidence.

Inferences from the Text	Textual Evidence Supporting the Inference
1.	
2.	
3.	
4.	

D

Name _____ Date _____ Selection _____

Citing Textual Evidence: Supporting an Inference

Use the left column of the following chart to make four inferences from the text. Then, in the right column, support each inference with textual evidence.

Inferences from the Text	Textual Evidence Supporting the Inference
1.	
2.	
3.	
4.	

E

Name _____ Date _____ Selection _____

Citing Textual Evidence: Supporting an Inference

Use the left column of the following chart to make four inferences from the text. Then, in the right column, support each inference with textual evidence.

Inferences from the Text	Textual Evidence Supporting the Inference
1.	
2.	
3.	
4.	

F

Informational Text 2

> 2. **Determine a central idea of a text and how it is conveyed through particular details; provide a summary of the text distinct from personal opinions or judgments.**

Explanation

The **central idea** is the most important point of a piece of writing. Sometimes the central idea is stated directly, but usually the reader has to figure it out by studying the supporting details in the text. **Supporting details** are pieces of information—such as examples, facts, reasons, or descriptions—that an author uses to make a convincing argument or point. Keep track of these details as you read. Ask yourself, why did the author include this detail? How does this detail help me understand the central idea of the text?

A good way to clarify the central idea of a text is to **summarize** it. A summary is a brief restatement in your own words of the key ideas in the text. A summary includes only the most important details, and it presents the information objectively without personal opinions or judgments. When writing a summary, state the main point of the text in the first sentence and give details to support it in the sentences that follow.

Examples

- **Summary**
  Here is a summary of a scientific article about the aloe vera plant.

  Aloe vera is a plant that is valued for its healing qualities. Many people grow aloe as a houseplant to use in treating wounds, burns, acne, insect bites, and other skin irritations. Because of its soothing qualities for the skin, manufacturers add aloe vera to many soaps, creams, and cosmetics. Some people drink aloe vera juice to relieve digestive problems.

- **Central Idea**
  Note that the summary begins by stating the central idea of the article: *Aloe vera is a plant that is valued for its healing qualities.* It then supports that idea with two important supporting details. One detail is that aloe is used to treat various skin problems. Another is that aloe is used as a digestive aid.

Academic Vocabulary

central idea the main idea or central message of a text

summary a statement of the central idea and important details in a work

Apply the Standard

Use the worksheets that follow to help you apply the standard as you read. Several copies of each worksheet have been provided for you to use with different informational texts.

- Summarizing Key Supporting Details
- Determining the Central Idea of a Work

Name _____ Date _____ Assignment _____

Summarizing Key Supporting Details

Use the following organizer to summarize a text. First, some present the central idea. Then, record the most important details. Use your own words, and write in full sentences.

Central Idea

....

....

....

1. Detail

....

....

....

2. Detail

....

....

....

....

3. Detail

....

....

4. Detail

....

....

....

For use with Informational Text 2

Name _____ Date _____ Assignment _____

Summarizing Key Supporting Details

Use the following organizer to summarize a text. First, some present the central idea. Then, record the most important details. Use your own words, and write in full sentences.

Central Idea

....

....

....

1. Detail

....

....

....

2. Detail

....

....

....

....

3. Detail

....

....

4. Detail

....

....

....

B

For use with Informational Text 2

Name _____ Date _____ Assignment _____

Summarizing Key Supporting Details

Use the following organizer to summarize a text. First, some present the central idea. Then, record the most important details. Use your own words, and write in full sentences.

Central Idea

....

....

....

1. Detail

....

....

....

2. Detail

....

....

....

....

3. Detail

....

....

4. Detail

....

....

....

C

For use with Informational Text 2

Name _____ Date _____ Assignment _____

Summarizing Key Supporting Details

Use the following organizer to summarize a text. First, some present the central idea. Then, record the most important details. Use your own words, and write in full sentences.

Central Idea

....

....

....

1. Detail

....

....

....

2. Detail

....

....

....

3. Detail

....

....

4. Detail

....

....

....

D

For use with Informational Text 2

Name _____ Date _____ Assignment _____

Summarizing Key Supporting Details

Use the following organizer to summarize a text. First, some present the central idea. Then, record the most important details. Use your own words, and write in full sentences.

Central Idea

....

....

....

1. Detail

....

....

....

2. Detail

....

....

....

3. Detail

....

....

4. Detail

....

....

....

E

Name _____ Date _____ Assignment _____

Summarizing Key Supporting Details

Use the following organizer to summarize a text. First, some present the central idea. Then, record the most important details. Use your own words, and write in full sentences.

Central Idea

....

....

....

1. Detail

....

....

....

2. Detail

....

....

....

3. Detail

....

....

4. Detail

....

....

....

For use with Informational Text 2

Name _____ Date _____ Assignment _____

Determining the Central Idea of a Work

Use the following graphic organizer to state the central idea of the text and to list important supporting details.

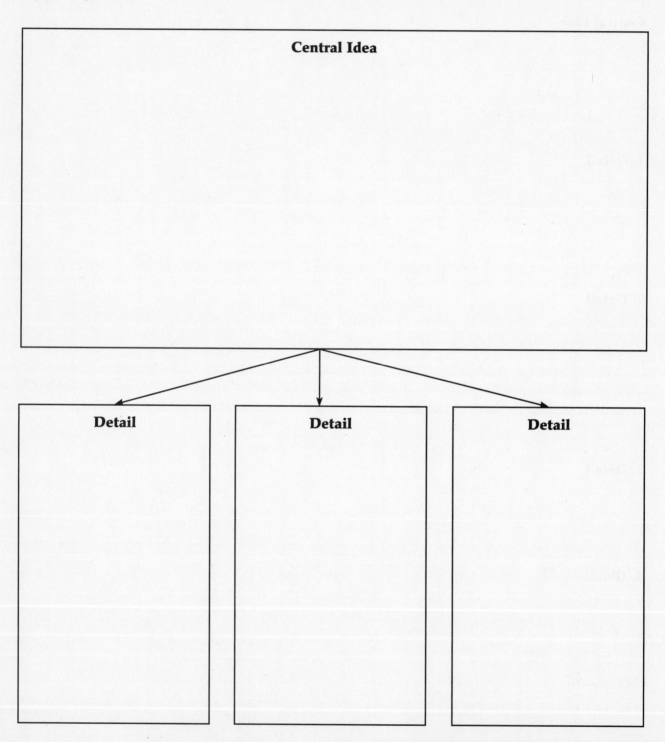

Central Idea

Detail

Detail

Detail

A

Name _____ Date _____ Assignment _____

Determining the Central Idea of a Work

Use the following graphic organizer to state the central idea of the text and to list important supporting details.

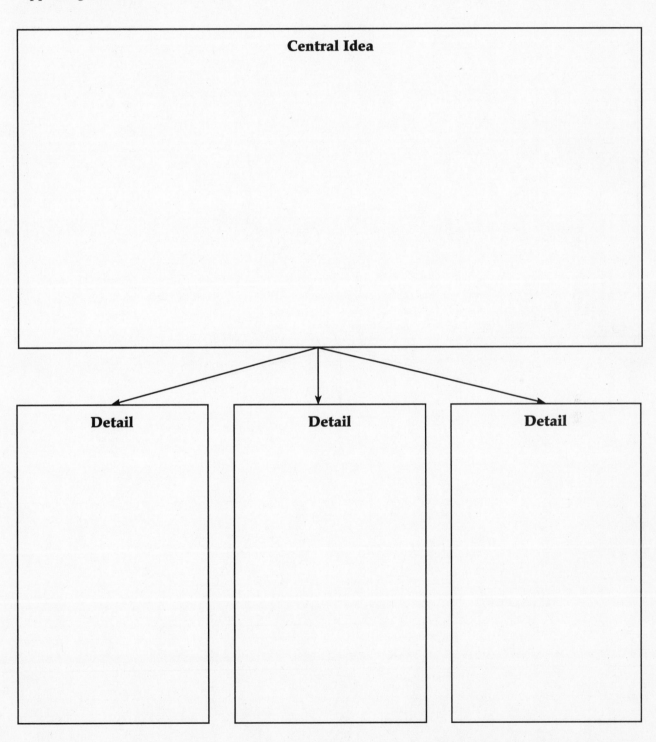

Central Idea

Detail

Detail

Detail

B

Name _____ Date _____ Assignment _____

Determining the Central Idea of a Work

Use the following graphic organizer to state the central idea of the text and to list important supporting details.

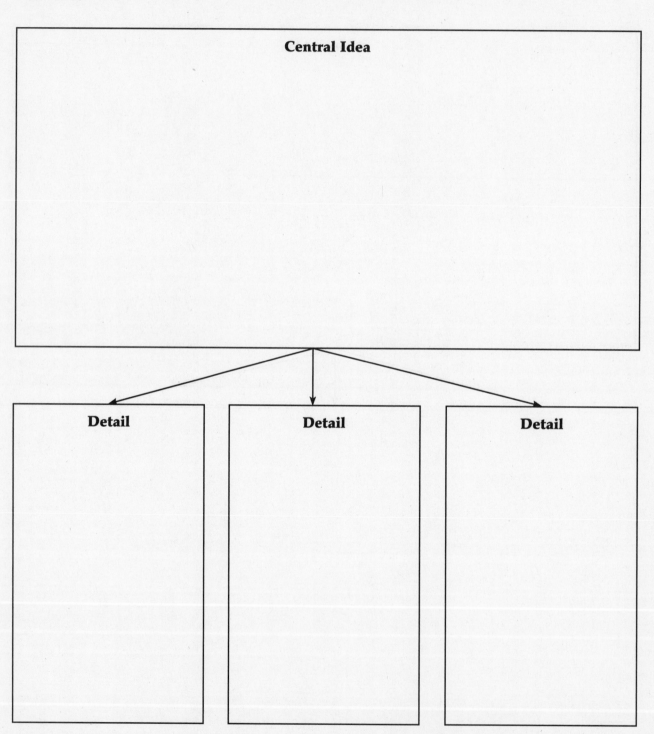

Central Idea

Detail

Detail

Detail

C

Name _____ Date _____ Assignment _____

Determining the Central Idea of a Work

Use the following graphic organizer to state the central idea of the text and to list important supporting details.

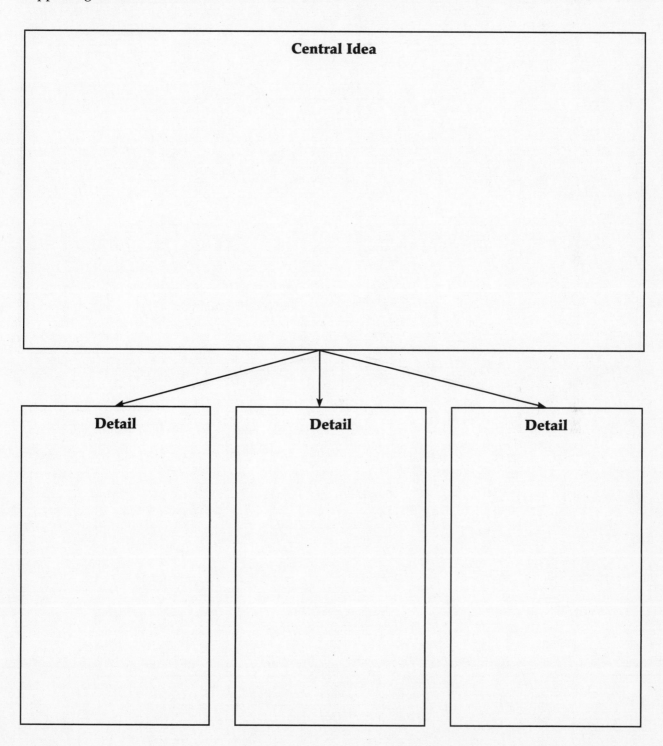

Central Idea

Detail

Detail

Detail

For use with Informational Text 2

Name _____ Date _____ Assignment _____

Determining the Central Idea of a Work

Use the following graphic organizer to state the central idea of the text and to list important supporting details.

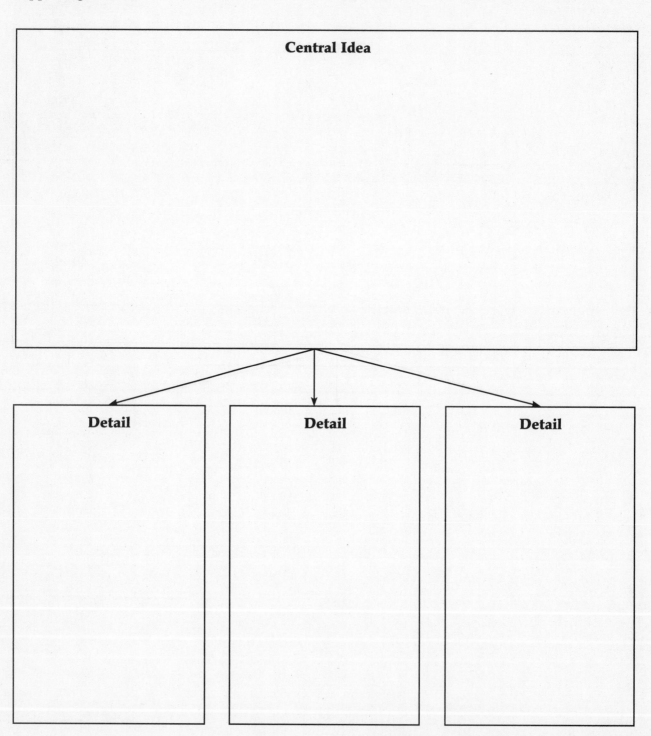

E

Name _____ Date _____ Assignment _____

Determining the Central Idea of a Work

Use the following graphic organizer to state the central idea of the text and to list important supporting details.

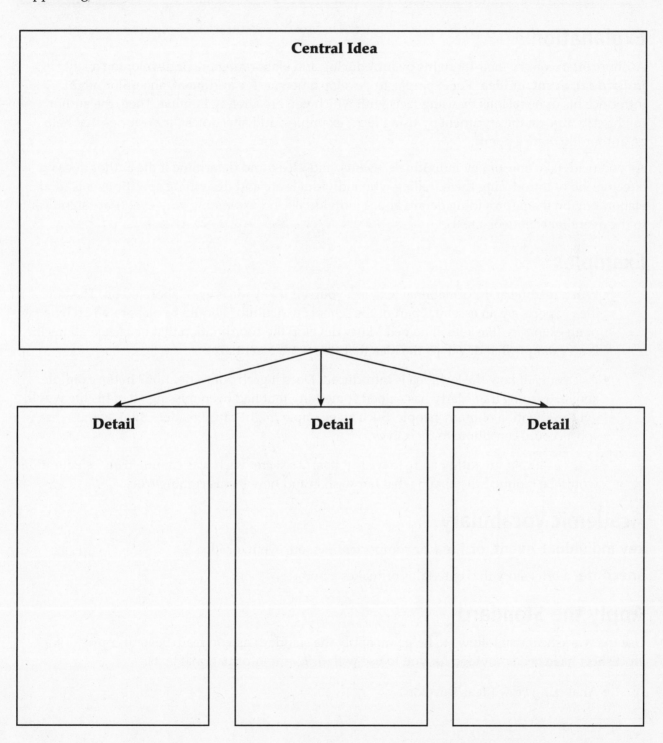

Central Idea

Detail

Detail

Detail

F

Informational Text 3

> **3. Analyze in detail how a key individual, event, or idea is introduced, illustrated, and elaborated in a text (e.g., through examples or anecdotes).**

Explanation

Authors often convey their thoughts by introducing and elaborating on, or developing a key **individual**, **event**, or **idea**. For example, to develop a persuasive argument, an author might introduce his or her claims by using facts with which you are already familiar. Then, the author might elaborate on the argument by using facts, examples, and anecdotes (brief stories that help an author illustrate a point).

As you read, take note of key individuals, events, and ideas, and determine if the author does an effective job of introducing them (telling who individuals are and describing specific events) and elaborating on them (providing details about individuals and explaining why events are significant to the overall meaning of a text).

Examples

- When reading an informational text, ask yourself if key ideas are elaborated on. The key idea "Sports are an essential part of the school curriculum" should be elaborated on by a fact or an example. "Basketball helped Marty develop the coordination that he lacked all his life" is an example that develops the idea that sports are essential.

- Ask yourself how the key idea is introduced. Does it grab your attention? In the example above, learning that Marty has gained something that had been missing all of his life would get the attention of many people. Such an example might cause readers think about what sports could contribute to their lives.

- If, for example, an author were to write, "Penny's secret wish was coming true," elaboration would be required to explain what her wish is and how it was coming true.

Academic Vocabulary

key individual, event, or idea any important person, event, or idea

anecdote a brief story that entertains or makes a point

Apply the Standard

Use the worksheet that follows to help you apply the standard as you read. Several copies of the worksheet have been provided for you to use with different informational texts.

- Analyzing How Ideas Develop

Name _____ Date _____ Assignment _____

Analyzing How Ideas Develop

Use the following organizer to analyze how key individuals, events, or ideas are developed in an informational text.

Individual, Event, or Idea	How it is Developed
1.	
2.	
3.	
4.	

A

Name _____ Date _____ Assignment _____

Analyzing How Ideas Develop

Use the following organizer to analyze how key individuals, events, or ideas are developed in an informational text.

Individual, Event, or Idea	How it is Developed
1.	
2.	
3.	
4.	

B

Name _____ Date _____ Assignment _____

Analyzing How Ideas Develop

Use the following organizer to analyze how key individuals, events, or ideas are developed in an informational text.

Individual, Event, or Idea	How it is Developed
1.	
2.	
3.	
4.	

C

Name _____ Date _____ Assignment _____

Analyzing How Ideas Develop

Use the following organizer to analyze how key individuals, events, or ideas are developed in an informational text.

Individual, Event, or Idea	How it is Developed
1.	
2.	
3.	
4.	

D

Analyzing How Ideas Develop

Use the following organizer to analyze how key individuals, events, or ideas are developed in an informational text.

Individual, Event, or Idea	How it is Developed
1.	
2.	
3.	
4.	

Name _____ Date _____ Assignment _____

Analyzing How Ideas Develop

Use the following organizer to analyze how key individuals, events, or ideas are developed in an informational text.

Individual, Event, or Idea	How it is Developed
1.	
2.	
3.	
4.	

For use with Informational Text 3

Informational Text 4

> 4. Determine the meaning of words and phrases as they are used in a text, including figurative, connotative, and technical meanings.

Explanation

Good writers choose their words carefully, using language that expresses exactly what they want to say and that conveys to the reader how they feel about their subject. When reading informational texts, you will come across words and phrases that are new to you or that are used in unfamiliar ways. To help determine their meanings, first think about whether the words and phrases are used figuratively or literally. **Figurative language** is writing that is used imaginatively, rather than literally. Words also have **connotative meanings**, or emotions and feelings that are associated with them. Connotations can be positive, neutral, or negative. Authors also use technical terms specifically related to a subject. If you encounter a technical term with which you are unfamiliar, use resources such as dictionaries or encyclopedias to help clarify its meaning.

Examples

- **Figurative meaning** goes beyond the literal, or dictionary defined meaning. The sentence "Mark ran as fast as lightning." doesn't mean that Mark actually moved that fast. However, the figurative language gives the reader a vivid picture of how quickly Mark ran.

- **Connotative meaning** refers to feelings and emotions associated with a word. If a scientist were described as *stubborn*, you would form a different opinion than if he or she were described as *persistent*.

- The **technical meaning** of a word is the meaning it has in a specific subject area. In the sentence "Earth's atmosphere rises 372 feet above its surface," the word *atmosphere* is used as a scientific term that specifically identifies the mixtures of gases surrounding the Earth or another planet.

Academic Vocabulary

figurative language writing that is not meant to be taken literally

connotations the positive or negative feelings associated with a word

technical meaning meaning specifically related to a subject

Apply the Standard

Use the worksheet that follows to help you apply the standard as you read. Several copies of the worksheet have been provided for you to use with different informational texts.

- Understanding Figurative Language, Connotations, and Technical Terms

Name _____ Date _____ Assignment _____

Understanding Figurative Language, Connotations, and Technical Terms

Use the organizer below to help you determine the figurative, connotative, or technical meaning of words and phrases you encounter while reading informational texts. In the left column, record words or phrases that contain figurative language; positive, negative, or neutral connotations; or one or more technical terms. In the right column, explain whether your word or phrase is an example of figurative language, connotation, or technical language and what it means. Use a dictionary, if necessary, to identify the meanings of technical terms.

Word or Phrase	Figurative, Connotative, or Technical Meaning
1.	
2.	
3.	

Name _____ Date _____ Assignment _____

Understanding Figurative Language, Connotations, and Technical Terms

Use the organizer below to help you determine the figurative, connotative, or technical meaning of words and phrases you encounter while reading informational texts. In the left column, record words or phrases that contain figurative language; positive, negative, or neutral connotations; or one or more technical terms. In the right column, explain whether your word or phrase is an example of figurative language, connotation, or technical language and what it means. Use a dictionary, if necessary, to identify the meanings of technical terms.

Word or Phrase	Figurative, Connotative, or Technical Meaning
1.	
2.	
3.	

Name _____ Date _____ Assignment _____

Understanding Figurative Language, Connotations, and Technical Terms

Use the organizer below to help you determine the figurative, connotative, or technical meaning of words and phrases you encounter while reading informational texts. In the left column, record words or phrases that contain figurative language; positive, negative, or neutral connotations; or one or more technical terms. In the right column, explain whether your word or phrase is an example of figurative language, connotation, or technical language and what it means. Use a dictionary, if necessary, to identify the meanings of technical terms.

Word or Phrase	Figurative, Connotative, or Technical Meaning
1.	
2.	
3.	

Name _____ Date _____ Assignment _____

Understanding Figurative Language, Connotations, and Technical Terms

Use the organizer below to help you determine the figurative, connotative, or technical meaning of words and phrases you encounter while reading informational texts. In the left column, record words or phrases that contain figurative language; positive, negative, or neutral connotations; or one or more technical terms. In the right column, explain whether your word or phrase is an example of figurative language, connotation, or technical language and what it means. Use a dictionary, if necessary, to identify the meanings of technical terms.

Word or Phrase	Figurative, Connotative, or Technical Meaning
1.	
2.	
3.	

Name _____ Date _____ Assignment _____

Understanding Figurative Language, Connotations, and Technical Terms

Use the organizer below to help you determine the figurative, connotative, or technical meaning of words and phrases you encounter while reading informational texts. In the left column, record words or phrases that contain figurative language; positive, negative, or neutral connotations; or one or more technical terms. In the right column, explain whether your word or phrase is an example of figurative language, connotation, or technical language and what it means. Use a dictionary, if necessary, to identify the meanings of technical terms.

Word or Phrase	Figurative, Connotative, or Technical Meaning
1.	
2.	
3.	

E

Name _____ Date _____ Assignment _____

Understanding Figurative Language, Connotations, and Technical Terms

Use the organizer below to help you determine the figurative, connotative, or technical meaning of words and phrases you encounter while reading informational texts. In the left column, record words or phrases that contain figurative language; positive, negative, or neutral connotations; or one or more technical terms. In the right column, explain whether your word or phrase is an example of figurative language, connotation, or technical language and what it means. Use a dictionary, if necessary, to identify the meanings of technical terms.

Word or Phrase	Figurative, Connotative, or Technical Meaning
1.	
2.	
3.	

Informational Text 5

> **5. Analyze how a particular sentence, paragraph, chapter, or section fits into the overall structure of a text and contributes to the development of the ideas.**

Explanation

Sentences, paragraphs, chapters, and sections are the building blocks of an informational text. Each component fits into the overall text structure and helps to develop the author's ideas. Sentences develop paragraphs, paragraphs develop chapters, and chapters may develop larger sections. As you read, pay attention to text aids such as chapter titles and subheadings. They show how the parts of a text fit together.

One way to understand how each part fits into the structure of a text is to create an **outline**. The process of outlining helps you see how all the ideas relate to one another as well as to the overall structure. A formal outline uses Roman numerals, capital letters, and Arabic numerals to label main and supporting ideas in a text. Because it both organizes and connects major ideas, an outline can be a useful study tool.

Examples

- A textbook about world cultures and geography might be divided into units, each covering a different broad region of the world. A unit on Latin America might be divided into chapters, each covering one country in that region. A chapter on Mexico might be divided into sections covering history, economics, government, and culture. A section on culture might contain individual paragraphs about foods, holidays, sports, and arts. Each component, from largest to smallest, fits into the overall structure of the text and contributes to the development of ideas.

- An essay about homelessness in Chicago might describe the problem and offer solutions. A paragraph introducing the problem might include sentences that give statistics about the number of people who are homeless. Another paragraph might discuss the causes of homelessness. A paragraph examining solutions might offer examples of successful programs. All the paragraphs contribute to the development of one central idea.

Academic Vocabulary

outline an organized summary of the most important information in a text

Apply the Standard

Use the worksheet that follows to help you apply the standard as you read. Several copies have been provided for you to use with different informational texts.

- Analyzing Text Structure

Name _____ Date _____ Assignment _____

Analyzing Text Structure

Use the following organizer to outline an informational text you have read. You may add or delete numbers and letters as needed. Then, complete the activity at the bottom of the page.

Title of Text:	
Topic of Text:	
Thesis (Main Idea) of Text:	
Outline:	

I. ....

      A. ....

      B. ....

II. ....

      A. ....

      B. ....

III. ....

      A. ....

      B. ....

Choose one sentence, paragraph, or section of the informational text you have read and explain how it develops the main idea of the text.

....

....

....

....

For use with Informational Text 5

Name _____ Date _____ Assignment _____

Analyzing Text Structure

Use the following organizer to outline an informational text you have read. You may add or delete numbers and letters as needed. Then, complete the activity at the bottom of the page.

Title of Text:	
Topic of Text:	
Thesis (Main Idea) of Text:	
Outline:	

I. ....

    A. ....

    B. ....

II. ....

    A. ....

    B. ....

III. ....

    A. ....

    B. ....

Choose one sentence, paragraph, or section of the informational text you have read and explain how it develops the main idea of the text.

....

....

....

....

B

For use with Informational Text 5

Name _____ Date _____ Assignment _____

Analyzing Text Structure

Use the following organizer to outline an informational text you have read. You may add or delete numbers and letters as needed. Then, complete the activity at the bottom of the page.

Title of Text:
Topic of Text:
Thesis (Main Idea) of Text:
Outline:

I. ....

      A. ....

      B. ....

II. ....

      A. ....

      B. ....

III. ....

      A. ....

      B. ....

Choose one sentence, paragraph, or section of the informational text you have read and explain how it develops the main idea of the text.

....

....

....

....

C

Name _____ Date _____ Assignment _____

Analyzing Text Structure

Use the following organizer to outline an informational text you have read. You may add or delete numbers and letters as needed. Then, complete the activity at the bottom of the page.

Title of Text:	
Topic of Text:	
Thesis (Main Idea) of Text:	
Outline:	

I. ....

     A. ....

     B. ....

II. ....

     A. ....

     B. ....

III. ....

     A. ....

     B. ....

Choose one sentence, paragraph, or section of the informational text you have read and explain how it develops the main idea of the text.

....

....

....

....

D

Name _____ Date _____ Assignment _____

Analyzing Text Structure

Use the following organizer to outline an informational text you have read. You may add or delete numbers and letters as needed. Then, complete the activity at the bottom of the page.

Title of Text:
Topic of Text:
Thesis (Main Idea) of Text:
Outline:

I. ....

      A. ....

      B. ....

II. ....

      A. ....

      B. ....

III. ....

      A. ....

      B. ....

Choose one sentence, paragraph, or section of the informational text you have read and explain how it develops the main idea of the text.

....

....

....

....

E

Name _____ Date _____ Assignment _____

Analyzing Text Structure

Use the following organizer to outline an informational text you have read. You may add or delete numbers and letters as needed. Then, complete the activity at the bottom of the page.

Title of Text:
Topic of Text:
Thesis (Main Idea) of Text:
Outline:

I. ....

      A. ....

      B. ....

II. ....

      A. ....

      B. ....

III. ....

      A. ....

      B. ....

Choose one sentence, paragraph, or section of the informational text you have read and explain how it develops the main idea of the text.

....

....

....

....

F

Informational Text 6

> **6. Determine an author's point of view or purpose in a text and explain how it is conveyed in the text.**

Explanation

An author's **point of view** is the perspective from which he or she writes. This perspective, or way of looking at the world, comes from the author's beliefs and background. The author's feelings and interest in a subject are revealed in his or her perspective.

The **author's purpose** is the author's reason for writing a specific work. Purposes can include to inform, to persuade, to entertain, and to reflect. Authors of informational texts sometimes have more than one purpose for writing a piece. For example, sometimes an author wants to inform readers about something and to persuade them to have a particular attitude at the same time. Details in the work give clues to the author's purpose or purposes.

Examples

- The author of a magazine article about endangered species of birds uses facts to inform readers about their environmental value and to persuade them to help protect the species. The author's perspective indicates positive feelings about wildlife in general.

- The author of a newspaper column uses reasons to persuade readers to support a particular candidate for office. The author's perspective is that of a long-time participant in local politics.

- A short book gives an author's reflections on wise living to encourage readers to reflect on their own lives. The author's perspective reveals a questioning, philosophic mind.

Academic Vocabulary

author's point of view the author's perspective, which is based on his or her feelings or personal interest in a topic

author's purpose the main reason an author writes a work

Apply the Standard

Use the worksheet that follows to help you apply the standard as you read. Several copies have been provided for you to use with different informational texts.

- Determining Point of View and Purpose

Name _____ Date _____ Assignment _____

Determining Point of View and Purpose

Complete the following organizer to determine the author's point of view and purpose in an informational text. First, write the title and topic of the selection. Then, in the left column, identify the author's point of view and purpose (or purposes) for writing. In the right column, provide details from the text that helped you determine the point of view and purpose.

Title of the Text:

Topic of the Text:

Author's Point of View:	Details from the Text:

Author's Purpose(s): ❏ to inform ❏ to persuade ❏ to entertain ❏ to reflect	Details from the Text:

A

Name _____ Date _____ Assignment _____

Determining Point of View and Purpose

Complete the following organizer to determine the author's point of view and purpose in an informational text. First, write the title and topic of the selection. Then, in the left column, identify the author's point of view and purpose (or purposes) for writing. In the right column, provide details from the text that helped you determine the point of view and purpose.

Title of the Text:

Topic of the Text:

Author's Point of View:	Details from the Text:

Author's Purpose(s): ❑ to inform ❑ to persuade ❑ to entertain ❑ to reflect	Details from the Text:

B

Name _____ Date _____ Assignment _____

Determining Point of View and Purpose

Complete the following organizer to determine the author's point of view and purpose in an informational text. First, write the title and topic of the selection. Then, in the left column, identify the author's point of view and purpose (or purposes) for writing. In the right column, provide details from the text that helped you determine the point of view and purpose.

Title of the Text:

Topic of the Text:

Author's Point of View:	Details from the Text:

Author's Purpose(s): ❏ to inform ❏ to persuade ❏ to entertain ❏ to reflect	Details from the Text:

C

For use with Informational Text 6

Name _____ Date _____ Assignment _____

Determining Point of View and Purpose

Complete the following organizer to determine the author's point of view and purpose in an informational text. First, write the title and topic of the selection. Then, in the left column, identify the author's point of view and purpose (or purposes) for writing. In the right column, provide details from the text that helped you determine the point of view and purpose.

Title of the Text:

Topic of the Text:

Author's Point of View:	Details from the Text:
Author's Purpose(s): ❑ to inform ❑ to persuade ❑ to entertain ❑ to reflect	**Details from the Text:**

For use with Informational Text 6

Name _____ Date _____ Assignment _____

Determining Point of View and Purpose

Complete the following organizer to determine the author's point of view and purpose in an informational text. First, write the title and topic of the selection. Then, in the left column, identify the author's point of view and purpose (or purposes) for writing. In the right column, provide details from the text that helped you determine the point of view and purpose.

Title of the Text:

Topic of the Text:

Author's Point of View:	Details from the Text:
Author's Purpose(s): ❏ to inform ❏ to persuade ❏ to entertain ❏ to reflect	**Details from the Text:**

E

Name _____ Date _____ Assignment _____

Determining Point of View and Purpose

Complete the following organizer to determine the author's point of view and purpose in an informational text. First, write the title and topic of the selection. Then, in the left column, identify the author's point of view and purpose (or purposes) for writing. In the right column, provide details from the text that helped you determine the point of view and purpose.

Title of the Text:

Topic of the Text:

Author's Point of View:	Details from the Text:
Author's Purpose(s): ❏ to inform ❏ to persuade ❏ to entertain ❏ to reflect	Details from the Text:

F

Informational Text 7

> **7. Integrate information presented in different media or formats (e.g., visually, quantitatively) as well as in words to develop a coherent understanding of a topic or issue.**

Explanation

When investigating a topic or an issue, **integrate**, or bring together, information from several resources to help you to develop a broad and clear understanding. You can accomplish this by examining different forms of **media**. For example, print media, which includes newspapers, books, and magazines, usually contains pictures, maps, charts, graphs, drawings, or other graphic aids to help explain ideas. The Internet and other electronic forms of media provide information in a variety of **formats** including written text, interactive maps or timelines, and video.

Examples

- **Visual** elements provide information not available from text sources. For example, in a science book, a chapter on the age of rocks might include a diagram with different layers of rock labeled with their ages. In addition, images can create emotional responses. For example, if you are studying the rainforest, seeing images of deforestation make you feel sad or upset. Images and video can be very persuasive, so you must analyze what you see, keeping in mind that a visual's purpose may be to make you feel a certain way.

- **Quantitative** information is presented in a format that makes complex data easy to understand. Charts and graphs are two formats that present quantitative information. For example, suppose you were studying worldwide population growth. A graph showing the estimated size of the human population from 10,000 BCE to today would quickly and easily communicate the explosion in population that has occurred only very recently. To interpret this kind of information, ask yourself, what information does the chart or graph provide? What can I conclude from the information?

Academic Vocabulary

format the way in which something is presented or organized

integrate information to put information together to create a new understanding

media various means of mass communication, such as television, radio, magazines and the Internet

Apply the Standard

Use the worksheet that follows to help you apply the standard as you read informational texts. Several copies of the worksheet have been provided for you.

- Integrating Information

Name _____ Date _____ Assignment _____

Integrating Information

In the left column of the following organizer, record the different forms of media you explored while investigating a topic or an issue. Then, in the right column, list the important ideas or information you found in each form of media. Finally, answer the question at the bottom of the page.

Topic or Issue ....

Resource	Important Ideas or Information
1.	
2.	
3.	
4.	

How did integrating, or bringing together, information from different forms of media help your overall understanding of the topic or issue?

....

....

....

For use with Informational Text 7

Name _____ Date _____ Assignment _____

Integrating Information

In the left column of the following organizer, record the different forms of media you explored while investigating a topic or an issue. Then, in the right column, list the important ideas or information you found in each form of media. Finally, answer the question at the bottom of the page.

Topic or Issue ....

Resource	Important Ideas or Information
1.	
2.	
3.	
4.	

How did integrating, or bringing together, information from different forms of media help your overall understanding of the topic or issue?

....

....

....

For use with Informational Text 7

Name _____ Date _____ Assignment _____

Integrating Information

In the left column of the following organizer, record the different forms of media you explored while investigating a topic or an issue. Then, in the right column, list the important ideas or information you found in each form of media. Finally, answer the question at the bottom of the page.

Topic or Issue ....

Resource	Important Ideas or Information
1.	
2.	
3.	
4.	

How did integrating, or bringing together, information from different forms of media help your overall understanding of the topic or issue?

....

....

....

For use with Informational Text 7

Name _____ Date _____ Assignment _____

Integrating Information

In the left column of the following organizer, record the different forms of media you explored while investigating a topic or an issue. Then, in the right column, list the important ideas or information you found in each form of media. Finally, answer the question at the bottom of the page.

Topic or Issue ....

Resource	Important Ideas or Information
1.	
2.	
3.	
4.	

How did integrating, or bringing together, information from different forms of media help your overall understanding of the topic or issue?

....

....

....

For use with Informational Text 7

Name _____ Date _____ Assignment _____

Integrating Information

In the left column of the following organizer, record the different forms of media you explored while investigating a topic or an issue. Then, in the right column, list the important ideas or information you found in each form of media. Finally, answer the question at the bottom of the page.

Topic or Issue ....

Resource	Important Ideas or Information
1.	
2.	
3.	
4.	

How did integrating, or bringing together, information from different forms of media help your overall understanding of the topic or issue?

....

....

....

Name _____ Date _____ Assignment _____

Integrating Information

In the left column of the following organizer, record the different forms of media you explored while investigating a topic or an issue. Then, in the right column, list the important ideas or information you found in each form of media. Finally, answer the question at the bottom of the page.

Topic or Issue ....

Resource	Important Ideas or Information
1.	
2.	
3.	
4.	

How did integrating, or bringing together, information from different forms of media help your overall understanding of the topic or issue?

....

....

....

For use with Informational Text 7

Informational Text 8

> 8. **Trace and evaluate the argument and specific claims in a text, distinguishing claims that are supported by reasons and evidence from claims that are not.**

Explanation

An author's **argument** or writing that expresses his or her position on an issue, consists of a **claim**—a statement about what the author believes to be true. The author supports a claim by giving **reasons** why the claim must be true. The author also supplies **evidence,** which is information that supports the reasons.

Evidence comes in the form of facts, examples, or statistics. When you read a persuasive argument, you should evaluate the author's conclusions, or claims. You should decide whether the evidence really supports the claim that the author made. To evaluate the evidence, ask some questions about it: Is the evidence based on real information, such as facts, statistics, and examples? Does the author identify the sources of the evidence? Can the evidence be verified? Does the evidence logically support the author's conclusions?

Examples

- An author writes an essay about the importance of saving money on a regular basis. He gives statistics that show how much money a person would have by the ages of twenty, thirty, fourty, and fifty after saving regularly starting at age fifteen. The author explains that he used the interest rate of 3 percent to figure out how much the savings will earn, even though the current rate is well under that amount, because the rate will rise over time. This writer's conclusions are well supported by reasons and evidence.

- A scientist writes a book to convince readers that the space program has valuable results for fields other than space exploration. She lists many inventions that had their roots in projects carried out for the space program. For each program, she gives the name of the program, the date, and the purpose of each scientific breakthrough that occurred as a result. She further names the scientists in charge and gives their job titles in the space program. This author's facts are well verified.

Academic Vocabulary

argument writing that expresses a position on an issue and supports it with evidence

claim the statement of an argument

evidence information that supports an author's reasons

Apply the Standard

Use the worksheet that follows to help you apply the standard as you read informational text selections. Several copies of the worksheet have been provided for you.

- Evaluate an Argument

Name _____ Date _____ Assignment _____

Evaluate an Argument

Use the organizer to evaluate an argument.

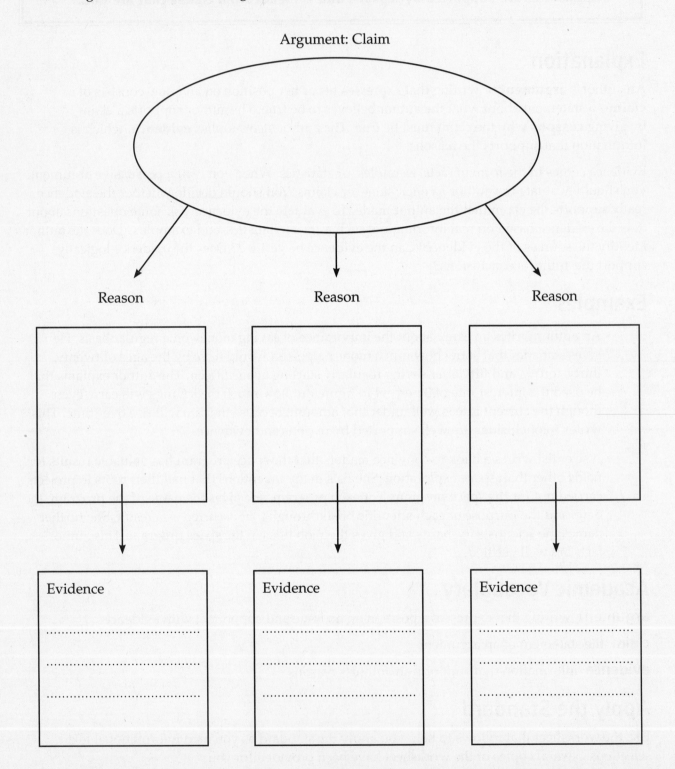

Argument: Claim

Reason

Reason

Reason

Evidence

Evidence

Evidence

A

Name _____   Date _____   Assignment _____

Evaluate an Argument

Use the organizer to evaluate an argument.

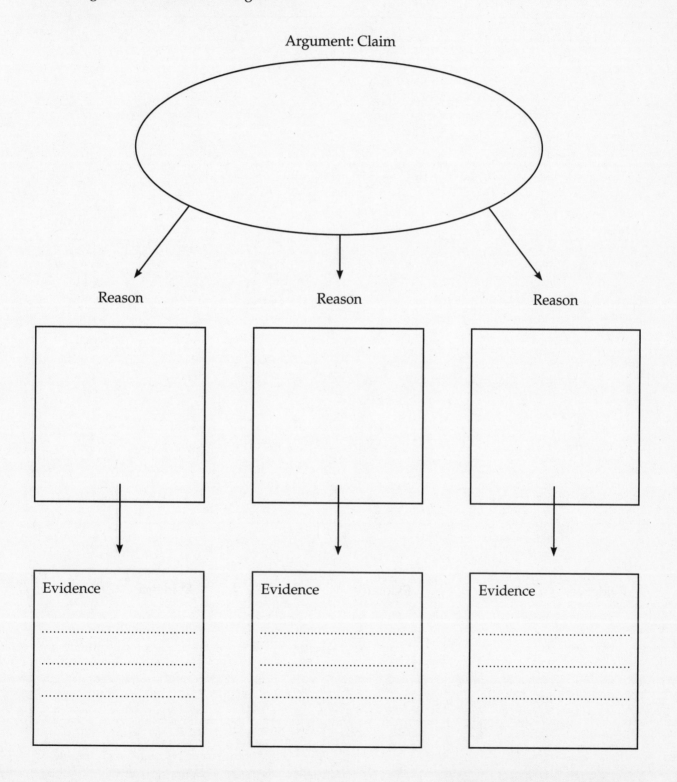

Argument: Claim

Reason   Reason   Reason

Evidence   Evidence   Evidence

....

....

....

B

Name _____ Date _____ Assignment _____

Evaluate an Argument

Use the organizer to evaluate an argument.

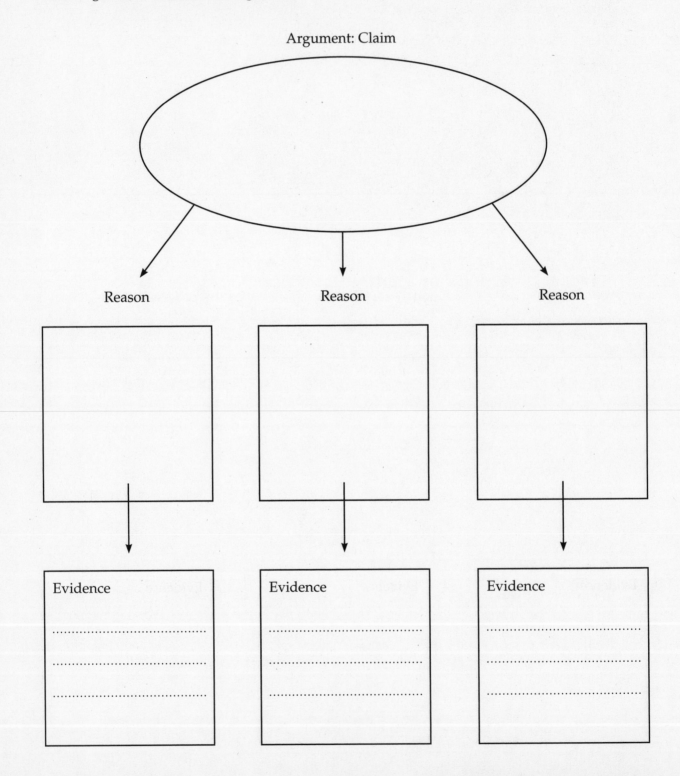

Argument: Claim

Reason

Reason

Reason

Evidence

....

....

....

Evidence

....

....

....

Evidence

....

....

....

C

Name _____ Date _____ Assignment _____

Evaluate an Argument

Use the organizer to evaluate an argument.

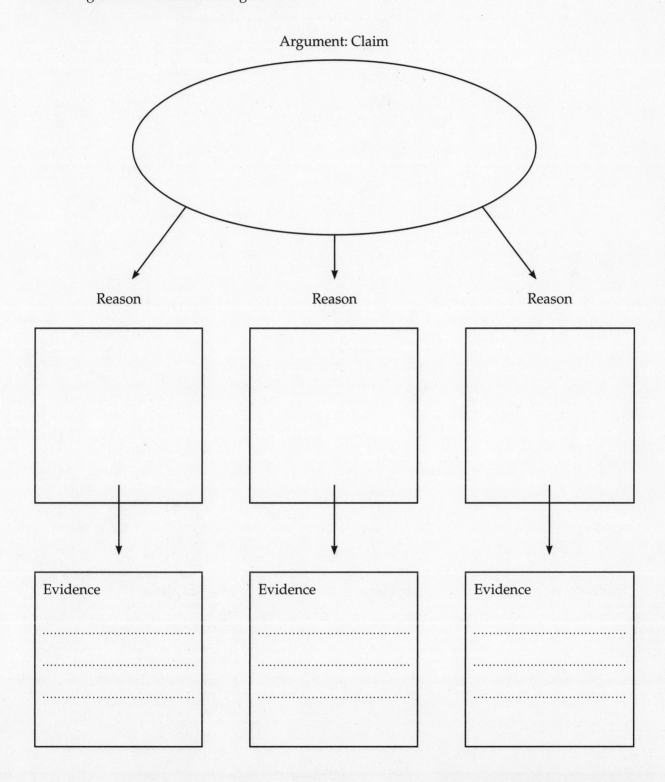

Argument: Claim

Reason

Reason

Reason

Evidence

....

....

....

Evidence

....

....

....

Evidence

....

....

....

For use with Informational Text 8

Name _____ Date _____ Assignment _____

Evaluate an Argument

Use the organizer to evaluate an argument.

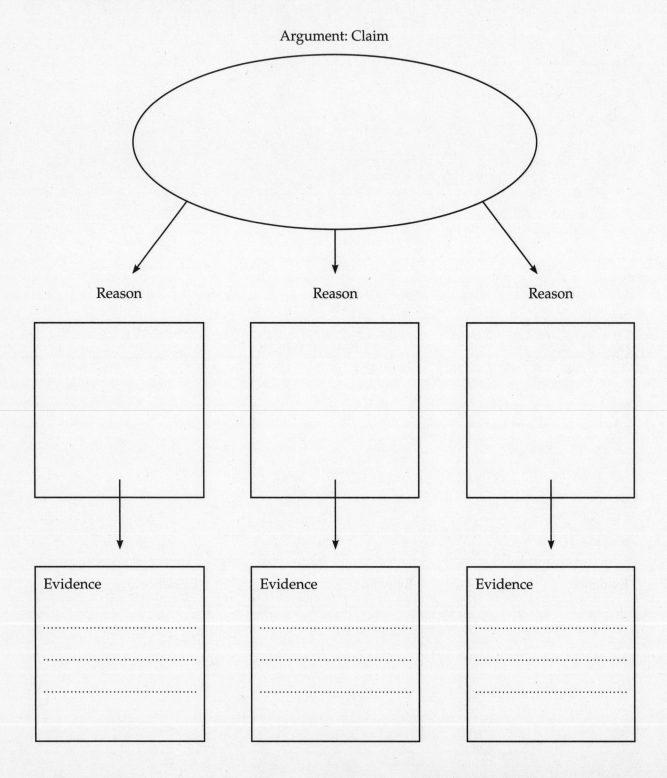

Argument: Claim

Reason

Reason

Reason

Evidence

Evidence

Evidence

E

156

Name _____ Date _____ Assignment _____

Evaluate an Argument

Use the organizer to evaluate an argument.

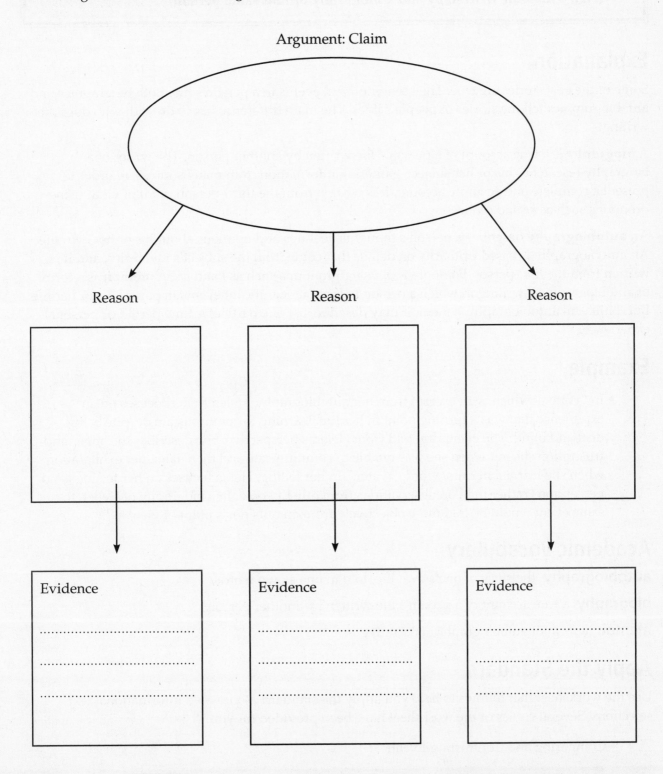

Argument: Claim

Reason   Reason   Reason

Evidence   Evidence   Evidence

F

Informational Text 9

9. **Compare and contrast one author's presentation of events with that of another (e.g., a memoir written by and a biography on the same person).**

Explanation

Some of the best stories are true. They center on real events in a person's life. Both biographies and autobiographies tell the stories of people's lives. The main difference has to do with who does the writing.

A **biography** is a true account of a person's life written by another person. The writer of a biography researches his or her subject, gathering information from many sources, in order to present a complete and accurate account. It is written from the third-person point of view, using pronouns such as *he* and *she*.

An **autobiography** describes a person's thoughts, feelings and opinions about his or her own life. An autobiography is based primarily on details that come from the subject's memories, and it is written from the first-person point of view, using pronouns such as *I* and *we*. A **memoir** is a form of autobiographical writing in which a person tells about significant events in part of his or her life. But, unlike an autobiography, a memoir may describe just one particular time period or personal experience.

Example

- In "Water," which is an excerpt from her autobiography, Helen Keller focuses on an experience that was a turning point in her life: learning to communicate despite being deaf and blind. The events are told from Helen's perspective. She describes the anger and frustration she felt when she was unable to communicate and then, later, her exhilaration when she learned her first word, "water." In her telling, Helen focuses on her feelings and perceptions rather than on observations from other people. In a biography of Keller, the same event would be told more objectively from an outsider's point of view.

Academic Vocabulary

autobiography the story of one's own life, told in one's own words

biography a true account of a person's life written by another person

memoir a form of autobiographical narrative

Apply the Standard

Use the worksheet that follows to help you apply the standard as you read informational text selections. Several copies of the worksheet have been provided for you.

- Comparing and Contrasting Events

Name _____ Date _____ Assignment _____

Comparing and Contrasting Events

Use the organizer to compare and contrast how key events are described in a biography and an autobiography. Consider point of view, objectivity, factual accuracy, and any other relevant points of comparison.

	How Events Are Presented in a Biography	**How Events Are Presented in an Autobiography**
Event		
Event		
Event		
Event		
Event		

A

Name _____ Date _____ Assignment _____

Comparing and Contrasting Events

Use the organizer to compare and contrast how key events are described in a biography and an autobiography. Consider point of view, objectivity, factual accuracy, and any other relevant points of comparison.

	How Events Are Presented in a Biography	**How Events Are Presented in an Autobiography**
Event		
Event		
Event		
Event		
Event		

Name _____ Date _____ Assignment _____

Comparing and Contrasting Events

Use the organizer to compare and contrast how key events are described in a biography and an autobiography. Consider point of view, objectivity, factual accuracy, and any other relevant points of comparison.

	How Events Are Presented in a Biography	**How Events Are Presented in an Autobiography**
Event		
Event		
Event		
Event		
Event		

D

Name _____ Date _____ Assignment _____

Comparing and Contrasting Events

Use the organizer to compare and contrast how key events are described in a biography and an autobiography. Consider point of view, objectivity, factual accuracy, and any other relevant points of comparison.

	How Events Are Presented in a Biography	How Events Are Presented in an Autobiography
Event		
Event		
Event		
Event		
Event		

E

Name _____ Date _____ Assignment _____

Comparing and Contrasting Events

Use the organizer to compare and contrast how key events are described in a biography and an autobiography. Consider point of view, objectivity, factual accuracy, and any other relevant points of comparison.

	How Events Are Presented in a Biography	How Events Are Presented in an Autobiography
Event		
Event		
Event		
Event		
Event		

F

Informational Text 10

> 10. **By the end of the year, read and comprehend literary nonfiction in the grades 6–8 text complexity band proficiently, with scaffolding as needed at the high end of the range.**

Explanation

Works of literary nonfiction vary widely in their **complexity.** The complexity of a work refers to how difficult it is to understand. Some essays and editorials have familiar subjects that are easy to understand. Others are written about unfamiliar subjects and present concepts that are difficult to understand. Some editorials use a simple style with conversational vocabulary and short sentences; others use advanced vocabulary featuring figurative language and long sentences. Similar situations exist for other types of literary nonfiction, such as journals, letters, biographies, and autobiographies.

As you read literary nonfiction, you will be expected to **comprehend,** or understand the meaning of, more complex texts than you have read before. To comprehend complex texts, use the reading strategies that are described here.

Examples

- To **monitor** your comprehension, stop and ask yourself questions about what you have just read. Do this whenever something happens that you might not have understood. For example, in Robert Fulghum's essay "The Lady and the Spider," you might stop and ask yourself what is going on. His neighbor has just walked out her front door and suddenly shouted very loudly. Clearly something unexpected has happened to her. Reread the paragraph until you understand what has happened. Then read ahead to see if you are right.
- When reading same essay, you can also use **context** to understand what is going on. Fulghum writes from the spider's point of view that a frenzied haystack is running around and making an unfamiliar sound. You can figure out what is going on by reading the context: the spider's web is torn loose, the haystack is "painted." These clues that are written from the spider's point of view tell you the haystack is the lady and the "paint" is her makeup she is wearing because she is on her way to work. The web is torn loose because she has run into it.
- **Visualize** what is going on from both points of view. The spider is watching its web being torn apart. The lady is frantic because there is a spider's web stuck onto her face. **Connect** these events to your own experiences. Have you ever run into a spider's web?

Academic Vocabulary

complexity the degree to which a work is difficult to understand
comprehend understand the meaning and importance of something

Apply the Standard

Use the worksheet that follows to help you apply the standard as you read. Several copies of the worksheet have been provided for you to use with different literature selections.

- Comprehending Complex Texts

Name _____ Date _____ Assignment _____

Comprehending Complex Texts

Explain what makes the literary nonfiction selection you are reading complex. Then explain how the strategy on the left in the chart can help you comprehend the selection.

What makes this selection complex?

....

....

Strategy	How the Strategy Helped Me Comprehend the Selection
monitoring comprehension	
using context	
visualizing	
connecting	

A

Name _____ Date _____ Assignment _____

Comprehending Complex Texts

Explain what makes the literary nonfiction selection you are reading complex. Then explain how the strategy on the left in the chart can help you comprehend the selection.

What makes this selection complex?

....

....

Strategy	How the Strategy Helped Me Comprehend the Selection
monitoring comprehension	
using context	
visualizing	
connecting	

B

Name _____ Date _____ Assignment _____

Comprehending Complex Texts

Explain what makes the literary nonfiction selection you are reading complex. Then explain how the strategy on the left in the chart can help you comprehend the selection.

What makes this selection complex?

....

....

Strategy	How the Strategy Helped Me Comprehend the Selection
monitoring comprehension	
using context	
visualizing	
connecting	

C

Name _____ Date _____ Assignment _____

Comprehending Complex Texts

Explain what makes the literary nonfiction selection you are reading complex. Then explain how the strategy on the left in the chart can help you comprehend the selection.

What makes this selection complex?

....

....

Strategy	How the Strategy Helped Me Comprehend the Selection
monitoring comprehension	
using context	
visualizing	
connecting	

Name _____ Date _____ Assignment _____

Comprehending Complex Texts

Explain what makes the literary nonfiction selection you are reading complex. Then explain how the strategy on the left in the chart can help you comprehend the selection.

What makes this selection complex?

....

....

Strategy	How the Strategy Helped Me Comprehend the Selection
monitoring comprehension	
using context	
visualizing	
connecting	

E

For use with Informational Text 10

Name _____ Date _____ Assignment _____

Comprehending Complex Texts

Explain what makes the literary nonfiction selection you are reading complex. Then explain how the strategy on the left in the chart can help you comprehend the selection.

What makes this selection complex?

....

....

Strategy	How the Strategy Helped Me Comprehend the Selection
monitoring comprehension	
using context	
visualizing	
connecting	

Writing Standards

Writing 1

> **1. Write arguments to support claims with clear reasons and relevant evidence.**

Writing Workshop: Argument

When you write an argument essay, you state a claim and then present reasons and evidence to support your claim. For example, an essay about bike helmets might state the claim that wearing a helmet should be the law for all bicycle riders, regardless of the rider's age. The details used to support that claim become the foundation of that argument. If the reasons make sense and the evidence is based on fact, then the argument will be sound. If the details are highly emotional or come from unreliable sources, the argument will be shaky at best.

Assignment

Write an argumentative essay about an issue that concerns people in your community or school. Include these elements:

✓ a claim, or clear opinion statement that presents your particular position on an issue

✓ reasons and evidence that support your position

✓ the use of reliable sources to give your argument credibility

✓ evidence to address readers' concerns and opposing positions

✓ clear and effective organization

✓ the use of transitions and conjunctions to clarify the relationship between ideas

✓ a consistent style and tone

✓ the use of language conventions, such as varied sentence patterns

*Additional Standards

Writing

1. Write arguments to support claims with clear reasons and relevant evidence.

1.a. Introduce claim(s) and organize the reasons and evidence clearly.

1.b. Support claim(s) with clear reasons and relevant evidence, using credible sources and demonstrating

an understanding of the topic or text.

1.c. Use words, phrases, and clauses to clarify the relationships among claim(s).

1.d. Establish and maintain a formal style.

1.e. Provide a concluding statement or section that follows from the argument presented.

4. Produce clear and coherent writing in which the development, organization, and style are appropriate to task, purpose, and audience.

6. Use technology, including the Internet, to produce and publish writing as well as to interact and collaborate with others.

Language

2. Demonstrate command of the conventions of standard English capitalization, punctuation, and spelling when writing.

3.a. Vary sentence patterns for meaning, reader/listener interest, and style.

3.b. Maintain consistency in style and tone.

Name _____ Date _____ Assignment _____

Prewriting/Planning Strategies

Choose a topic. Find a topic for your essay. Look through the newspaper or online to find stories about current issues. Read letters to the editor. Watch and listen to local television and radio news programs. Choose a topic that grabs your attention.

You can also meet with a group of classmates to discuss places and people that are important to you. Talk about the issues that affect these locations and people. Note the issues that prompt the most discussion. Choose one of these issues as a topic.

Select an issue that has at least two clear sides. For example, an essay on dropping out of school would not be a good topic, because no one is in favor of students dropping out of school. However, the need for more afterschool programs that encourage children to stay in school is a good topic. People may have good reasons to support or oppose it.

Narrow your topic. Make sure your topic is not too big for a brief essay. **Narrow** your topic by focusing on a specific part of the issue. Keep focusing until your topic is manageable.

Broad: Example: We can make our city safer.

↓

Narrower: Example: We can make our streets safer for people.

↓

Narrower: Example: We can make our sidewalks safer for pedestrians.

↓

Focused: Example: We can make our sidewalks safer for pedestrians by banning skateboarding on city sidewalks.

Name _____ Date _____ Assignment _____

Supporting a Claim

Consider all sides of an issue. Collect evidence from credible sources. Focus on the most current up-to-date information and try to find a minimum of two sources for each detail. Look ahead to questions and objections that your readers may have. Gather evidence to address questions and opposing points of view. Once you have completed your chart, review the evidence to make sure it is clear and relevant.

- If any idea you list is not **clear,** look for more facts and details to clarify and strengthen your ideas.

- If any evidence contradicts another piece of evidence, delete it, or put a question mark next to it until you can confirm which evidence is accurate.

- If any idea is not **relevant,** or directly related to your topic, delete it.

Reasons and Evidence That Support My Claim	Sources Used
Reasons and Evidence That Address Counterarguments	

Name _____ Date _____ Assignment _____

Drafting Strategies

Create a structure for your draft. Make an organizational plan for your essay that is both logical and persuasive.

- Use the graphic organizer below to build a convincing argument. Begin by writing a thesis statement that identifies the issue and the specific point about the issue that you are making.

- Review the reasons and evidence you have gathered to support your claim. Rank reasons in order of importance, starting with number 1 for least important. List reasons in this order in the organizer. Choose one counterargument to address.

Claim/ Thesis Statement:	
Supporting Reason #1 (least important):	**Evidence** **A.** **B.**
Supporting Reason #2:	**Evidence** **A.** **B.**
Supporting Reason #3 (most important):	**Evidence** **A.** **B.**
Counterargument:	**Evidence** **A.** **B.**

For use with Writing 1

Name _____ Date _____ Assignment _____

Developing and evaluating your claim. Consider the age of your audience and how much they are likely to know about your topic. Keep your task, purpose, and audience in mind as you write.

1. Introduce your claim in a thesis statement. State your position in clear, memorable terms. Use precise language that sets a serious, formal tone for your essay.

2. As you draft your claim, make your position clear. Be sure readers will recognize which side of an issue you support. Use powerful language to emphasize well-supported points.

3. Use your notes as a guide. Include transitions to make the relationship between your claim and supporting details clear and obvious.

4. Present counterarguments fairly and reasonably. Give factual evidence that shows why an opposing point of view should not be supported.

5. Conclude with a strong statement that summarizes your argument and gives readers something new to think about.

My Claim	Evaluating the Claim
	❏ Is the claim clearly stated?
	❏ Is there any doubt which side of the issue my argument supports?
	❏ Are the reasons logical and serious?
	❏ Is all the evidence relevant?
	❏ Does the argument consider the audience's knowledge?
Counterarguments	
	❏ Have I addressed a counterargument fairly and reasonably?
	❏ Have I used sufficient evidence to disprove the counterargument?

Style

Establish and maintain a formal style. A relaxed, informal style is acceptable for classroom discussions. A formal style is more appropriate for a written argument. A formal style tells your readers that you are serious about your topic. It says that you want readers to give your ideas serious thought.

Examples

Claim: Students should be allowed to have cell phones at school for emergency purposes only.

Informal: Parents will go nuts if they can't get a hold of their kids when something bad happens at home.

Formal: When there is an emergency at home, parents should feel confident that they can reach students directly and quickly.

Here are some guidelines for maintaining a formal style as you draft your essay:

- A formal style creates a distance between the writer and the reader.

- It is direct and objective and never overly emotional.

- It uses facts, reasons, and examples to support key ideas.

- It uses precise language and strong images.

- It uses standard English and avoids contractions and slang.

Clarify the relationships among ideas. Transitional words, phrases, and clauses can help you show the relationships among claims and reasons in your essay. As you draft, use transitions to link ideas.

- Cause and effect: *as a result, for this reason, therefore, so, then*

- Comparison and contrast: *on the one hand, in the same way, however, otherwise*

- Emphasizing: *in fact, for this reason, especially*

- Adding information: *for example, besides, in addition, also*

- Summarizing: *finally, in conclusion, to sum up, after all*

Varied sentence structure can add interest to your essay. Sentence structure can also help you clarify the relationships between ideas, as in these examples:

- A complex sentence can clarify the relationship between claims and reasons: *Students are more likely to develop better eating habits if they are given healthy food choices in the cafeteria.*

- A compound sentence can clarify the relationships between reasons and evidence: *Recently, Leverett Middle School began serving whole grain breads, fresh vegetables, and other low-fat, high-fiber foods at lunch, and students quickly began choosing these healthier options over less-nutritious foods.*

Name _____ Date _____ Assignment _____

Conclusion

Provide a strong conclusion. Your written argument should end with a strong conclusion that follows logically from reasons and evidence presented in the body of the essay. Use the following strategy to construct your conclusion.

- Begin with a summary statement of the claim: *Homework does serve a useful purpose for many students and should not be eliminated.*

- Then review the main points of the argument: *As I have shown, homework is a good way to check students' understanding of what has been taught in class. Teachers can use it to assess students' progress and determine which students need help with certain concepts. In addition, homework can be used to extend classroom instruction for students interested in learning more about a subject.*

- End by restating the claim in a memorable way. Consider referring to ideas presented earlier in the essay, such as opposing points of view: *As long as homework is never assigned as busy work or as a substitute for classroom instruction, homework offers students a greater chance at success in school.*

My Conclusion	Evaluating My Conclusion
	❑ Does it begin with a restatement of my claim?
	❑ Does it sum up the main points of my argument?
	❑ Does it end with a memorable statement that gives readers something new or more to think about?

Name _____ Date _____ Assignment _____

Revising Strategies

Put a checkmark beside each question as you revise.

	Questions to Ask as You Revise
Writing Task	❏ Have I written an essay that argues for my position on an issue? ❏ Does my topic have at least two sides? ❏ Does my essay have a clear and effective beginning, middle, and end?
Purpose	❏ Does my introduction contain a thesis statement that clearly states my claim or position? ❏ Do I give reasons and evidence to support my claim? ❏ Are the reasons clear and logical? ❏ Do I have enough facts, quotations, and examples and other evidence to support my claim? ❏ Do I use only relevant evidence to strengthen my argument? ❏ Does my conclusion follow logically from ideas presented in my argument?
Audience	❏ Do I use precise language and details that are appropriate for the age and knowledge level of my readers? ❏ Is my argument easy to follow and understand? ❏ Do I use transitions to clarify relationships between ideas? ❏ Do I address questions and concerns my readers might have about my topic? ❏ Does my argument appeal to reason and not just to emotion? ❏ Do I vary sentence structure to add interest to my ideas? ❏ Will my audience be persuaded to agree with my position?

Revising

Revise for varied sentence structure. You can add interest to your essay by varying the structure and length of sentences in your paragraphs.

Vary beginnings. One way to vary sentence structure is to use different beginnings.

- Begin with the subject: <u>Students</u> *will be more satisfied and have more energy if they eat high-protein, high-fiber food at lunch.*

- Begin with an adverb: <u>Additionally,</u> *bright green vegetables are visually appealing*

- Begin with a phrase: <u>In reality,</u> *no one wants to makes unhealthy choices.*

- Begin with a clause: <u>Because students enjoyed the new menu choices,</u> *they began to pass up the french fries and pizza.*

Balance short and long sentences. As you revise, check to see that you have used a variety of sentence lengths. A series of short, choppy sentences can make writing dull. A series of long, complicated sentences can make ideas difficult for readers to follow. A mix of long and short sentences is much more appealing and more likely to hold readers' interest. Notice the differences in these examples.

- **Short, choppy sentences:** *Children should wear bike helmets. Adults should wear bike helmets. This will lower the number of head injuries. Statistics prove it.*

- **Long, complicated sentences:** *In spite of the factual evidence that proves that most serious head injuries that happen during a bike accident could be prevented if the riders were wearing helmets, many adults continue to ride without helmets. Aside from the fact that they are endangering their own lives, such irresponsible actions also set a terrible example for younger children.*

- **Balance of short and long sentences:** *Everyone agrees that young children should wear bike helmets. Helmets can help prevent serious head injuries. Statistics prove it. These same statistics should motivate adults to wear helmets. Not only will adults be ensuring their own safety, but they will also be setting an excellent example for children.*

When you revise to combine short, choppy sentences into compound and complex sentences, use conjunctions, such as *and, but, or, so, although, since,* and *because* to link related ideas.

Revision Checklist

❏ Are there a variety of sentence patterns?

❏ Is there a balanced mix of sentence lengths?

❏ Are conjunctions used to combine related ideas in compound and complex sentences?

Editing and Proofreading

Review your draft to correct errors in capitalization, spelling, and punctuation.

Focus on Capitalization: Review your draft carefully to find and correct capitalization errors. If your argumentative essay names places, people, or official groups and organizations, be sure that you have capitalized the proper name correctly.

Incorrect capitalization	**Correct capitalization**
Di franco middle school	Di Franco Middle School

Focus on Spelling: An argumentative essay that includes spelling errors is distracting and annoying for readers. Distracted and annoyed readers are not going to give your argument serious thought. Check the spelling of each word. Look for words that you tend to misspell or are unsure about and make sure that they are correct. Pay particular attention to the spelling of irregular plurals. Check a dictionary if you are unsure of the spelling of an irregular plural. Irregular plurals are usually listed right after the pronunciation of the word. If you have typed your draft on a computer, use the spell-check feature to double-check for errors. Keep in mind that spell-checkers will not find words that are typed incorrectly but spell another word, for example, *form* instead of *from*. Proofread carefully, even after you run spell-check.

Focus on Punctuation: Commas Proofread your writing to find and correct punctuation errors. Specifically, look for places in your writing where you have used compound and complex sentences. Be sure you punctuate these sentences correctly.

Rule: Use a comma between two independent clauses that are joined by *and, but, or, nor,* and *yet* in a compound sentence: *People should not use cell phones in restaurants, and they should remember to turn off their ringers.*

Rule: Use a comma after an introductory clause in a complex sentence: *In cases of emergency, people should politely excuse themselves to use their cell phones.*

Revision Checklist

❑ Have you reviewed your essay for words, titles, or names that should be capitalized?

❑ Have you read each sentence and checked that no words are misspelled?

❑ Do you have compound or complex sentences that need commas to separate clauses?

Name _____ Date _____ Assignment _____

Publishing and Presenting

Consider one of the ways shown below to present your writing:

Deliver a speech. Use your argumentative essay as a basis for a speech that you give to classmates. Set aside some time before you present your speech to practice. Print out a copy and highlight details that you want to emphasize for persuasive effect. Rehearse with a peer, and pay particular attention to your pacing. Ask your listener where you should raise and lower your voice for the greatest effect.

Post your essay. Print out a final copy of your essay and post it on a community bulletin board. Or publish your essay electronically by uploading a copy to the class or school website. Create links in your file to other information about your topic.

Rubric for Self-Assessment

Find evidence in your writing to address each category. Then use the rating scale to grade your work.

Evaluating Your Argument	not very					very
Focus: How clearly is your position stated?	1	2	3	4	5	6
Organization: How clearly and logically have you organized ideas in your argument?	1	2	3	4	5	6
Support/Elaboration: How relevant and suited to your audience is your evidence?	1	2	3	4	5	6
Style: How well have you maintained a formal style throughout your argument?	1	2	3	4	5	6
Conventions: How free of errors in grammar, usage, spelling, and punctuation is your argument?	1	2	3	4	5	6

Writing 2

> **2. Write informative/explanatory texts to examine a topic and convey ideas, concepts, and information through the selection, organization, and analysis of relevant content.**

Writing Workshop: Comparison-and-Contrast Essay

When you develop a comparison-and-contrast essay, you show how two or more subjects are alike and how they are different. For example, a comparison-and-contrast essay might compare famous athletes, kinds of music, American cities, historical events, fictional characters, and so on. A comparison-and-contrast essay does not examine every single thing about each subject. Instead, it focuses on important features about the subjects that make the comparison interesting and sometimes surprising.

Assignment

Write a comparison-and-contrast essay that compares two subjects of interest to you. Include these elements:

- ✓ a topic, involving two subjects that are similar and different in notable ways
- ✓ a thesis, or purpose, stated in a strong opening paragraph
- ✓ an organizational pattern that highlights similarities and differences between the two subjects
- ✓ facts, descriptions, and examples that develop the similarities and differences
- ✓ a conclusion that follows from the comparison and contrast
- ✓ a formal style
- ✓ correct use of language conventions

*Additional Standards

Writing

2. Write informative/ explanatory texts to examine a topic and convey ideas, concepts, and information through the selection, organization and analysis of relevant content.

2.a. Introduce a topic; organize idea, concepts, and information, using strategies such as definition, classification, comparison/ contrast, and cause/ effect; include formatting (e.g., headings), graphics (e.g., charts, tables), and multimedia when useful to aiding comprehension.

2.b. Develop the topic with relevant facts, definitions, concrete details, quotations, or other information and examples.

2.c. Use appropriate transitions to clarify the relationships among ideas and concepts.

2.d. Use precise language and domain-specific vocabulary to inform about or explain the topic.

2.e. Establish and maintain a formal style.

2.f. Provide a concluding statement or section that

follows from the information or explanation presented.

4. Produce clear and coherent writing in which the development, organization, and style are appropriate to task, purpose, and audience.

6. Use technology, including the Internet, to produce and publish writing as well as to interact and collaborate with others.

Language

2. Demonstrate command of the conventions of standard English capitalization,

punctuation, and spelling when writing.

3.a. Vary sentence patterns for meaning, reader/listener interest, and style.

6. Acquire and use accurately grade-appropriate general academic and domain-specific words and phrases; gather vocabulary knowledge when considering a word or phrase important to comprehension or expression.

Name _____ Date _____ Assignment _____

Prewriting/Planning Strategies

Choose a topic. Make a short list of categories that interest you, such as movies, sports, food, travel, literature, music, science, or history. Choose the three categories that interest you most. Then use the chart below to list people, places, animals, objects, and other ideas associated with the categories you chose. When you have finished, review each list. Look for topic ideas that it suggests, such as two types of music you enjoy, two athletes you admire, or two places you have visited or would like to visit. Make sure you choose subjects that are similar in some specific ways.

Category 1:	Category 2:	Category 3:

Narrow your topic. Some topics are too broad to compare in a short essay. For example, you could write a book comparing and contrasting everything about Mexico and Spain. To make a broad topic more manageable, divide it into smaller subtopics, such as Mexican and Spanish food. Then focus your essay on one of these subtopics.

Broad Topic	Subtopic 1	Subtopic 2
Subject a:	Subject a:	Subject a:
Subject b:	Subject b:	Subject b:

Name _____ Date _____ Assignment _____

Prewriting/Planning Strategies

Gather details. Use the diagram below to gather facts, definitions, descriptions, quotations, and examples related to your two subjects. Use the middle section where the circles overlap to record details that show how the subjects are alike. Record details that show how each subject is different in the outside sections. Look for interesting points of comparison that will engage your audience and may also surprise them. Try to include an equal number of points for each subject so that your comparison-and-contrast essay will be balanced.

Subject 1. ....   **Subject 2.** ....

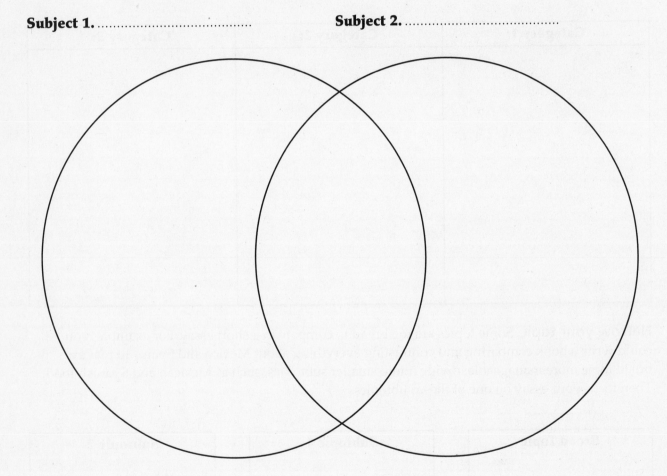

Name _____ Date _____ Assignment _____

Drafting Strategies

Choose an organizational pattern. Most comparison-and-contrast essays are organized in one of two ways.

- **Block Method:** Present all of your details about one subject first. Then, present all of your details about the second subject. This method works well when you are comparing more than two things, or when you are including many types of details.

- **Point-by-Point Method:** Discuss each feature of your subjects in turn. For example, if you are comparing two types of dinosaurs, first discuss the diet of each dinosaur. Then move on to their size, and then compare their mobility.

Use the following organizers to help you decide whether the block method or the point-by-point method is better for your essay.

Block Method   **Point-by-Point Method**

List all details about **Subject 1:**   Subject 1   Subject 2

List all details about **Subject 2:**

Name _____ Date _____ Assignment _____

Develop your comparison and contrast essay.

1. Start with a catchy introduction and strong thesis statement.

a) Draw your audience in with the first sentence. For example, if you're comparing two athletes, start with a surprising fact or quotation about one or both of them.

b) Include a strong thesis statement that identifies your subjects and makes a key point about both of them.

c) Hint at what your audience can expect to learn in the rest of the essay.

2. Use specific details. The more you can pinpoint the similarities and differences between your subjects, the more interesting and effective your essay will be. For example, instead of saying one basketball player is a great shooter and one plays great defense, provide statistics and percentages that illustrate those concepts.

3. Use transitions. Use transitional words and phrases to signal when you are discussing either a similarity or a difference. Transitions that show similarities include *similarly, also, both,* and *like.* Transitions that show differences include *in contrast, unlike, on the other hand, but,* and *however.*

4. Note formatting ideas. Jot down formatting ideas you might use to highlight important points in your essay. Include a variety of elements, such as headings or bold print for key terms, photographs, illustrations, charts, diagrams, and video and audio clips. Choose elements that help readers better understand your ideas.

My Comparison-Contrast		Formatting Notes
Subject 1:	Subject 2:	

Style

Establish a formal style. A formal style that shows respect for your readers is appropriate for a written essay. Here are some guidelines for establishing a formal style as you write your comparison-and-contrast essay.

- Express ideas clearly and logically, without relying on emotion or personal opinions.

- Use specific facts and examples to support key ideas.

- Use precise language.

- Use standard English and avoid contractions, dialect, and slang.

Examples:

Informal: You probably think rap fans and rock fans are way different, but you're so wrong.

Formal: Surprisingly, rap music fans and rock music fans have many things in common.

Use precise language and subject-specific vocabulary. Supporting ideas with precise language and domain-specific vocabulary gives your writing a knowledgeable voice. Precise language not only makes you sound like an authority on the subject, it also adds impact to your ideas.

Not Precise: Bill Russell played in a lot of All-Star games during his career.

Precise: During his career with the Boston Celtics, basketball legend Bill Russell played in 12 consecutive All-Star Games from 1958 to 1969.

Domain-specific terms are words and phrases that are specific to a subject area. When using subject-specific vocabulary, consider your readers. If you think that they may not recognize or understand a specific term, then provide a definition.

Audience of Students: The first poem is written in four-line stanzas called quatrains. *(Students may not know what quatrains are, so the writer includes the definition "four-line stanzas.")*

Audience of English Teachers: The first poem is written in quatrains. *(The writer knows that English teachers are familiar with poetry terms.)*

Name _____ Date _____ Assignment _____

Conclusion

Provide a strong conclusion. Your comparison-and-contrast essay should end with a strong conclusion that flows logically from the ideas you explained in the essay. Here is one strategy for writing a strong conclusion.

- Begin with a summary statement that reminds readers of your thesis: *Charleston, South Carolina, and Boston, Massachusetts, are two historic cities that attract thousands of tourists every year.*

- Briefly review the main points of the comparison: *Restored waterfront areas, classic architecture, narrow streets, and colorful neighborhoods add to the small-town charm of both cities.*

- Add a new piece of information that your audience will find interesting: *Although Charleston streets are lined with palm trees and Boston streets are often covered in snow, tourists to these cities find themselves steeped in the history of our country everywhere they turn.*

Planning My Conclusion	**My Conclusion**
Main idea: .... Summary of main points: .... New piece of information:	

Name _____ Date _____ Assignment _____

Revising

Evaluate organization and balance. Your essay should have one organizational pattern from start to finish and should give equal space to each of your subjects. To check the balance of your essay, review it point by point.

You can use different colored markers to underline or highlight details for each subject.

- If there is too much of one color, revise to add more details about the other subject.

- If the colors first appear in large blocks, and then the colors alternate, you may have started your essay with block organization and then switched to a point-by-point pattern. Revise to use one organizational pattern throughout the essay.

Use the chart to evaluate organization and balance.

Subject 1: ....

Subject 2: ....

Organizational Pattern: ....

	Subject 1	Subject 2
Point 1:		
Point 2:		
Point 3:		

Name _____ Date _____ Assignment _____

Revising Strategies

Put a checkmark beside each question as you revise

	Questions to Ask as You Revise
Writing Task	❏ Have I written an essay that compares and contrasts two subjects? ❏ Do I use specific details to show how the two subjects are similar? ❏ Do I use specific details to show how the two subjects are different?
Purpose	❏ Does my introduction contain a thesis statement that identifies my two subjects and focuses on a key point between them? ❏ Do I develop the comparison with relevant facts, definitions, concrete details, quotations, examples, or other information? ❏ Does all the information support or develop my thesis statement? ❏ Is my essay balanced, with an equal number of details for each subject? ❏ Do I use one pattern of organization throughout the essay? ❏ Does my conclusion follow logically from ideas presented in my essay?
Audience	❏ Do I use precise language and subject-specific terms that are appropriate for my audience? ❏ Is my comparison easy to follow and understand? ❏ Do I vary sentence lengths? ❏ Do I use transitions to signal similarities and differences? ❏ Is there anywhere that I can add a surprising comparison to heighten interest? ❏ Is there anywhere that I can add formatting to make my ideas clearer?

Revising

Revise choppy sentences. Short sentences are often used to emphasize an idea or quicken the pace of a piece of writing. However, too many short sentences in a row can make your writing sound choppy. You can combine choppy sentences by using **compound complements.**

Understanding Complements

Complements are words that are needed to complete the meaning of a sentence. Complements depend on the type of verb in the sentence. **Action verbs** take direct and indirect objects. **Linking verbs** take predicate adjectives and predicate nouns.

Combining Sentences Using Complements

This chart shows how compound complements can eliminate choppy sentences.

Complement	Choppy Sentences	Compound Complements
predicate adjective	Tennis is fast-paced. It is fun.	Tennis is **fast-paced and fun.**
predicate noun	One great sport is tennis. Another is badminton.	Two great sports are **tennis and badminton.**
direct object	Playing tennis well requires equipment. It requires practice.	Playing tennis well requires **equipment and practice.**
indirect object	Tennis gives me great exercise. Tennis gives my friends exercise.	Tennis gives **my friends and me** exercise.

Fixing Choppy Sentences

Reread the draft of your essay aloud. Listen for pairs of choppy sentences that compare or contrast your subjects. Look at the complements that follow each verb. Then combine the sentences with compound complements when it makes sense to do so. Use the rules and examples above to guide your revisions.

Revision Checklist

❏ Are there short, choppy sentences that can be combined?

❏ Can I combine these sentences by using compound complements?

Editing and Proofreading

Review your draft to correct errors in capitalization, spelling, and punctuation.

Focus on Capitalization: Review your draft carefully to find and correct capitalization errors. If your comparison-and-contrast essay names places or people, check that you have capitalized each proper name correctly.

Incorrect capitalization	**Correct capitalization**
Wrigley field	Wrigley Field

Focus on Spelling: After working hard on your essay, do not let careless spelling mistakes spoil your work. Check the spelling of each word. Look for words that you tend to misspell and make sure that they are correct. If you have typed your draft on a computer, use the spell-check feature to double-check for errors. Keep in mind that spell-checkers will not find words that are typed incorrectly but spell a different word, such as *hour* instead of *our*. Proofread carefully even after you run spell-check.

Pay special attention to comparative adjectives, which often appear in comparison-and-contrast essays. For example, when adding *-er or -est* to one-syllable words that end in a consonant, double the final consonant: *big, bigger, biggest*. For adjectives that end in *y*, you usually have to change the *y* to *i* before adding *-er* or *–est: happy, happier, happiest*.

Check your essay for double comparisons. Never use *-er* or *-est* and *more* or *most* in the same sentence.

    Incorrect: The Great Dane was the *most biggest* dog in the show.

    Correct: The Great Dane was the *biggest* dog in the show.

Focus on Punctuation: Quotations Proofread your writing to make sure every sentence begins with a capital letter and ends with a punctuation mark. If you have used quotations, check that you have placed quotation marks around someone's exact words.

Revision Checklist

❏ Have you reviewed your essay for words, including proper names, that should be capitalized?

❏ Have you read each sentence and checked that all of the words are spelled correctly?

❏ Have you checked for double comparisons?

❏ Do all your sentences have the correct end punctuation?

Name _____ Date _____ Assignment _____

Publishing and Presenting

Consider one of the following ways to present your writing:

Make a recording. Practice reading your essay aloud a few times. Read slowly and clearly, emphasizing the strongest points of comparison. Ask a partner to listen and give you advice on how to improve your presentation. Then record your reading and share it with a group of classmates.

Share with your family. If you have compared two subjects of interest to your family—two birthdays, two holiday traditions, two vacations—read your essay at a family gathering. Invite other members of the family to add details to your comparison that you may have forgotten or did not know. Later, you can add these details.

Rubric for Self-Assessment

Find evidence in your writing to address each category. Then use the rating scale to grade your work. Circle the score that best applies for each category.

Evaluating Your Argument	not very					very
Focus: How clearly have you stated how two or more subjects are alike and different?	1	2	3	4	5	6
Organization: How effectively are points of comparison organized?	1	2	3	4	5	6
Support/Elaboration: How well do you use facts, descriptions, and examples to describe similarities and differences?	1	2	3	4	5	6
Style: How precise is your language and how well have you maintained a formal style?	1	2	3	4	5	6
Conventions: How free of errors in grammar, usage, spelling, and punctuation is your essay?	1	2	3	4	5	6

Writing 3

> **3. Write narratives to develop real or imagined experiences or events using effective technique, relevant descriptive details, and well-structured event sequences.**

Writing Workshop

When you write a short story, you use your imagination, your personal experiences, and your knowledge of the real world to bring to life made-up characters, settings, and events. A short story develops around a conflict that the main character or characters face. At the end of the story, readers discover how the conflict is settled and how the characters feel about it. The purpose of a short story is to entertain, but short stories often also teach a lesson about life that readers can identify with.

Assignment

Write a short story about a person who faces a difficult challenge or decision. Include these elements:

✓ one or more well-developed characters

✓ an interesting conflict, or problem

✓ a plot that moves in a natural sequence of events toward a satisfactory conclusion

✓ a clear and accurate point of view, or perspective

✓ concrete and sensory language

✓ narrative techniques, including dialogue and descriptive details

✓ effective use of transitions

✓ correct use of language conventions, especially the use of consistent verb tenses

*Additional Standards

Writing
3. Write narratives to develop real or imagined experiences or events using effective technique, relevant descriptive details, and well-structured event sequences.

3.a. Engage and orient the reader by establishing a context and introducing a narrator and/or characters; organize an event sequence that unfolds naturally and logically.

3.b. Use narrative techniques, such as dialogue, pacing, and description, to develop experiences, events, and/or characters.

3.c. Use a variety of transition words, phrases, and clauses to convey sequence and signal shifts from one time frame or setting to another.

3.d. Use precise words and phrases, relevant

descriptive details, and sensory language to convey experiences and events.

3.e. Provide a conclusion that follows from the narrated experiences or events.

6. Use technology, including the Internet, to produce and publish writing as well as to interact and collaborate with others; demonstrate sufficient command of key

boarding skills to type a minimum of three pages in a single sitting.

Language
2. Demonstrate command of the conventions of standard English capitalization, punctuation, and spelling when writing.

3.a. Vary sentence patterns for meaning, reader/listener interest, and style.

Name _____ Date _____ Assignment _____

Prewriting/Planning Strategies

Choose a topic. Freewrite for five minutes. Start with an image of a person in a boat in the middle of the sea; a girl standing on a corner waiting for a bus; a young boy carrying a large, mysterious box. Or start with a feeling, such as curiosity, fear, joy, excitement, or disappointment. As you freewrite, focus on the flow of ideas rather than on spelling or grammar. When five minutes have passed, stop writing and review your ideas. Circle the most interesting details. Think about how you might turn these details into a story.

Your own life experiences can also provide you with ideas for a short story. To recall these experiences, flip through family photo albums, read entries in your personal journal, and talk to family members. Jot down experiences as you recall them. Choose one as the basis for your story.

Explore the conflict. The basic elements of a short story are characters, setting, and plot. The plot consists of the main conflict, or struggle, and the events that show how the conflict is solved. Once you have a chosen an idea for a story, take some time to explore and develop the conflict. Keep in mind that a conflict can be a difficult challenge the character must face, a decision the character must make, or a goal the character wants to achieve. Answer the questions in the chart.

1. What does my character want or have to do?	
2. Who or what is getting in the way?	
3. What will the character do to overcome the person or thing that is getting in the way?	

Name _____ Date _____ Assignment _____

Understand your main character. Get to know your main character before you write. Then you will know what he or she is likely to do and say in certain situations. Use the web to explore your character's physical appearance, likes, dislikes, traits, special interests, and goals. Feel free to add additional categories as you develop your character.

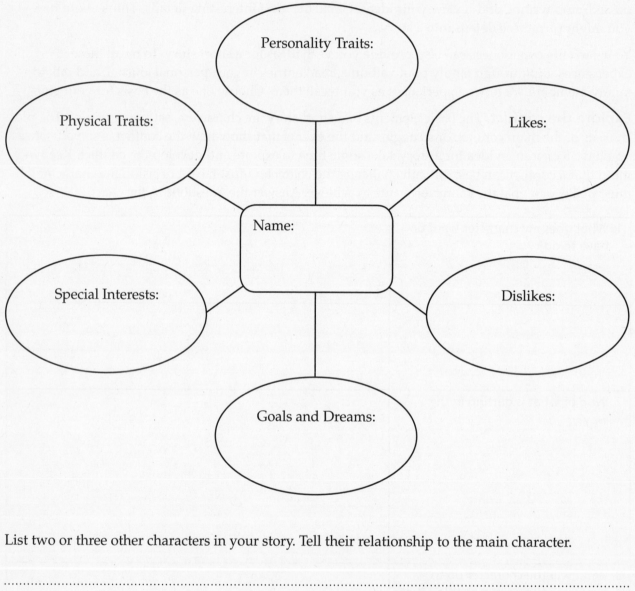

List two or three other characters in your story. Tell their relationship to the main character.

....

....

....

Name _____ Date _____ Assignment _____

Drafting Strategies

Identify Setting: In some stories, the setting simply provides a background for the story action. Other times, the setting adds to the conflict. For example, if the conflict involves a character struggling to find her way home through a forest, then the forest becomes an important part of the conflict. Use the chart to establish a setting for your story.

Where and when does the story take place?	What details help describe the setting?	What does the setting mean to the conflict?

Develop a plot outline. Use the plot diagram below to organize events in your short story. Plot usually follows this pattern:

- **Exposition** introduces the characters, setting, and conflict.

- The **rising action** includes two or three important events that show how the character tries to solve the conflict. These events lead to the climax.

- The **climax** is the most exciting or most suspenseful part of the story. It is where the main character finally deals with the conflict.

- During **falling action,** events and emotions wind down and lead to the final outcome.

- In the **resolution,** the conflict is resolved and the story comes to a conclusion.

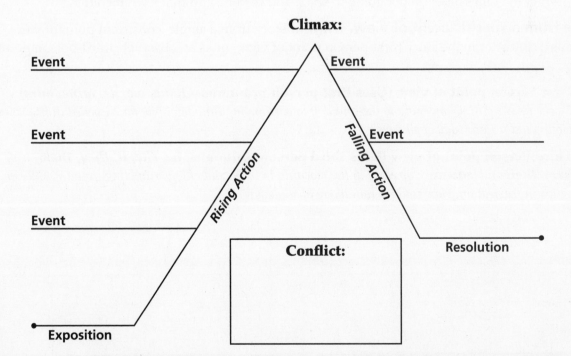

Narrative Techniques

Good writers show readers what is happening in a story instead of simply telling them. As you draft your story, make your characters, setting, and events come to life with precise language, vivid sensory details, and lively dialogue.

Use precise language and sensory details. An effective narrative uses precise words and phrases and vivid sensory details to engage readers and help them visualize or "see" what is happening. **Sensory details** describe how things look, sound, feel, taste, and smell.

> **Vague:** Jake was unhappy when the teacher returned his test. (*How did Jake show that he was unhappy? Who is Jake's teacher? What kind of test was it?*)

> **Precise:** Jake put his head over his eyes and groaned when Mr. Lee dropped the graded Math test on Jake's desk. (*Instead of telling readers that Jake was unhappy, the writer shows what Jake does so readers can see Jake's misery. The writer also uses precise details—Mr. Lee, Math test, and desk—to describe the scene.*)

> **Dull:** The sky looked stormy.

> **Vivid:** The sky boiled with black clouds and loud, rumbling thunder. (*The writer sensory details—boiled, black, loud, rumbling—to help readers see and hear the setting.*)

Use dialogue. The way a person speaks often reflects his or her background, education, and personality. Use lively, natural-sounding dialogue to give your characters their own voice. Keep in mind that realistic characters do not usually speak formally to each other. They often use contractions, slang, and may interrupt each other, as in the examples below. When writing dialogue, try to vary speaker tags; instead of using *said* every time, use more precise words such as *whispered, muttered, grumbled*, and so on.

> "I'm so sorry," Mark gasped, running up to Lila. "First the bus was late and then …"

> "Forget it," Lila said. "I'm not going to spaz. You're here, and that's what counts."

Write from a specific point of view. Tell your story from a single, consistent point of view, either as a character in the story (first-person point of view) or as an observer (third-person point of view.)

> **First Person point of view (Uses first person pronouns—*I, me, we, us, mine, ours*):**
> *I woke up early in the morning to the sound of low, rumbling thunder. "No, no," I yelled in frustration. How could it rain today of all days?*

> **Third Person point of view (Uses third person pronouns, *he, she, it, they, them, his, hers, theirs*):** *Harry woke up early in the morning to the sound of low, rumbling thunder. "No, no," he yelled in frustration. How could it rain today of all days?*

Name _____ Date _____ Assignment _____

Organize your narrative. Now that you have a good idea of who your characters are, what your setting is, and how your plot unfolds, use the graphic organizer to organize your narrative. As you write, use transitional words, phrases, and clauses to show a logical sequence of events and to signal shifts from one time frame or setting to another.

- **Transitional words:** *first, next, then, meanwhile, before, during, now, yesterday, finally*

- **Transitional phrases:** *at the same time, last week, a month ago, some years back*

- **Transitional clauses:** *Before this event took place, While he was sleeping, When I was a child, After she left, As I walked into another room*

.... **(Title)**	1. Give your story a title. It should convey the real meaning of your story and capture your readers' interest. 2. Introduce your main characters, the setting, and the conflict. 3. Describe what happens up to and including the climax of the story. Remember to • establish and maintain a consistent point of view. • use vivid, precise language, sensory details, and dialogue. • use transitions to show sequence.

Name _____ Date _____ Assignment _____

Conclusion

Provide a strong, satisfactory conclusion. Readers want a satisfactory conclusion to a story. They want to know what the main characters do and feel after they deal with the conflict. They do not want to be left wondering about any details introduced into the plot. These tips can help you write a strong conclusion that satisfies your readers.

- End with emphasis, not abruptly or vaguely by trailing off. The last event you narrate or scene you describe should help to summarize the narrative by clearly showing the results of what has happened. For example, if through the events in the story, the main character has changed in some significant way, then the last scene should show this change. If the character has learned a specific lesson, then the last scene should show how the character applies or plans to apply this lesson to his or her life in the future.

- Tie up loose ends. Unless you are planning to write a sequel to your story, you should not leave readers wondering what happened to an important character or whether solving the conflict made any difference to the character's life. Be careful not to cram unnecessary or unrelated details into the resolution. The resolution should tell the final outcome of the story and flow naturally from the events leading up to it.

My Conclusion	Evaluating My Conclusion
	❑ Does my conclusion show what happens to the main character after the conflict is resolved? ❑ Does it flow logically from story events? ❑ Does it wrap up all the loose ends in the story?

Name _____ Date _____ Assignment _____

Revising Strategies

Evaluate your story

Use the organizer to explain how you plan to revise and edit your story to make it better. If you wish you can give a partner a copy of your draft and this graphic organizer and have your partner suggest ways to improve your story.

Focus Questions		How to Revise
Does my title capture the essence of my story and my readers' interest?	Yes .... No	
Do I introduce characters, setting, and conflict early in the story?	Yes .... No	
Do I use precise language, sensory details, and dialogue to help readers see the setting, characters, and events?	Yes .... No	
Do I use natural-sounding dialogue that makes my characters believable?	Yes .... No	
Do all the events show how the main character deals with the conflict?	Yes .... No	
Do I use transitions to make the sequence of events clear and to show shifts in time and place?	Yes .... No	
Does the ending leave readers with any unanswered questions?	Yes .... No	
Do I maintain either a first-person point of view or a third-person point of view throughout?	Yes .... No	
Do I use a variety of words and sentence lengths?	Yes .... No	

Revising

Revise to maintain verb tense. Most stories are told in the past tense. A **verb tense** tells the time—past, present, or future—of an action or a state of being. Using different verb tenses in a story can help explain the sequence and shifts in time, but it can also lead to errors.

Present tense indicates an action or a condition in the present. It may also indicate an action or a condition that occurs regularly.

> Ian *is helping* his uncle build a deck. Carla *teaches* swimming.

Past tense tells that an action took place in the past.

> The Lanfords *traveled* to Turkey last March.

Future Tense tells that an action will take place in the future.

> I *will rearrange* my bedroom furniture this weekend.

Indentifying Mistakes in Verb Tense

Jumping from one verb tense to another can confuse readers. Look at these examples.

Incorrect use of verb tenses: As Carlos *waited* outside the gym, he *sees* his friend Raul. *(The verb* waited *is past tense, but the verb* sees *is present tense.)*

Correct use of verb tenses: As Carlos *waited* outside the gym, he *saw* his friend Raul. *(Both verbs are in past tense.)*

Correct use of different tenses to show sequence of events: Amy *finished* her report early so she *will attend* the concert. *(The verb* finished *is past tense, and the verb* will attend *is future tense.)*

Fixing Mistakes in Verb Tense

Follow these steps to fix errors in verb tense.

> 1. **Review your story, noting shifts in verb tenses within a sentence or paragraph.**
>
> 2. **Make sure that you have used changes in verb tenses for a good reason.** You may have chosen to show a relationship between events or to show the order of events.
>
> 3. **Rewrite sentences that contain incorrect shifts in tenses.**

Editing and Proofreading

Review your draft to correct errors in capitalization, spelling, and punctuation.

Focus on Capitalization: Review your draft carefully to find and correct capitalization errors. Make sure you have capitalized the title of your story correctly. Remember that the first and last word of a title are always capitalized. Articles (*a, an, the*) and short prepositions (*in, on, of*) are not capitalized.

Incorrect capitalization:	A Walk through A Dark Tunnel
Correct capitalization	A Walk Through a Dark Tunnel

Focus on Spelling: Check the spelling of each word in your story. Pay particular attention to the spelling of homophones. **Homophones** are words that sound the same but have different spellings and meanings. A spell checker will not find an error if a word is spelled correctly but used incorrectly; therefore, proofread carefully. Here are examples of easily confused words: *our/are, than/then, know/no, lose/loose, accept/except, it's/its*. Check a dictionary if you are unsure of the spelling of any word in your story.

Focus on Punctuation: Proofread your writing to find and correct punctuation errors. Specifically, make sure you have punctuated dialogue correctly. Follow these rules.

Rule: Use a comma to separate a character's exact words from the other parts of the sentence.

Rule: Use quotation marks to enclose the speaker's exact words. Place commas inside the quotation marks.

Rule: Always place a period inside quotation marks. Place a question mark or an exclamation point inside the quotation marks if the dialogue is a question or exclamation.

Rule: Place question marks and exclamation points outside the quotation marks when they punctuate the entire sentence.

Examples:

"My mom will drive us to practice," Mike said, "and then pick us up later."

Janet laughed and said, "That is the most outrageous idea I have ever heard!"

Do you wonder what might have happened to them if Ed had said, "I trust you."?

Revision Checklist

❏ Have you reviewed your story to make sure your title, names, and other proper nouns are capitalized?

❏ Have you read each sentence and checked that all of the words are spelled correctly, especially homophones?

❏ Have you punctuated dialogue correctly?

Name _____ Date _____ Assignment _____

Publishing and Presenting

Consider one of the following ways to present your writing:

Submit your story. Submit your story to your school's literary magazine, a national magazine, or an e-zine, or enter a contest that publishes student writing. Many publishers have writer's guidelines on their Web sites. Print out the guidelines and follow them. If you cannot find guidelines, take the time to make your manuscript look professional by using plain white paper and double spacing, and be sure to put your name, story title, and page number on each page. Include a cover sheet with your name, address, telephone number, e-mail address, word count of your story, a two-or three-sentence summary of the story's plot, and a brief explanation of why you think your story should be published.

Give a reading. Get together with a group of classmates and present a literary reading for an audience at your school. To enhance your reading, find and play soft background music appropriate for the content of the story.

Rubric for Self-Assessment

Find evidence in your writing to address each category. Then use the rating scale to grade your work.

Evaluating Your Short Story	not very				very	
Focus: How well drawn are the characters?	1	2	3	4	5	6
Organization: How clearly organized is the story's plot?	1	2	3	4	5	6
Support/Elaboration: How well do the details and language establish the setting and describe the characters?	1	2	3	4	5	6
Style: How consistently have you used point of view?	1	2	3	4	5	6
Conventions: How correct is your grammar, especially your use of verb tenses?	1	2	3	4	5	6

Writing 4

> **4. Produce clear and coherent writing in which the development, organization, and style are appropriate to task, purpose, and audience.**

Explanation

A writer's main goal is to produce writing that is clear and coherent. Readers quickly lose interest in writing that is vague, illogical, or difficult to follow. To accomplish this goal, consider your task, purpose, and audience.

- Your **task** is the specific reason you are writing. For example, your task may be to write a comparison-contrast essay or a descriptive paragraph.

- Your **purpose** is why you are writing or the effect you want your writing to have. For example, your purpose may be to explain the similarities and differences between lions, tigers, and other large cats; or it may be to create a feeling of excitement through a vivid description of a sporting event.

- Your **audience** is the people for whom you are writing. Often you will write for your teachers and classmates. You may also write for younger students, friends and family, or a wider reading audience, such as your entire school community.

Your specific task, purpose, and audience will affect the choices you make as you write. For example, if you are writing a report for your teacher, you will likely organize it by writing an introduction, several body paragraphs, and a conclusion. You will develop your topic fully and will write in a formal style that is straightforward. If your task is to write an email to a friend, however, your **organization,** development, and **style** will be very different. And just imagine how your writing would need to change if you were working on a short story, a letter to the editor, or a set of directions. To produce clear and coherent writing, you must always consider how your task, purpose, and audience affect the development, organization, and style of your writing.

Academic Vocabulary

organization the way in which details are arranged in a piece of writing

style the way in which the writer uses language

Apply the Standard

Use the worksheet that follows to help you apply the standard as you write. Several copies of the worksheet have been provided for you to use with a number of different assignments.

- Writing to a Specific Task, Purpose, and Audience

Name _____ Date _____ Selection _____

Writing to a Specific Task, Purpose, and Audience

Use the organizer to identify the task, purpose, and audience for your writing assignment. Note how each will affect your choice of details, organization, and style.

Assignment:	
Task	**Note:**
Purpose	**Note:**
Audience	**Note:**

A

Name _____ Date _____ Selection _____

Writing to a Specific Task, Purpose, and Audience

Use the organizer to identify the task, purpose, and audience for your writing assignment. Note how each will affect your choice of details, organization, and style.

Assignment:	
Task	**Note:**
Purpose	**Note:**
Audience	**Note:**

B

Name _____ Date _____ Selection _____

Writing to a Specific Task, Purpose, and Audience

Use the organizer to identify the task, purpose, and audience for your writing assignment. Note how each will affect your choice of details, organization, and style.

Assignment:	
Task	**Note:**
Purpose	**Note:**
Audience	**Note:**

For use with Writing 4

Name _____ Date _____ Selection _____

Writing to a Specific Task, Purpose, and Audience

Use the organizer to identify the task, purpose, and audience for your writing assignment. Note how each will affect your choice of details, organization, and style.

Assignment:	
Task	**Note:**
Purpose	**Note:**
Audience	**Note:**

Name _____ Date _____ Selection _____

Writing to a Specific Task, Purpose, and Audience

Use the organizer to identify the task, purpose, and audience for your writing assignment. Note how each will affect your choice of details, organization, and style.

Assignment:	
Task	**Note:**
Purpose	**Note:**
Audience	**Note:**

E

Name _____ Date _____ Selection _____

Writing to a Specific Task, Purpose, and Audience

Use the organizer to identify the task, purpose, and audience for your writing assignment. Note how each will affect your choice of details, organization, and style.

Assignment:	
Task	**Note:**
Purpose	**Note:**
Audience	**Note:**

Writing 5

> **5. With some guidance and support from peers and adults, develop and strengthen writing as needed by planning, revising, editing, rewriting, or trying a new approach.**

Explanation

Successful writers understand the importance of each stage of the writing process. Few writers can produce a flawless piece of writing with no preparation. Most good writers take the time before they write to use prewriting strategies to gather details, develop and expand ideas, and plan the structure of a piece of writing. Yet, even with planning, most writers expect their first draft to need some revisions.

With a good writing plan in place, you should produce a decent first draft, but it will still need some work. You may, however, be too close to your writing to see where it fails. Your teacher and **peers** can offer a fresh point of view. They can help you identify weak spots in your writing and suggest ways to make it stronger. Here are some ideas on how to get guidance and support from your teacher and peers:

- Make an appointment to review your teacher's written comments on your draft. Discuss how **revising** specific parts will strengthen your writing.

- Read aloud your writing to a partner and ask for feedback. Provide a checklist that will help your partner focus on the main goals of the assignment.

- Share your writing in a group. Ask peers to point out where your writing succeeds and where it needs work. Discuss alternative approaches to improve your writing.

- Ask a peer to review your writing for errors in **conventions** and to check for varied sentence patterns and consistency in style and tone.

Occasionally, your teacher or peers may suggest that you start over. Having to rewrite can be discouraging, but producing a successful piece of writing will make the extra work worth it. Try to be open to their suggestions, even if it will require more work on your part.

Academic Vocabulary

peer a person who is the same age or has the same status as another person

revising rewriting to improve and strengthen writing

conventions correct use of punctuation, capitalization, grammar, and spelling

Apply the Standard

Use the worksheets that follow to help you apply the standard as you write. Several copies of the worksheets have been provided for you to use with a number of different assignments.

- Evaluating Writing with Peers

- Revising and Editing

Name _____ Date _____ Assignment _____

Evaluating Writing with Peers

Have your peers use this organizer to evaluate your first draft.

Focus Questions		Peer Comments and Suggestions for Revising
Does my writing have a clear focus or controlling idea?	Yes .... No	
Is the organizational plan clear?	Yes .... No	
Is the relationship between ideas in sentences and paragraphs clear and easy to follow?	Yes .... No	
Do I provide enough details to support each important idea?	Yes .... No	
Do I use transitions effectively?	Yes .... No	
Do I use precise nouns and vivid adjectives, adverbs, and verbs to create clear, strong images?	Yes .... No	
Do I vary sentence patterns and length effectively?	Yes .... No	
Are my task, purpose, and audience clear?	Yes .... No	

Name _____ Date _____ Assignment _____

Evaluating Writing with Peers

Have your peers use this organizer to evaluate your first draft.

Focus Questions		Peer Comments and Suggestions for Revising
Does my writing have a clear focus or controlling idea?	Yes .... No	
Is the organizational plan clear?	Yes .... No	
Is the relationship between ideas in sentences and paragraphs clear and easy to follow?	Yes .... No	
Do I provide enough details to support each important idea?	Yes .... No	
Do I use transitions effectively?	Yes .... No	
Do I use precise nouns and vivid adjectives, adverbs, and verbs to create clear, strong images?	Yes .... No	
Do I vary sentence patterns and length effectively?	Yes .... No	
Are my task, purpose, and audience clear?	Yes .... No	

B

Name _____ Date _____ Assignment _____

Evaluating Writing with Peers

Have your peers use this organizer to evaluate your first draft.

Focus Questions		Peer Comments and Suggestions for Revising
Does my writing have a clear focus or controlling idea?	Yes .... No	
Is the organizational plan clear?	Yes .... No	
Is the relationship between ideas in sentences and paragraphs clear and easy to follow?	Yes .... No	
Do I provide enough details to support each important idea?	Yes .... No	
Do I use transitions effectively?	Yes .... No	
Do I use precise nouns and vivid adjectives, adverbs, and verbs to create clear, strong images?	Yes .... No	
Do I vary sentence patterns and length effectively?	Yes .... No	
Are my task, purpose, and audience clear?	Yes .... No	

Name _____ Date _____ Assignment _____

Evaluating Writing with Peers

Have your peers use this organizer to evaluate your first draft.

Focus Questions		Peer Comments and Suggestions for Revising
Does my writing have a clear focus or controlling idea?	Yes .... No	
Is the organizational plan clear?	Yes .... No	
Is the relationship between ideas in sentences and paragraphs clear and easy to follow?	Yes .... No	
Do I provide enough details to support each important idea?	Yes .... No	
Do I use transitions effectively?	Yes .... No	
Do I use precise nouns and vivid adjectives, adverbs, and verbs to create clear, strong images?	Yes .... No	
Do I vary sentence patterns and length effectively?	Yes .... No	
Are my task, purpose, and audience clear?	Yes .... No	

D

For use with Writing 5

Name _____ Date _____ Assignment _____

Evaluating Writing with Peers

Have your peers use this organizer to evaluate your first draft.

Focus Questions		Peer Comments and Suggestions for Revising
Does my writing have a clear focus or controlling idea?	Yes .... No	
Is the organizational plan clear?	Yes .... No	
Is the relationship between ideas in sentences and paragraphs clear and easy to follow?	Yes .... No	
Do I provide enough details to support each important idea?	Yes .... No	
Do I use transitions effectively?	Yes .... No	
Do I use precise nouns and vivid adjectives, adverbs, and verbs to create clear, strong images?	Yes .... No	
Do I vary sentence patterns and length effectively?	Yes .... No	
Are my task, purpose, and audience clear?	Yes .... No	

E

For use with Writing 5

Name _____ Date _____ Assignment _____

Evaluating Writing with Peers

Have your peers use this organizer to evaluate your first draft.

Focus Questions		Peer Comments and Suggestions for Revising
Does my writing have a clear focus or controlling idea?	Yes .... No	
Is the organizational plan clear?	Yes .... No	
Is the relationship between ideas in sentences and paragraphs clear and easy to follow?	Yes .... No	
Do I provide enough details to support each important idea?	Yes .... No	
Do I use transitions effectively?	Yes .... No	
Do I use precise nouns and vivid adjectives, adverbs, and verbs to create clear, strong images?	Yes .... No	
Do I vary sentence patterns and length effectively?	Yes .... No	
Are my task, purpose, and audience clear?	Yes .... No	

F

Name _____ Date _____ Assignment _____

Revising and Editing

Use the organizer to explain how you plan to revise and edit your writing.

Sentence or passage from writing (For a long passage, note where it appears. For example, "second and third paragraphs.")	How I will revise or edit to improve and strengthen my writing?

A

Name _____ Date _____ Assignment _____

Revising and Editing

Use the organizer to explain how you plan to revise and edit your writing.

Sentence or passage from writing (For a long passage, note where it appears. For example, "second and third paragraphs.")	How I will revise or edit to improve and strengthen my writing?

B

For use with Writing 5

Name _____ Date _____ Assignment _____

Revising and Editing

Use the organizer to explain how you plan to revise and edit your writing.

Sentence or passage from writing (For a long passage, note where it appears. For example, "second and third paragraphs.")	**How I will revise or edit to improve and strengthen my writing?**

For use with Writing 5

Name _____ Date _____ Assignment _____

Revising and Editing

Use the organizer to explain how you plan to revise and edit your writing.

Sentence or passage from writing (For a long passage, note where it appears. For example, "second and third paragraphs.")	How I will revise or edit to improve and strengthen my writing?

D

Revising and Editing

Use the organizer to explain how you plan to revise and edit your writing.

Sentence or passage from writing (For a long passage, note where it appears. For example, "second and third paragraphs.")	How I will revise or edit to improve and strengthen my writing?

E

Name _____ Date _____ Assignment _____

Revising and Editing

Use the organizer to explain how you plan to revise and edit your writing.

Sentence or passage from writing (For a long passage, note where it appears. For example, "second and third paragraphs.")	How I will revise or edit to improve and strengthen my writing?

Writing 6

> 6. Use technology, including the Internet, to produce and publish writing as well as to interact and collaborate with others; demonstrate sufficient command of keyboarding skills to type a minimum of three pages in a single sitting.

Explanation

Computers, word processing software, the Internet, and other **technology** can make it easier for you to apply the steps of the writing process.

- During prewriting, you can use computer software to create graphic organizers.

- When you write a first draft, you can compose two or three versions of an introduction. Then, with just a click or two of a mouse, you can delete all but the best one.

- During revising and editing, you can easily replace a dull word with a vivid one, add and delete details, or reorganize them. You can also find and correct errors in spelling, grammar, punctuation, and capitalization by using spell check.

- Finally, you can use technology to publish a final copy enhanced with appropriate photographs, charts, graphs, videos, and sound.

The Internet can enhance how you **collaborate,** or work together, with other writers. If your class or school has a Web site, you can use it to upload drafts for peer review, post comments on other students' writing, and publish your work. When working with a partner or a group, you can use e-mail and group chats to share ideas, discuss progress, and offer advice.

Whenever you use a computer, remember to practice proper **keyboarding skills,** such as maintaining good posture and correctly placing your hands and fingers. You should be able to use both hands to type at least three pages of text in a sitting.

Academic Vocabulary

technology advanced electronic tools, such as computers, scanners, printers, word-processing and design programs, and the Internet

collaborate work with others to achieve a goal or goals

keyboarding pressing the keys on a computer to enter text

Apply the Standard

Use the worksheets that follow to help you apply the standard as you write. Several copies of each worksheet have been provided for you to use with different assignments.

- Using Technology in the Writing Process

- Using Technology to Collaborate with Other Writers

- Evaluating Keyboarding Skills

Name _____ Date _____ Assignment _____

Using Technology in the Writing Process

Use the organizer to plan how you can use technology during each stage of the writing process.

Stage	What technology can I use?	What is its purpose?
Prewriting		
Drafting		
Writing		
Revising and Editing		
Publishing		

A

Name _____ Date _____ Assignment _____

Using Technology in the Writing Process

Use the organizer to plan how you can use technology during each stage of the writing process.

Stage	What technology can I use?	What is its purpose?
Prewriting		
Drafting		
Writing		
Revising and Editing		
Publishing		

B

For use with Writing 6

Name _____ Date _____ Assignment _____

Using Technology in the Writing Process

Use the organizer to plan how you can use technology during each stage of the writing process.

Stage	What technology can I use?	What is its purpose?
Prewriting		
Drafting		
Writing		
Revising and Editing		
Publishing		

C

For use with Writing 6

Name _____ Date _____ Assignment _____

Using Technology in the Writing Process

Use the organizer to plan how you can use technology during each stage of the writing process.

Stage	What technology can I use?	What is its purpose?
Prewriting		
Drafting		
Writing		
Revising and Editing		
Publishing		

D

Name _____ Date _____ Assignment _____

Using Technology in the Writing Process

Use the organizer to plan how you can use technology during each stage of the writing process.

Stage	What technology can I use?	What is its purpose?
Prewriting		
Drafting		
Writing		
Revising and Editing		
Publishing		

E

Name _____ Date _____ Assignment _____

Using Technology in the Writing Process

Use the organizer to plan how you can use technology during each stage of the writing process.

Stage	What technology can I use?	What is its purpose?
Prewriting		
Drafting		
Writing		
Revising and Editing		
Publishing		

F

For use with Writing 6

Name _____ Date _____ Assignment _____

Using Technology to Collaborate with Other Writers

Use the organizer to plan how you will use technology to collaborate with other students. After you complete the assignment, use the organizer to evaluate your efforts.

Plan

What technology will I use to interact and collaborate with others for this assignment?

❏ E-mail

❏ Group chat

❏ Web page

❏ Blog

❏ Peer editing software

❏ Other (Explain) ....

....

Review

How well did I use technology to collaborate with other students? (For each item, circle an appropriate number.)

	poor ⟶ excellent					
Gathering information	1	2	3	4	5	6
Organizing details	1	2	3	4	5	6
Sharing feedback on drafts	1	2	3	4	5	6
Revising	1	2	3	4	5	6
Editing	1	2	3	4	5	6
Publishing	1	2	3	4	5	6

Choose one item from the rating scale. Use the space below to explain why you gave it the rating that you did.

For use with Writing 6

Name _____ Date _____ Assignment _____

Using Technology to Collaborate with Other Writers

Use the organizer to plan how you will use technology to collaborate with other students. After you complete the assignment, use the organizer to evaluate your efforts.

Plan

What technology will I use to interact and collaborate with others for this assignment?

❏ E-mail

❏ Group chat

❏ Web page

❏ Blog

❏ Peer editing software

❏ Other (Explain) ....

....

Review

How well did I use technology to collaborate with other students? (For each item, circle an appropriate number.)

	poor ————————————————➤ excellent					
Gathering information	1	2	3	4	5	6
Organizing details	1	2	3	4	5	6
Sharing feedback on drafts	1	2	3	4	5	6
Revising	1	2	3	4	5	6
Editing	1	2	3	4	5	6
Publishing	1	2	3	4	5	6

Choose one item from the rating scale. Use the space below to explain why you gave it the rating that you did.

Name _____ Date _____ Assignment _____

Using Technology to Collaborate with Other Writers

Use the organizer to plan how you will use technology to collaborate with other students. After you complete the assignment, use the organizer to evaluate your efforts.

Plan

What technology will I use to interact and collaborate with others for this assignment?

❑ E-mail

❑ Group chat

❑ Web page

❑ Blog

❑ Peer editing software

❑ Other (Explain) ....

....

Review

How well did I use technology to collaborate with other students? (For each item, circle an appropriate number.)

	poor ——————————————➤ excellent					
Gathering information	1	2	3	4	5	6
Organizing details	1	2	3	4	5	6
Sharing feedback on drafts	1	2	3	4	5	6
Revising	1	2	3	4	5	6
Editing	1	2	3	4	5	6
Publishing	1	2	3	4	5	6

Choose one item from the rating scale. Use the space below to explain why you gave it the rating that you did.

C

For use with Writing 6

Name _____ Date _____ Assignment _____

Using Technology to Collaborate with Other Writers

Use the organizer to plan how you will use technology to collaborate with other students. After you complete the assignment, use the organizer to evaluate your efforts.

Plan

What technology will I use to interact and collaborate with others for this assignment?

❏ E-mail

❏ Group chat

❏ Web page

❏ Blog

❏ Peer editing software

❏ Other (Explain) ....

....

Review

How well did I use technology to collaborate with other students? (For each item, circle an appropriate number.)

	poor ⟶ excellent					
Gathering information	1	2	3	4	5	6
Organizing details	1	2	3	4	5	6
Sharing feedback on drafts	1	2	3	4	5	6
Revising	1	2	3	4	5	6
Editing	1	2	3	4	5	6
Publishing	1	2	3	4	5	6

Choose one item from the rating scale. Use the space below to explain why you gave it the rating that you did.

For use with Writing 6

Name _____ Date _____ Assignment _____

Using Technology to Collaborate with Other Writers

Use the organizer to plan how you will use technology to collaborate with other students. After you complete the assignment, use the organizer to evaluate your efforts.

Plan

What technology will I use to interact and collaborate with others for this assignment?

❑ E-mail

❑ Group chat

❑ Web page

❑ Blog

❑ Peer editing software

❑ Other (Explain) ....

....

Review

How well did I use technology to collaborate with other students? (For each item, circle an appropriate number.)

	poor ⟶ excellent					
Gathering information	1	2	3	4	5	6
Organizing details	1	2	3	4	5	6
Sharing feedback on drafts	1	2	3	4	5	6
Revising	1	2	3	4	5	6
Editing	1	2	3	4	5	6
Publishing	1	2	3	4	5	6

Choose one item from the rating scale. Use the space below to explain why you gave it the rating that you did.

For use with Writing 6

Name _____ Date _____ Assignment _____

Using Technology to Collaborate with Other Writers

Use the organizer to plan how you will use technology to collaborate with other students. After you complete the assignment, use the organizer to evaluate your efforts.

Plan

What technology will I use to interact and collaborate with others for this assignment?

❏ E-mail

❏ Group chat

❏ Web page

❏ Blog

❏ Peer editing software

❏ Other (Explain) ....

....

Review

How well did I use technology to collaborate with other students? (For each item, circle an appropriate number.)

	poor ⟶ excellent					
Gathering information	1	2	3	4	5	6
Organizing details	1	2	3	4	5	6
Sharing feedback on drafts	1	2	3	4	5	6
Revising	1	2	3	4	5	6
Editing	1	2	3	4	5	6
Publishing	1	2	3	4	5	6

Choose one item from the rating scale. Use the space below to explain why you gave it the rating that you did.

Name _____ Date _____ Assignment _____

Evaluating Keyboarding Skills

Use the organizer to evaluate your keyboarding skills and to determine where you need improvement. Place a check in the appropriate box.

	Always	Usually	Hardly Ever
Posture Do I sit up straight with my feet flat on the floor?			
Hand Placement Are both my hands on the keyboard, with my wrists and forearms level with the keys and parallel to the floor?			
Finger Placement Are all my fingers on the center row of the keyboard as I type?			
Rate Can I produce a minimum of 3 pages in one sitting?			
Pace Do I keep up an even pace as I type long passages?			
Accuracy Do I have a minimal number of errors in my finished work (for example, 3 or less typing errors per page)?			

A

Name _____ Date _____ Assignment _____

Evaluating Keyboarding Skills

Use the organizer to evaluate your keyboarding skills and to determine where you need improvement. Place a check in the appropriate box.

	Always	Usually	Hardly Ever
Posture Do I sit up straight with my feet flat on the floor?			
Hand Placement Are both my hands on the keyboard, with my wrists and forearms level with the keys and parallel to the floor?			
Finger Placement Are all my fingers on the center row of the keyboard as I type?			
Rate Can I produce a minimum of 3 pages in one sitting?			
Pace Do I keep up an even pace as I type long passages?			
Accuracy Do I have a minimal number of errors in my finished work (for example, 3 or less typing errors per page)?			

Name _____ Date _____ Assignment _____

Evaluating Keyboarding Skills

Use the organizer to evaluate your keyboarding skills and to determine where you need improvement. Place a check in the appropriate box.

	Always	Usually	Hardly Ever
Posture Do I sit up straight with my feet flat on the floor?			
Hand Placement Are both my hands on the keyboard, with my wrists and forearms level with the keys and parallel to the floor?			
Finger Placement Are all my fingers on the center row of the keyboard as I type?			
Rate Can I produce a minimum of 3 pages in one sitting?			
Pace Do I keep up an even pace as I type long passages?			
Accuracy Do I have a minimal number of errors in my finished work (for example, 3 or less typing errors per page)?			

For use with Writing 6

Name _____ Date _____ Assignment _____

Evaluating Keyboarding Skills

Use the organizer to evaluate your keyboarding skills and to determine where you need improvement. Place a check in the appropriate box.

	Always	Usually	Hardly Ever
Posture Do I sit up straight with my feet flat on the floor?			
Hand Placement Are both my hands on the keyboard, with my wrists and forearms level with the keys and parallel to the floor?			
Finger Placement Are all my fingers on the center row of the keyboard as I type?			
Rate Can I produce a minimum of 3 pages in one sitting?			
Pace Do I keep up an even pace as I type long passages?			
Accuracy Do I have a minimal number of errors in my finished work (for example, 3 or less typing errors per page)?			

D

For use with Writing 6

Name _____ Date _____ Assignment _____

Evaluating Keyboarding Skills

Use the organizer to evaluate your keyboarding skills and to determine where you need improvement. Place a check in the appropriate box.

	Always	Usually	Hardly Ever
Posture Do I sit up straight with my feet flat on the floor?			
Hand Placement Are both my hands on the keyboard, with my wrists and forearms level with the keys and parallel to the floor?			
Finger Placement Are all my fingers on the center row of the keyboard as I type?			
Rate Can I produce a minimum of 3 pages in one sitting?			
Pace Do I keep up an even pace as I type long passages?			
Accuracy Do I have a minimal number of errors in my finished work (for example, 3 or less typing errors per page)?			

For use with Writing 6

Name _____ Date _____ Assignment _____

Evaluating Keyboarding Skills

Use the organizer to evaluate your keyboarding skills and to determine where you need improvement. Place a check in the appropriate box.

	Always	Usually	Hardly Ever
Posture Do I sit up straight with my feet flat on the floor?			
Hand Placement Are both my hands on the keyboard, with my wrists and forearms level with the keys and parallel to the floor?			
Finger Placement Are all my fingers on the center row of the keyboard as I type?			
Rate Can I produce a minimum of 3 pages in one sitting?			
Pace Do I keep up an even pace as I type long passages?			
Accuracy Do I have a minimal number of errors in my finished work (for example, 3 or less typing errors per page)?			

For use with Writing 6

Writing 7

> **7. Conduct short research projects to answer a question, drawing on several sources and refocusing the inquiry when appropriate.**

Explanation

Your teacher may ask you to conduct a short research project about a topic that interests you. To get started, write a question that you have about the topic. (Your teacher may assign a question.) Then do some initial research. Look for answers to your question in several different print or online sources. Locate **primary sources**—firsthand original accounts, such as interview transcripts and newspaper articles. In addition, find **secondary sources**—accounts that are not original, such as encyclopedia entries. Utilize a variety of media, such as newspapers, magazines, textbooks, and reliable websites Your goal at this point is to focus your **inquiry,** or process of looking for information, to make it suitable for a short research project. Based on how little or how much information you find, you may want to refocus the inquiry by asking one or two closely related questions.

For example, imagine you are researching science fiction author Ray Bradbury. You might focus or refocus your research with these questions:

- How did Ray Bradbury begin writing science fiction?

- What common themes do many of Ray Bradbury's short stories share?

If you are researching graphic novels, you might focus or refocus your research with these questions:

- What is a graphic novel?

- What are some well-known graphic novels? Who are well-known authors?

Once you have a focus for your inquiry, conduct your research and take notes. Use no more than three or four different sources, and make sure to record only facts and details that will help you answer your questions. Then answer your questions by **synthesizing**, or combining, the information you have gathered with your own words and ideas.

Academic Vocabulary

inquiry the process of looking for information to answer specific questions about a topic

synthesizing combining information from different sources and presenting it in a new way

primary source firsthand or original accounts

secondary source accounts that are not original

Apply the Standard

Use the worksheets that follow to help you apply the standard as you write. Several copies of each worksheet have been provided for you to use with different assignments.

- Researching to Answer a Question

- Synthesizing Information from Different Sources

Name _____ Date _____ Assignment _____

Researching to Answer a Question

Use the organizer to gather information about your topic. Write your original question, your question after refocusing your inquiry, and your sources. Then list the information you gather from each source.

Original Question: **Refocused Question:**	
Source:	
Source:	
Source:	

Name _____ Date _____ Assignment _____

Researching to Answer a Question

Use the organizer to gather information about your topic. Write your original question, your question after refocusing your inquiry, and your sources. Then list the information you gather from each source.

Original Question: **Refocused Question:**	
Source:	
Source:	
Source:	

Name _____ Date _____ Assignment _____

Researching to Answer a Question

Use the organizer to gather information about your topic. Write your original question, your question after refocusing your inquiry, and your sources. Then list the information you gather from each source.

Original Question: **Refocused Question:**	
Source:	
Source:	
Source:	

Name _____ Date _____ Assignment _____

Synthesizing Information from Different Sources

Use the organizer to synthesize information from different sources.

```
┌─────────────────────────────────────────────────────────────────────┐
│ Your Question:                                                        │
│                                                                       │
│                                                                       │
└─────────────────────────────────────────────────────────────────────┘

┌─────────────────────────────────────────────────────────────────────┐
│ Information from source 1:                                            │
│                                                                       │
│                                                                       │
│                                                                       │
└─────────────────────────────────────────────────────────────────────┘
                                    ↓
┌─────────────────────────────────────────────────────────────────────┐
│ Information from source 2:                                            │
│                                                                       │
│                                                                       │
│                                                                       │
└─────────────────────────────────────────────────────────────────────┘
                                    ↓
┌─────────────────────────────────────────────────────────────────────┐
│ Information from source 3:                                            │
│                                                                       │
│                                                                       │
│                                                                       │
└─────────────────────────────────────────────────────────────────────┘
                                    ↓
┌─────────────────────────────────────────────────────────────────────┐
│ Answer your question by synthesizing, or combining, information       │
│ from your sources:                                                    │
│                                                                       │
│                                                                       │
│                                                                       │
│                                                                       │
│                                                                       │
└─────────────────────────────────────────────────────────────────────┘
```

A

Name _____ Date _____ Assignment _____

Synthesizing Information from Different Sources

Use the organizer to synthesize information from different sources.

Your Question:

Information from source 1:

Information from source 2:

Information from source 3:

Answer your question by <u>synthesizing,</u> or combining, information from your sources:

Name _____ Date _____ Assignment _____

Synthesizing Information from Different Sources

Use the organizer to synthesize information from different sources.

Your Question:

Information from source 1:

Information from source 2:

Information from source 3:

Answer your question by <u>synthesizing</u>, or combining, information from your sources:

C

For use with Writing 7

Writing 8

> **8.** Gather relevant information from multiple print and digital sources; assess the credibility of each source; and quote or paraphrase the data and conclusions of others while avoiding plagiarism and providing basic bibliographic information for sources.

Writing Workshop

When you write a research report, you ask questions about a topic that interests you. Then you do research to find the answers to those questions. A **research report** presents facts and information gathered from multiple sources, which you check to be true and accurate. You are most likely to write a research report as a school assignment. However, learning how and where to find the answers to important questions can benefit you in just about any field of work you choose after you leave school.

Assignment

Write a research report to gain more knowledge about a topic that interests you. Include these elements:

✓ a topic for inquiry that is narrow enough to cover thoroughly

✓ a strong introduction that clearly defines the topic

✓ facts, details, and examples from a variety of credible print and digital sources

✓ information that is accurate, relevant, valid, and current

✓ a clear method of organization, including a strong conclusion

✓ a *bibliography* containing accurate and complete citations

✓ correct use of language conventions, including the proper punctuation of citations and titles of referenced works

*Additional Standards

Writing
8. Gather relevant information from multiple print and digital sources; assess the credibility of each source; and quote or paraphrase the data and conclusions of others while avoiding plagiarism and providing basic bibliographic information for sources.

2. Write informative/explanatory texts to examine a topic and convey ideas, concepts, and information through the selection, organization, and analysis of relevant content.

6. Use technology, including the Internet, to produce and publish writing as well as to interact and collaborate with others; demonstrate sufficient command of keyboarding skills to type a minimum of three pages in a single sitting.

9. Draw evidence from literary or informational texts to support analysis, reflection, and research.

Language
2. Demonstrate command of the conventions of standard English capitalization, punctuation, and spelling when writing.

Name _____ Date _____ Assignment _____

Prewriting/Planning Strategies

Choose a general idea. Begin the search for a good topic for your report. First think about what interests you. Do you enjoy learning about historic people or events? Are you intrigued by ancient cultures, scientific discoveries, sports, weather or space exploration? If you cannot come up with an idea, browse through textbooks, books, magazines, or an encyclopedia. List the names of people, places, events, or any other ideas that interest you. Then scan your notes and circle the idea that interests you the most.

Use a topic web to narrow your topic. After you have a general idea for a topic, do some quick research. If you find a huge amount of information, your topic is too broad for a research report. Narrow your topic to make it more specific and more manageable. Use the topic web to narrow your topic. Each row should contain smaller and smaller aspects of your general topic. For example, the topic of "Ancient Rome" is too broad for a research report. Instead you could continue to narrow that down until you reach a much more specific topic, such as "The Colosseum," a building in Ancient Rome.

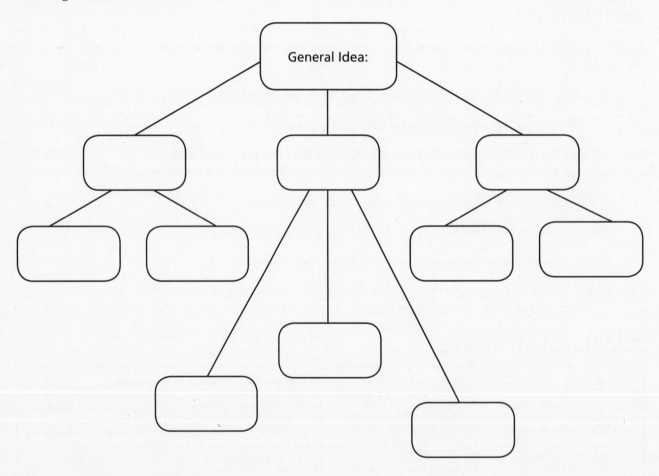

General Idea:

Write your narrowed topic: ....

Ask questions about your topic. Decide what you want your report to explain about your topic. Then ask questions that will help you help you focus your research. For example, in a report about the Colosseum, you might ask questions about its architecture, construction, and purpose in Ancient Rome. Next make a list of primary and secondary sources where you plan to look to find information that answers your questions.

Primary sources: firsthand or original accounts. Examples include interviews and personal observations recorded in news reports, journals, diaries, and letters.

Secondary sources: accounts that are not first hand or original. Examples include encyclopedia entries, documentaries, the Internet, books, television, and magazine articles.

Use the graphic organizer to write your research questions and list specific sources. List both primary and secondary sources.

Topic:				
	Question 1:	**Question 2:**	**Question 3:**	**Question 4:**
Source 1				
Source 2				
Source 3				
Source 4				

Evaluating Sources

The information in your research report should be interesting, relevant, and accurate. You can ensure the accuracy of the facts and details in your report if you use credible, accurate sources. Take time to evaluate the credibility and accuracy of your sources.

Print Sources. You can usually find accurate information in encyclopedia articles; textbook articles; nonfiction books; autobiographies; articles in specialized magazines, such as science journals; printed interviews, and brochures and pamphlets, published by respected organizations, such as the National Parks system.

Digital Sources: You can also use a variety of digital sources for your research. These include informational CDs; radio and television documentaries, sponsored by respected institutions, such as the Smithsonian; videos and slide programs; and the Internet.

Be careful when researching the Internet. Some Web sites are written by individuals who are not experts on the topic. Information on these sites may or may not be accurate. Other sites are sponsored by companies or organizations that want you to support their causes or buy their products. Facts on these sites may be biased or skewed to suit the purpose of these sponsors. Internet sources sponsored by the government (ending in *.gov*) or educational institutions (ending in *.edu*) are generally more credible than those put up by businesses (ending in *.com*).

To save time when doing Internet searches, use specific terms that will focus your results. For example, using "dog" as a search term will yield thousands and thousands of hits. Using a search term such as "guide dogs," is more focused and should yield relevant hits.

To evaluate the accuracy of print and digital sources, ask yourself these questions:

- Is this a primary source or a secondary source?

- Is the information the most up-to-date information available?

- Is the author or subject of the interview an expert in the field?

- Is the information presented objectively and fairly?

- Does the source have any hidden purpose, such as wanting me to support a cause or buy a product?

- Is the information accurate? Can I confirm it in at least one other source?

News Media Sources: The news should be presented objectively and accurately. Yet many news outlets slant their reports so that they favor specific groups or policies. Before using facts from a news outlet, confirm the facts with at least two other sources.

Name _____ Date _____ Assignment _____

Record source information. At the end of your report, you will provide a bibliography of every source you cite in your report. This task will be easier if you keep accurate details about your sources as you conduct your research.

Use the **source cards** to record details about each source you use. Include the title, author, publication date and place, and page numbers on which you find information. Use the "Other" line, to list a Web address if the source is an Internet site, or other notes about the source, for example, if it is a CD or an interview. Use as many source cards as you need. Be sure to record information carefully and accurately.

Title:
Author:
Publication Date and Place:
Page Numbers:
Other:

Title:
Author:
Publication Date and Place:
Page Numbers:
Other:

Name _____ Date _____ Assignment _____

Taking Notes. Follow these guidelines for taking notes efficiently.

- Take complete and accurate notes. This will save you from having to go back and check every source when you draft and revise.

- Keep your notes organized and focused. Write one of your research questions at the top of each card. Use different colored markers to highlight each question. Then write only facts and details that answer that question on the note card. If your note cards get mixed up, you can see at a glance by the color which notes go together.

- Use a new note card for each new source. Go back and number your source cards. Then write that source number on the note card. If you prefer, you can write an abbreviated form of the title of the source or the author's last name.

- Use quotation marks when you copy words exactly. Indicate the author's last name and page number on which the quotation appears in parenthesis after the quotation. This will be helpful if you have go back to check the quotation when you draft, and if you decide to use the exact quotation in your report.

- In most cases, you should take notes in your own words. This will protect you from accidentally **plagiarizing,** or copying someone else's ideas and words, when you write your draft.

Record fact, details, examples, and explanations about your topic on note cards like this. Use as many note cards as you need.

Research Question:
Source notation:

Name _____ Date _____ Assignment _____

Drafting Strategies

Create an outline to organize information. When your notes are complete, use the graphic organizer to create an outline for your draft. A solid, detailed outline will serve as a map when you write your draft.

- For the Introduction (I) write an interesting thesis statement that states your main idea. This sentence should clearly point out what special point you plan to make about your topic in your report.

- Next, group your notes by categories that break your main topic into subtopics. Your research questions should help suggest these subtopics. For example, if you asked a question about the architecture of the Colosseum, then "Architecture" is a reasonable subtopic. Write subtopics next to the Roman Numerals (II, III, IV). Write details and facts related to each subtopic next to the letters (A, B,).

- For the conclusion, write a sentence that restates your main idea.

Introduction   I. ....

....

(Subtopic 1) II. ....

(Detail) A. ....

(Detail) B. ....

(Subtopic 2) III. ....

(Detail) A. ....

(Detail) B. ....

(Subtopic 3) IV. ....

(Detail) A. ....

(Detail) B. ....

Conclusion   V. ....

....

....

Match your draft to your outline. Use your outline to guide the writing of your draft. The headings with Roman numerals indicate main sections of your report. You may need to write several paragraphs to cover each Roman numeral topic fully. Organize your paragraphs around the topics with capital letters.

Write an interesting beginning. Draft an introduction that grabs readers' attention and leads to your thesis statement. Try one or more of these approaches:

- Look through your notes for an interesting fact, surprising detail, or quotation. Use this to begin your introduction.

- Ask a thoughtful question. Try to recall something you wondered about as you researched your topic. Begin your introduction with the words "Have you ever wondered why—?" Make sure that you answer that question in the report.

- Tell a touching or amusing anecdote—a very brief story—about your subject that leads logically into your thesis statement.

Develop topic sentences for body paragraphs. Each paragraph in the body of your report should have a clear topic sentence that states the main idea of the paragraph. All other sentences in the paragraph should contain facts, examples, and details that support the topic sentence. Using your outline, write topic sentences to express each main idea in the body of your report. Leave space in between each paragraph for supporting details.

Support main ideas with facts. Fill in the spaces in the body paragraphs with supporting facts, details, examples, and explanations from your notes. Try to **paraphrase** the information, or put it into your own words. Using your own words shows that you understand how the information relates to the topic. It also helps you to avoid **plagiarism**—presenting another's work as your own.

Cite sources as you draft. You must include documentation every time you use another writer's ideas. As you draft, circle ideas that come directly from your sources. Use these tips to give proper credit within your report.

- For *paraphrased information* or facts that are not common knowledge, insert parentheses for the author's last name and the page number(s) from which the information came:
  The Colosseum could hold 50,000 spectators (Smith 87-88).

- For a *direct quotation*, use quotation marks. After the end quotation mark, insert in parentheses the author's last name and the page number(s) from which the quotation came:
  "It is a supreme work of architecture." (Jones 92).

Crediting Sources

A **bibliography** at the end of your report provides readers with full bibliographic information of each source you cited in your report. The author and page number citations within your report will lead your reader to the specific source in your bibliography. Interested readers can use that information to learn more about your topic.

This chart shows the Modern Language Association (MLA) format for crediting sources.

MLA Style for Listing Sources

Book with one author	Pyles, Thomas. *The Origins and Development of the English Language.* 2nd ed. New York: Harcourt Brace Jovanovich, Inc., 1971.
Book with two or three authors	McCrum, Robert, William Cran, and Robert MacNeil. *The Story of English.* New York: Penguin Books, 1987.
Book with an editor	Truth, Sojourner: *Narrative of Sojourner Truth.* Ed. Margaret Washington. New York: Vintage Books, 1993.
Signed article in a weekly magazine	Wallace, C. (2000, February 14). A Vodacious Deal. *Time*, 155, 63.
Signed article in a Monthly magazine	Gustatitis, Joseph. "The Sticky History of Chewing Gum." *American History* Oct. 1998: 30-38.
Unsigned editorial o	"Selective Silence" Editorial. *Wall Street Journal* 11 Feb. 2000: A14.
Filmstrips, slide programs, videocassettes, DVDS	*The Diary of Anne Frank.* Dir. George Stevens. Perf. Millie Perkins, Shelly Winters, Joseph Schildkraut, Lou Jacobi, and Richard Beymer. Twentieth Century Fox, 1959.
Internet	"Fun Facts About Gum." NACGM site. National Association of Chewing Gum Manufacturers. 19 Dec. 1999 <http://www.nacgm.org/consumer/funfacts.html>
Newspaper	Thurow, Roger. "South Africans Who Fought for Sanctions Now Scrap for Investors." *Wall Street Journal* 11 Feb. 2000: A1+
Personal Interview	Smith, Jane. Personal interview. 10 Feb. 2000.
CD (with multiple publishers)	Simms, James, ed. *Romeo and Juliet.* By William Shakespeare. CD-ROM. Oxford: Attica Cybernetics Ltd.; London: BBC Education; London: HarperCollins Publishers, 1995.
Signed article from an encyclopedia	Askeland, Donald R. (1991)."Welding." *World Book Encyclopedia.* 1991 ed.

Name _____ Date _____ Assignment _____

Create a bibliography. Use the graphic organizer to create a bibliography for your research report. Use the entries in the MLA style sheet on the previous page as a model. Arrange your sources in the order that you cited them for the first time in your report.

Bibliography

Name _____ Date _____ Assignment _____

Revising Strategies

Revise for effective paragraph structure. Review each paragraph in your draft to make sure it has a clear topic sentence that expresses the main idea of the paragraph. Check that all the other sentences in the paragraph support the topic sentence. Follow the steps in the chart to revise for effective paragraph structure.

1. Circle each topic sentence.
2. Underline supporting sentences.
3. Cross out any sentence that does not elaborate on the topic sentence.
4. Cross out any sentence that does not contain a fact, detail, or example that illustrates the topic sentence.
5. If you discover that a paragraph does not have a topic sentence, write one now.
6. If you have only one or two sentences left in a paragraph after deleting irrelevant details, add new details; or combine the remaining sentences with another paragraph.

Revise for unity and organization. A research report that has unity is focused on one central idea. It covers that idea completely. It does not suddenly introduce any new ideas about the topic, nor does it veer off onto a totally different topic. A unified research report is organized clearly and logically. Ideas flow smoothly from one paragraph to the next, from the introduction through the conclusion. Use the following questions to check your report's unity and organization. Make revisions based on your responses.

Does every paragraph develop the thesis statement in my introduction?	❑ Yes	❑ No
Do all of my paragraphs contain topic sentences that express the main idea of the paragraph?	❑ Yes	❑ No
Do I introduce any ideas that are not related to my thesis statement?	❑ Yes	❑ No
Do I repeat words and phrases at the end of one paragraph and at the beginning of the next to show how ideas are connected?	❑ Yes	❑ No
Do I use transitions such as *first, then,* and *finally* between paragraphs to create a smooth flow of ideas?	❑ Yes	❑ No
Does the conclusion sum up ideas in the body of my essay and restate my thesis?	❑ Yes	❑ No

Punctuating Citations and Titles of Reference Works

Check that you have presented the titles of works and the words from various sources accurately in your report. Follow these guidelines.

- **Underlining and italicizing.** Underline or italicize the titles of long written works and the titles of periodicals.

- **Using quotation marks.** Titles of short written works and Internet sites should be set off in quotation marks.

Underlined/Italicized	Quotation Marks
Title of a Book	Title of a Short Story
Title of a Play	Chapter From a Book
Title of a Long Poem	Title of a Short Poem
Title of a Magazine	Title of an Article
Title of a Newspaper	Title of a Web Site

Including direct quotations. A **direct quotation** conveys the exact words that another person wrote or said.

- Introduce short quotations with a comma, and follow with your own sentences, setting them off with quotation marks.

- Introduce quotations that are five lines or longer with a colon. Set them off from your text by starting a new line and indenting the quotation. *Do not use* quotation marks.

Fixing errors. To find and fix errors involving quotation marks, underlining, and italics, follow these steps.

1. **Check the quoted material you have used.**

2. **Make sure that the quotations are copied exactly from the source.** Enclose these words in quotation marks.

3. **Punctuate correctly.** Follow the punctuation rules for the use of quotation marks and underlining or italicizing of titles.

Editing and Proofreading

Review your draft to correct errors in capitalization, spelling, and punctuation.

Focus on Capitalization: Review your draft carefully to find and correct capitalization errors. Make sure every sentence begins with a capital letter. Make sure titles of sources cited in your report and bibliography are capitalized correctly. If you have made specific references to experts on your topic who have titles, make sure you have capitalized their titles correctly

Dr. Francis Fiore   **Mayor Eva Gomez**

Focus on Spelling: Check the spelling of each word in your story. Pay particular attention to the spelling of authors' names. When in doubt, go back to source materials to double check for accuracy. Remember that a spell checker cannot offer corrections for proper names. In addition, a spell checker will not find words that are spelled correctly but used incorrectly, such as *they're, their,* and *there.* Therefore, proofread carefully.

Focus on Punctuation: Proofread your writing to find and correct punctuation errors. make sure every sentence has end punctuation. Check that you have put parentheses around citations that appear within your report. Make sure that you have used quotation marks around direct quotations and short works, and that you have underlined or italicized long written works or periodicals. Make sure that all the entries in your bibliography are punctuated correctly.

Revision Checklist

❏ Have you reviewed your research report for correct capitalization?

❏ Have you read each sentence and checked that all of the words are spelled correctly?

❏ Have you punctuated all your sentences and the bibliography correctly?

Name _____ Date _____ Assignment _____

Publishing and Presenting

Consider one of the following ways to present your writing:

Create a mini-lesson. Use your report as the basis for a short lesson on your topic that includes an activity related to the topic. Have on hand graphs, charts, maps, photographs, videos, or any other visuals that will enhance your lesson and further explain important ideas in your report. If your report is about an important person from recent times, you may be able to find a recording in his or her voice that you can play as a dramatic introduction to the lesson.

Offer your report to an organization. Find out if members of a local organization, club, or local library would benefit from your research. Plan a multi-media presentation with visuals, such as posters, photographs, videos or music to accompany your presentation. If any of your classmates have chosen topics that would be suitable for a joint presentation, invite them to participate.

Rubric for Self-Assessment

Find evidence in your writing to address each category. Then use the rating scale to grade your work.

Evaluating Your Research Report	not very					very
Focus: How well defined is the topic?	1	2	3	4	5	6
Organization: How clear is the method of organization?	1	2	3	4	5	6
Support/Elaboration: How well have you used a variety of credible sources?	1	2	3	4	5	6
Style: How well do facts, details, examples and explanations support the main idea?	1	2	3	4	5	6
Conventions: How accurate and complete are citations in the bibliography?	1	2	3	4	5	6

Writing 9a

> **9a. Draw evidence from literary or informational texts to support analysis, reflection, and research**
>   • Apply *grade 6 Reading standards to literature* (e.g., "Compare and contrast texts in different forms or genres [e.g., stories and poems; historical novels and fantasy stories] in terms of their approaches to similar themes and topics").

Explanation

To understand a topic, it is often necessary to consult different sources on the same subject. Many times, those sources are works from different genres. To explore the theme, you may be asked to write an essay comparing and contrasting how the theme is treated in two works from different genres. A **theme** is the central idea in a literary work about life and human nature. You might have noticed that many topics and themes appear in different **genres** of literature. For example,

   • a short story and a poem could both explore the theme that love is a powerful force;

   • a historical novel and a fantasy story might both focus on the message that the desire to do good can lead to unexpected results.

To write a comparison-contrast essay, choose two works from different genres that share the same theme. Take notes on how each writer develops the theme. For example, to compare and contrast a short story and a poem that have similar themes, ask yourself such questions as: *How does the short story writer use setting, characterization, and plot events to develop the theme? How does the poet use imagery and language to express the theme?*

Choose one of these patterns to organize details in the body of your essay.

   • **Block Method:** Explain how the theme is developed in one work. Then describe how it is developed in the second work.

   • **Point-by-Point Method:** Explain how a specific element develops the theme in one work, then in the other. Use this alternating comparison for other elements.

Transitional words and phrases such as *both, also, unlike, on the other hand*, and *in contrast* can help make the similarities and differences between the two works clear.

Academic Vocabulary

theme the central idea or message about life and human nature in a literary work

genres categories of literary works, such as short story, poem, historical novel, and drama

Apply the Standard

Use the worksheet that follows to help you apply the standard as you write. Several copies have been provided for you to use with different assignments.

   • Comparing and Contrasting Themes

Name _____ Date _____ Assignment _____

Comparing and Contrasting Themes

Choose two selections with similar themes for a comparison-and-contrast essay. Use the organizer to note evidence from each work that shows the development of theme.

	Title: Author: Genre:	Title: Author: Genre:
How are the themes in both works alike?		
Think about the characters. How do their words, actions, thoughts, and feelings help develop the theme?		
How does the setting contribute to the theme?		
What events help develop the theme?		
How does the mood contribute to the theme?		
What words or figures of speech help develop the theme?		

A

For use with Writing 9a

Name _____ Date _____ Assignment _____

Comparing and Contrasting Themes

Choose two selections with similar themes for a comparison-and-contrast essay. Use the organizer to note evidence from each work that shows the development of theme.

	Title: Author: Genre:	Title: Author: Genre:
How are the themes in both works alike?		
Think about the characters. How do their words, actions, thoughts, and feelings help develop the theme?		
How does the setting contribute to the theme?		
What events help develop the theme?		
How does the mood contribute to the theme?		
What words or figures of speech help develop the theme?		

For use with Writing 9a

Name _____ Date _____ Assignment _____

Comparing and Contrasting Themes

Choose two selections with similar themes for a comparison-and-contrast essay. Use the organizer to note evidence from each work that shows the development of theme.

	Title: Author: Genre:	Title: Author: Genre:
How are the themes in both works alike?		
Think about the characters. How do their words, actions, thoughts, and feelings help develop the theme?		
How does the setting contribute to the theme?		
What events help develop the theme?		
How does the mood contribute to the theme?		
What words or figures of speech help develop the theme?		

For use with Writing 9a

Writing 9b

> **9b. Draw evidence from literary or informational texts to support analysis, reflection, and research.**
>
> • Apply *grade 6 Reading standards* to literary nonfiction (e.g., "Trace and evaluate the argument and specific claims in a text, distinguishing claims that are supported by reasons and evidence from claims that are not").

Explanation

In an argument, a writer states a position on an issue. This position is called the **claim.** When you write an evaluation of an argument, you examine the evidence the writer uses to support the claim. You check to determine whether the claim is valid or not. Based on the evidence in the text, you decide if the writer's argument is sound.

Choose a text that contains an argument to evaluate, such as an editorial or a speech. Then take notes for your essay. Here are some points to keep in mind as you take notes:

- A sound argument contains a clearly stated opinion.

- A valid claim is supported by reasons and **evidence**, such as facts, examples, expert opinions, and statistics.

- The writer provides verifiable sources for his or her evidence.

- Reasons are logical and presented in an order that makes sense.

- The writer considers and then gives evidence against opposing points of view.

- The writer does not use claims that rely solely on readers' emotions.

Before you write, look over your notes. Determine whether the writer's argument is sound and the claim is valid. Then decide which examples you will use to support your evaluation. Use your notes as a guide as you write.

To begin your draft, state the writer's position. Then, write a thesis statement that expresses your opinion of the writer's argument and claim. In the body of your essay, show how the writer develops the argument. Explain why the claim is or is not valid. Use examples from the text to support your ideas. Finally, write a conclusion that restates your thesis and sums up your ideas.

Academic Vocabulary

claim the writer's position on an issue

evidence factual details that support a claim

Apply the Standard

Use the worksheet that follows to help you apply the standard as you write. Several copies have been provided for you to use with different assignments.

- Evaluating an Argument

Name _____ Date _____ Assignment _____

Evaluating an Argument

Use the organizer to take notes for an essay in which you evaluate a writer's argument. Use specific details from the text to explain your responses.

Title:		Form (e.g. essay, speech):
Writer's position:		
What does the writer want readers to believe or do?		

Evaluation Questions	Response	Explain
Is an opinion clearly stated?	❏ Yes ❏ No	
Is the claim supported by reasons and evidence?	❏ Yes ❏ No	
Does the author provide sources than can be verified?	❏ Yes ❏ No	
Do the reasons make sense? Are they logical?	❏ Yes ❏ No	
Are reasons and evidence presented in an order that makes sense?	❏ Yes ❏ No	
Are transitions used to make the argument easy to follow?	❏ Yes ❏ No	
Does the writer acknowledge and give evidence against an opposing point of view?	❏ Yes ❏ No	
Are readers likely to agree or disagree with the writer's position?	❏ Yes ❏ No	

A

For use with Writing 9b

Name _____ Date _____ Assignment _____

Evaluating an Argument

Use the organizer to take notes for an essay in which you evaluate a writer's argument. Use specific details from the text to explain your responses.

Title:	Form (e.g. essay, speech):

Writer's position:

What does the writer want readers to believe or do?

Evaluation Questions	Response	Explain
Is an opinion clearly stated?	❏ Yes ❏ No	
Is the claim supported by reasons and evidence?	❏ Yes ❏ No	
Does the author provide sources than can be verified?	❏ Yes ❏ No	
Do the reasons make sense? Are they logical?	❏ Yes ❏ No	
Are reasons and evidence presented in an order that makes sense?	❏ Yes ❏ No	
Are transitions used to make the argument easy to follow?	❏ Yes ❏ No	
Does the writer acknowledge and give evidence against an opposing point of view?	❏ Yes ❏ No	
Are readers likely to agree or disagree with the writer's position?	❏ Yes ❏ No	

For use with Writing 9b

Name _____ Date _____ Assignment _____

Evaluating an Argument

Use the organizer to take notes for an essay in which you evaluate a writer's argument. Use specific details from the text to explain your responses.

Title:	Form (e.g. essay, speech):

Writer's position:

What does the writer want readers to believe or do?

Evaluation Questions	Response	Explain
Is an opinion clearly stated?	❏ Yes ❏ No	
Is the claim supported by reasons and evidence?	❏ Yes ❏ No	
Does the author provide sources than can be verified?	❏ Yes ❏ No	
Do the reasons make sense? Are they logical?	❏ Yes ❏ No	
Are reasons and evidence presented in an order that makes sense?	❏ Yes ❏ No	
Are transitions used to make the argument easy to follow?	❏ Yes ❏ No	
Does the writer acknowledge and give evidence against an opposing point of view?	❏ Yes ❏ No	
Are readers likely to agree or disagree with the writer's position?	❏ Yes ❏ No	

Writing 10a

10. **Write routinely over extended time frames (time for research, reflection, and revision) and shorter time frames (a single sitting or a day or two) for a range of discipline-specific task, purposes, and audiences.**

Explanation

Writing is a routine part of every student's life. Some writing assignments, such as multi-page essays or research reports, require a week or more to complete. Other writing activities can be finished in one class period or over a day or two. Emails and **blog** entries are examples of writing that can be completed in shorter time frames.

Technology makes emails and blog entries quick to write and easy to share. However, for your messages to be successful, they require thought and planning, like other kinds of writing. Here are strategies to use in planning and completing these shorter writing assignments successfully.

- Identify your task, purpose, and audience. Ask: Why am I writing? Who will be reading this? Keep your answers in mind as you write. If you have been given a **writing prompt**, read it carefully to make sure you understand the assignment.

- Plan how you will use the time available. If you have 40 minutes, you might use 10 minutes to plan, 20 minutes to write, and 10 minutes to revise and edit.

- If you are writing an email, fill in the email heading with the email address and a brief subject line that relates to the main idea of your email. If you are writing a blog entry, focus on a single topic, include an eye-catching headline, and bookmark any links you plan to embed in your post.

- Take a few minutes to jot down the main points you want to make about your subject. Then number your ideas in the order that you will discuss them.

- Draft your email or blog entry. Keep the tone informal and conversational, but use proper grammar and avoid slang and inappropriate language.

- Before you send your email or post your blog entry, reread it to make sure your message is complete and your ideas make sense. Compare your work against your outline. Check that your links work and correct any errors in punctuation, capitalization, spelling, and grammar.

Academic Vocabulary

blog web log; a common form of online writing, similar to a journal, to which writers post entries on a regular basis

writing prompt a sentence or sentences that provide a specific writing idea

Apply the Standard

Use the worksheet that follows to help you apply the standard as you write.

- Writing Emails or Blog Entries

Name _____ Date _____ Assignment _____

Writing Emails or Blog Entries

Use the organizer to plan and organize your email or blog entry.

Task: ❏ Email 　　　 ❏ Blog	Purpose: _____	Audience: _____
Plan your time: Prewrite _____ minutes	Draft _____ minutes	Revise and Edit _____ minutes

Organize Ideas

Email Message
To:
Subject:

- (greeting)
- (Body: Tell purpose of email)
- (Body-important idea)
- (Body-important idea)
- (closing)
  (signature)

Blog entry
Focus of blog
Topic of entry:

- (topic sentence that states main idea)
- (supporting detail)
- (supporting detail)
- (supporting detail)
- (conclusion)

Writing 10

10. **Write routinely over extended time frames (time for research, reflection, and revision) and shorter time frames (a single sitting or a day or two) for a range of discipline-specific tasks, purposes, and audiences.**

Explanation

A **summary** is a brief retelling of a text's main ideas in your own words. Students are often asked to summarize a text to show their grasp of these ideas. Summaries are short and can usually be done in a single class period or as an after school assignment.

If asked to write a summary in a short time frame, decide how many minutes you will spend on prewriting, drafting, revising, and editing. Allow a few minutes for copying a final draft. Your method depends on whether you are to summarize fiction or nonfiction.

- **Summarizing fiction:** Decide which characters, events, and details are key to explaining the plot. Begin by introducing the main characters and the story's conflict. Then, present the important events in the order in which they occur. Give enough information for readers to understand the general ideas and flow of the drama. End by explaining how the conflict is solved and what happens to the main character.

- **Summarizing nonfiction:** Scan the text, highlighting key details. Look for one or two sentences at the beginning of the text that tell the topic and main idea. A good place to look for other key ideas is in subheadings and the topic sentence of each supporting paragraph. Begin by giving the main idea. Then, present the most important ideas in the order in which they appear. End by restating the main idea.

When you write a summary, keep it brief and objective. Do not give your own opinion about the topic or the work itself. Just tell what is in the selection. Remember to use your own words and leave out any details that do not support the main ideas.

Academic Vocabulary

summary a brief retelling of a text's main ideas in one's own words

Apply the Standard

Use the worksheet that follows to help you apply the standard as you write. Several copies have been provided for you to use with different assignments.

- Writing a Summary

Name _____ Date _____ Assignment _____

Writing a Summary

Use the organizer below to help write a summary. First, identify your task, purpose, and audience. Then, plan your time. Next, list the key ideas, details, or events from the selection. Finally, use the information in the organizer to write a brief, objective summary.

Task: _____	Purpose: _____	Audience: _____	
Plan your time Prewrite: _____ minutes	Draft: _____ minutes	Revise and Edit: _____minutes	
Organize Ideas			
Key idea, detail, or event:	Key idea, detail, or event:	Key idea, detail, or event:	Key idea, detail, or event:

Summary

For use with Writing 10b

Writing 10

> **10. Write routinely over extended time frames (time for research, reflection, and revision) and shorter time frames (a single sitting or a day or two) for a range of discipline-specific tasks, purposes, and audiences.**

Explanation

When you write creatively, you use your imagination to express thoughts and feelings. In creative writing, you may choose to entertain, to explore ideas, or to tell truths about life. Poems and dramatic scenes are two kinds of creative writing. Each has its own form and way of conveying meaning.

- A poem is arranged in lines and stanzas. When you write a poem, appeal to readers' senses. Writers use **sound devices**, like rhyme, **rhythm**, and **onomatopoeia**; **figurative language**, like simile, symbolism, and metaphor; and imagery to appeal to the reader's senses.

- A dramatic scene conveys meaning through characters' words, actions, gestures, and interactions on the stage. When writing a dramatic scene, tell a story through dialogue and stage directions. Decide who will speak in the scene and use stage directions in brackets to show their actions.

  Theater Usher: Please follow me, Mr. President. Your seat is right this way. Mrs. Lincoln has already been seated.
  [Usher points and starts walking toward private theater box.]
  President Lincoln: [apologetically] I am sorry to have kept everyone waiting.

Be sure you know what your assignment is and how much time you have to complete it. Then make a plan that allows time for prewriting, drafting, revising, editing, and producing a clean final copy.

Academic Vocabulary

figurative language figures of speech such as similes, metaphors, and personification

sound devices rhythm, rhyme, alliteration, and other techniques that contribute to the effect of a poem

rhythm the pattern of stressed and unstressed syllables

onomatopoeia the use of words that imitate sounds

Apply the Standard

Use the worksheet that follows to help you apply the standard as you write.

- Writing a Poem or Scene

Name _____ Date _____ Assignment _____

Writing a Poem or Scene

Use the organizer to plan a dramatic scene.

Task:	Purpose:	Audience: ....

Gather ideas for a dramatic scene

Describe the setting, characters, and conflict you plan to include:

....

....

....

What idea or message about life do you want the scene to convey?

....

....

....

Make notes on the dialogue and actions in your scene.

Characters' Dialogue	Characters' Actions

A

Writing 10d

> 10. **Write routinely over extended time frames (time for research, reflection, and revision) and shorter time frames (a single sitting or a day or two) for a range of discipline-specific tasks, purposes, and audiences.**

Explanation

A **how-to essay** describes a **process** or explains how something is done. Process writing has a wide practical use in your daily life. Examples include recipes, guides for playing a game, instruction booklets for using a phone, and travel directions.

When writing a how-to paper, choose a topic that interests you. Be sure you know the topic well enough to explain it clearly and completely in a series of steps. Next, identify your audience. What might your readers already know? An informed audience may not need as much information to follow a process. Then write a draft with these elements:

- a list of materials, if needed

- a sequence of steps, listed in exact order

- transitional words and phrases to make the order clear; for example, *first of all, after you have, while you, at the same time, once you have*, and *finally*.

- helpful diagrams or illustrations, if needed

- explanation of any unfamiliar terms

- a specific, clear result

Make a plan that allows time for prewriting, drafting, revising, editing, and producing a final, clean copy. When you revise, make sure the introduction grabs readers' attention. Look to see that the middle includes all the steps of the process in the correct order. Check your modifiers to be sure they are used correctly. You may wish to set off the actual directions in a numbered or bulleted list. Finally, check the conclusion and make sure it sums up the process clearly.

Academic Vocabulary

how-to essay a short, focused piece of expository writing that explains a process

process series of steps or actions that lead to a specific result

Apply the Standard

Use the worksheet that follows to help you apply the standard as you write.

- Writing a How-to Paper

Name _____ Date _____ Assignment _____

Writing a How-to Paper

Use the organizer to gather and organize details for your how-to paper.

Task:	Purpose:	Audience: ....
Plan your time Prewrite: ....minutes	Draft: ....minutes	Revise and Edit: ....minutes

Gather Details

List of Materials Readers Need to Complete Process

Organize Directions Step-by-Step

Step 1	→	Step 2	→	Step 3

Step 6	←	Step 5	←	Step 4

A

Speaking and
Listening Standards

Speaking and Listening 1

> **1. Engage effectively in a range of collaborative discussions (one-on-one, in groups, and teacher-led) with diverse partners on grade 6 topics, texts, and issues, building on others' ideas and expressing their own clearly.***

Workshop: Deliver a Research Presentation

A research presentation is very much like a written research report. It shares many of the same characteristics. Both involve researching for reliable sources to support your ideas, outlining, and writing your report. One major difference is that with a research presentation, you present your report to the class orally, rather than turning in a written copy. You can include eye-catching graphics (such as charts, diagrams, or even a slide show) to help convey your main points.

Assignment

Present a research report on a topic of your choosing. Include these elements:

- a clearly stated main idea

- research that supports your main idea

- a coherent, logical organization

- graphics, such as charts or diagrams, to help illuminate important points

- appropriate eye contact, adequate volume, and clear pronunciation

- language that is formal and precise and that follows the rules of standard English

*Additional Standards

Speaking and Listening

1.a. Come to discussions prepared, having read or studied required material; explicitly draw on that preparation by referring to evidence on the topic, text, or issue to probe and reflect on ideas under discussion.

1.b. Follow rules for collegial discussions, set specific goals

and deadlines, and define individual roles as needed.

1.c. Pose and respond to specific questions with elaboration and detail by making comments that contribute to the topic, text, or issue under discussion.

1.d. Review the key ideas expressed and demonstrate understanding of multiple

perspectives through reflection and paraphrasing.

4. Present claims and findings, sequencing ideas logically and using pertinent descriptions, facts, and details to accentuate main ideas or themes; use appropriate eye contact, adequate volume, and clear pronunciation.

5. Include multimedia components (e.g., graphics, images, music, sound) and visual displays in presentations to clarify information.

6. Adapt speech to a variety of contexts and tasks, demonstrating command of formal English when indicated or appropriate.

Research and Organize Your Report

After you've decided on a topic, you need to perform research and then organize your information into a logical presentation.

Main idea Decide on the main idea of your report. For example, you may want to investigate the topic of high-speed trains. You could focus your topic to learn about the benefits and drawbacks of high-speed train travel. Try to state your main idea in one clear topic sentence.

Then, with a small group, take turns reading topic sentences aloud to be sure that each group member's topic is clear enough and focused enough. If a topic is too broad or too narrow, offer suggestions for focusing or clarifying the main idea. Finally, provide ideas for research questions that should be answered in the report and for finding information to support each topic.

Research your main idea Gather information about your main idea from several sources, such as books, magazines, and the Internet. This information will provide the supporting details for your presentation. Make sure the sources you use are valid and reliable. Ask yourself the following questions to determine if a source is trustworthy and legitimate:

- Is the information current (within the past two years)?

- Is the source well known for correct facts?

- Does the source provide specific details about where its facts or information came from?

- If the source makes an argument, does it also present opposing views and seem unbiased?

Use precise and concise language Make sure your main idea sentence is clear and specific. Avoid using extra words that might confuse the audience. Your supporting details should be equally precise and easy to understand. Look at the following example:

> **Wordy, imprecise language:** *High-speed trains are really fast and can make getting from one place to another cost a lot less money.*

> **Clear, precise language:** *High-speed train travel saves time and money.*

Conclusion As you plan your report, remember that you must end your presentation with a strong conclusion. The conclusion should restate your main idea and one or two of your main supporting details. Try to close with a statement or question that will engage the listener. Make sure you leave time to answer your classmates' questions.

Name _____ Date _____ Assignment _____

Organize Your Research Presentation

Fill in the following chart to help organize your presentation. Write your topic sentence in the box at the top of the chart. Then, jot down three main points in the boxes below your topic sentence, supporting each point with facts, details, examples, and explanations gathered through research. Finally, briefly restate your main idea and one or two of your main points in the "Conclusion" box.

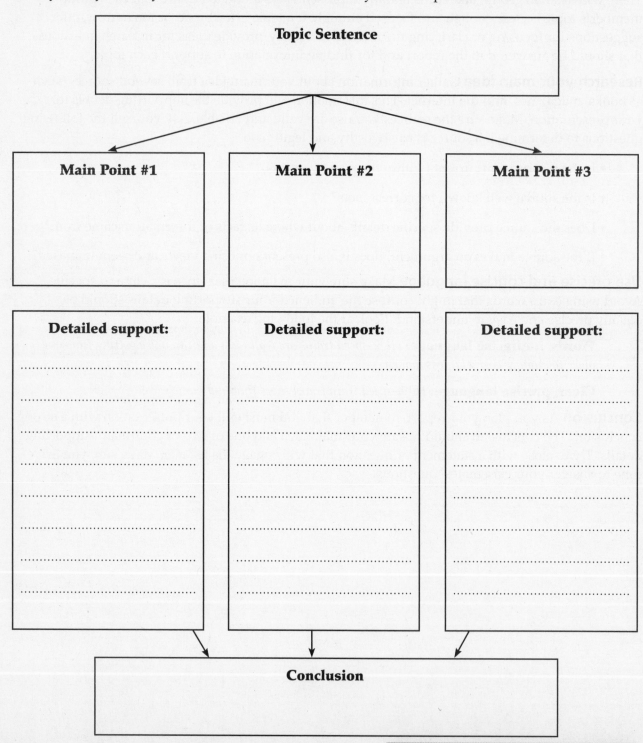

Topic Sentence

Main Point #1

Main Point #2

Main Point #3

Detailed support:

Detailed support:

Detailed support:

Conclusion

Name _____ Date _____ Assignment _____

Visuals and Multimedia

Make your presentation visually engaging by using charts, graphs, diagrams, and other multimedia.

Use visual displays and multimedia components. Visuals and multimedia components can grab your audience's attention and help clarify complex information and ideas. Graphs and diagrams can show your audience how something works or illustrate relationships between different ideas. Audio or video clips can help highlight or explain elements of your presentation. You don't want to overdo the visuals and multimedia components—they are most effective when used to emphasize important points. Integrate these items into your presentation by introducing each one and explaining how it supports your point.

Collaborate with a small group to brainstorm ideas for visuals and multimedia to use in your presentation. Everyone should discuss the main idea and major points of their presentations so the group can generate ideas. When you have decided on the visuals and multimedia components you want to use in your presentation, complete this chart to help you integrate them into your presentation:

Visual or Multimedia Component	Main Point It Supports	Where to Include It and How to Introduce It

Name _____ Date _____ Assignment _____

Presentation Techniques

How you present your research to your audience is as important as how well you have organized and written it.

Use presentation techniques. Keep these tips in mind as you rehearse your presentation. You can use the rubric that follows to evaluate yourself.

- **Eye contact:** Maintain eye contact with members of your audience so they feel that you are speaking directly to them.

- **Volume:** Make sure you speak loudly enough for everyone to hear you. When appropriate, increase or decrease your volume when making an important point.

- **Pronunciation:** Speak at an even pace and clearly enunciate your words so your audience can understand what you are saying. Be careful not to rush. If you have trouble pronouncing a word, practice it so you avoid stumbling over it when presenting your report.

- **Natural gestures:** Stand straight and face your audience. Avoid moving your hands in a nervous or distracting manner. The natural gestures you normally use in conversation can help you maintain a friendly but appropriately formal tone.

- **Language conventions:** The language you use should follow the rules of written English. Errors in grammar or inappropriate slang will distract listeners from your message.

Use the rubric below to assess fellow students' presentation techniques.

Presentation Technique	Listening Rubric
Eye contact	❑ Did the speaker maintain eye contact? ❑ Did you feel the speaker was speaking directly to you?
Speaking volume	❑ Was the speaker loud enough for everyone to hear? ❑ Did he or she vary tone for effect or to make a point?
Pronunciation	❑ Was the speaker's delivery evenly paced and easy to understand? ❑ Did he or she exhibit control over language in the report?
Gestures	❑ Did the speaker use effective hand gestures to emphasize important points in the presentation?
Language conventions	❑ Did the speaker use standard English? ❑ Was the language clear and precise?

Name _____ Date _____ Assignment _____

Discuss and Evaluate

After you and your classmates have presented your reports, discuss the content of your report and your delivery with classmates.

Discuss and evaluate the presentation. Survey your classmates to see if your main idea was clear and your research supported the main idea. Ask them to describe specific strengths and weaknesses of your presentation. Listen for a consensus among your classmates' responses. Try to summarize the points of agreement and disagreement. Refer to the guidelines below to make your discussion as productive as possible.

Guidelines for Discussion

Prepare for the discussion by reviewing the rubric for evaluating a presentation, which appears below.

- Help the group set goals for the discussion and assign specific roles, such as leader or note-taker, as necessary.

- Ask detailed questions and answer questions in a way that helps the group stay focused and meet its goals.

- Listen for new ideas suggested by others, and, when appropriate, change your own thinking to take such ideas into account.

Guidelines for Group Discussion

Discussion Rubric	Notes
❑ Did everyone in the group participate in the discussion? ❑ Was everyone able to express his or her opinion freely?	
❑ Was there a leader guiding the discussion? ❑ Was someone taking notes to share with the group at the end of the discussion?	
❑ Did participants ask detailed questions? ❑ Did participants answer and elaborate on questions asked by others? ❑ Did the group's questions and answers stay focused on the topic?	
❑ Were participants open to comments from others? ❑ Were people in the group open to new ideas and different perspectives suggested by others?	

For use with Speaking and Listening 1

Name _____ Date _____ Assignment _____

Self-Assessment

When the class discussion and evaluation is completed, take a few moments to reflect on your presentation. How do you think it went? Consider how your classmates reacted to the presentation—did the group discussion help you to realize anything about your presentation?

Using a rubric for self-assessment. Based on your own and your classmates' opinions of your performance, fill out the following rubric. Try to assess your presentation and delivery as if you were an audience member instead of the person who gave the presentation. Use the rating scale to grade your work. Circle the score that best applies for each category.

Criteria	Rating Scale
	not very very
Focus: How clearly did my presentation state the main idea? How easily were the most important points recognized?	1 2 3 4 5
Organization: How well was my presentation organized? How easily could listeners follow it?	1 2 3 4 5
Research and Support: How well did I support the main idea and important points with strong research, clear visual displays, and engaging and appropriate multimedia components?	1 2 3 4 5
Delivery: How often did I make eye contact with listeners? Did I maintain an adequate volume and speak clearly?	1 2 3 4 5
Conventions: How free of grammatical errors was my presentation?	1 2 3 4 5

Speaking and Listening 2

> **2. Interpret information presented in diverse media and formats (e.g., visually, quantitatively, orally) and explain how it contributes to a topic, text, or issue under study.**

Explanation

When you are studying a particular topic or text, you may need to gather information from several different sources to increase your understanding. You can find information in print by looking in books, magazines, newspapers, or other texts. You can also check a variety of non-print **media** sources, such as video newscasts, Internet articles, television programs, and music CD.

Both print and non-print media present information in a variety of **formats,** including

- visual elements, such as pictures and videos
- quantitative information, such as charts and graphs
- oral elements, such as interviews, narration, or song lyrics

Successful listeners and speakers are able to **interpret** information found in all kinds of media and formats. When you interpret information, you should be able to explain what you learned and tell how the information expanded your understanding of a particular topic, text, or issue. It should also help you better explain how the ideas in the source clarified or enhanced your understanding.

Examples

- **Visual** elements provide information not available from text sources. Images also create emotional responses. For example, if you are studying gorillas, images of their destroyed habitats may make you feel sad, upset, or angry. Images can be very persuasive. Remember that the visual's purpose may be to make you feel a certain way.

- **Quantitative** information is often presented in a format that makes complex data easy to understand. Charts and graphs are two ways to present quantitative information. For example, in your study of gorillas, you may find a chart that shows the decline in the gorilla population worldwide over the last 100 years.

- **Oral** elements refer to information that is spoken or sung. Often you will find audio clips within news articles on the Web. For example, you might find an article about gorillas that includes an interview with a researcher who studies the animals.

Academic Vocabulary

format the way in which something is presented and published

interpret to explain or understand the meaning of a work

media various forms of mass communication (e.g., TV, radio, newspapers, Internet)

Apply the Standard

Use the worksheet that follows to help you apply the standard.

- Interpreting Information from Different Media

Name _____ Date _____ Selection _____

Interpreting Information from Different Media

Use the organizer to analyze information on a single topic from different media sources. Then answer the question that follows.

Topic:		
Type of Media	**Format(s) Used**	**Information Provided**
1.		
2.		
3.		

How does each source contribute to your understanding of the topic? ....

....

....

A

Name _____ Date _____ Selection _____

Interpreting Information from Different Media

Use the organizer to analyze information on a single topic from different media sources. Then answer the question that follows.

Topic:		
Type of Media	**Format(s) Used**	**Information Provided**
1.		
2.		
3.		

How does each source contribute to your understanding of the topic? ....

....

....

For use with Speaking and Listening 2

Name _____ Date _____ Selection _____

Interpreting Information from Different Media

Use the organizer to analyze information on a single topic from different media sources. Then answer the question that follows.

Topic:		
Type of Media	**Format(s) Used**	**Information Provided**
1.		
2.		
3.		

How does each source contribute to your understanding of the topic? ....

....

....

C

Speaking and Listening 3

> **3. Delineate a speaker's argument and specific claims, distinguishing claims that are supported by reasons and evidence from claims that are not.**

Explanation

Some speakers try to convince you to do something, some want you to believe what they believe, and still others just want you to purchase what they are selling. With any media message whose purpose is to persuade you, it is important to discern what is factual and what is opinion.

Successful listeners are able to **delineate,** or clearly describe and define, the argument and specific claims a speaker is making.

Examples

- A strong argument makes a specific **claim** and provides clear reasons and reliable evidence to support the claim. A weak argument, or one based on opinion, rarely contains strong support. When listening to a speaker or media message, listen for the specific claim being made. Look for cause and effect words or phrases, like *as a result, because, cause,* and *due to.* A claim may also begin such as, "It appears that . . ." or "Evidence shows that . . ."

- Distinguish claims supported by reason and evidence from claims that are not. Direct quotes from experts, research by reputable institutions, and specific numbers from scientific studies are generally reliable sources in a strong argument.

- Verify the evidence from a speaker or media message by looking it up yourself. See if the evidence the speaker provided is legitimate or from a trustworthy source (Web sites that end in *.org* or *.edu* are usually reliable sources.).

Academic Vocabulary

delineate to specifically describe and define

claim an assertion of an idea or belief

Apply the Standard

Use the worksheets that follow to help you apply the standard.

- Understanding a Speaker's Argument

- Evaluating Evidence and Reasoning

Name _____ Date _____ Selection _____

Understanding a Speaker's Argument

Use the organizer to help delineate a speaker's argument and identify specific claims. Then answer the question at the bottom of the page.

```
┌─────────────────────────────────────────────────┐
│                  Main Claim                       │
│                                                   │
│   .............................................   │
│                                                   │
│   .............................................   │
│                                                   │
│   .............................................   │
│                                                   │
│   Ask: Is this claim supported by reasons or evidence? │
└─────────────────────────────────────────────────┘
```

```
┌──────────────────┐  ┌──────────────────┐  ┌──────────────────┐
│ Secondary/Supporting│  │ Secondary/Supporting│  │ Secondary/Supporting│
│      Claim        │  │      Claim        │  │      Claim        │
│                   │  │                   │  │                   │
│  ...............  │  │  ...............  │  │  ...............  │
│                   │  │                   │  │                   │
│  ...............  │  │  ...............  │  │  ...............  │
│                   │  │                   │  │                   │
│  ...............  │  │  ...............  │  │  ...............  │
│                   │  │                   │  │                   │
│ Ask: Is this claim│  │ Ask: Is this claim│  │ Ask: Is this claim│
│ supported by      │  │ supported by      │  │ supported by      │
│ reasons or evidence?│  │ reasons or evidence?│  │ reasons or evidence?│
└──────────────────┘  └──────────────────┘  └──────────────────┘
```

How do the secondary claims in the speaker's argument support the main claim?

....

....

....

....

A

Name _____ Date _____ Selection _____

Understanding a Speaker's Argument

Use the organizer to help delineate a speaker's argument and identify specific claims. Then answer the question at the bottom of the page.

Main Claim

....

....

....

Ask: Is this claim supported by reasons or evidence?

Secondary/Supporting Claim	**Secondary/Supporting Claim**	**Secondary/Supporting Claim**
....	....	....
Ask: Is this claim supported by reasons or evidence?	Ask: Is this claim supported by reasons or evidence?	Ask: Is this claim supported by reasons or evidence?

How do the secondary claims in the speaker's argument support the main claim?

....

....

....

....

B   For use with Speaking and Listening 3

Name _____ Date _____ Selection _____

Understanding a Speaker's Argument

Use the organizer to help delineate a speaker's argument and identify specific claims. Then answer the question at the bottom of the page.

Main Claim

....

....

....

Ask: Is this claim supported by reasons or evidence?

Secondary/Supporting Claim

....

....

....

Ask: Is this claim supported by reasons or evidence?

Secondary/Supporting Claim

....

....

....

Ask: Is this claim supported by reasons or evidence?

Secondary/Supporting Claim

....

....

....

Ask: Is this claim supported by reasons or evidence?

How do the secondary claims in the speaker's argument support the main claim?

....

....

....

....

C

Name _____ Date _____ Selection _____

Evaluating Evidence and Reasoning

Use the organizer to evaluate the evidence and reasoning in a speaker's argument. Research to verify the validity of the author's claims. Then answer the question at the bottom of the page.

Evidence/Reasoning Offered	Facts Cited	Facts Verified
1.		
2.		
3.		

How would you characterize the strength of the argument based on the evidence and reasoning?

....

....

....

....

....

A

Name _____ Date _____ Selection _____

Evaluating Evidence and Reasoning

Use the organizer to evaluate the evidence and reasoning in a speaker's argument. Research to verify the validity of the author's claims. Then answer the question at the bottom of the page.

Evidence/Reasoning Offered	Facts Cited	Facts Verified
1.		
2.		
3.		

How would you characterize the strength of the argument based on the evidence and reasoning?

....

....

....

....

....

For use with Speaking and Listening 3

Name _____ Date _____ Selection _____

Evaluating Evidence and Reasoning

Use the organizer to evaluate the evidence and reasoning in a speaker's argument. Research to verify the validity of the author's claims. Then answer the question at the bottom of the page.

Evidence/Reasoning Offered	Facts Cited	Facts Verified
1.		
2.		
3.		

How would you characterize the strength of the argument based on the evidence and reasoning?

....

....

....

....

....

C

Speaking and Listening 4

> **4. Present claims and findings, sequencing ideas logically and using pertinent descriptions, facts, and details to accentuate main ideas or themes; use appropriate eye contact, adequate volume, and clear pronunciation.**

Explanation

When you give a presentation to an audience, start by clearly making a claim about your topic. Support your claim with evidence. Use **pertinent,** or relevant, descriptions, facts, and details to **accentuate** your main points, and present them in a logical **sequence**. Your audience should be able to understand your claim and follow along with your presentation. Effective speakers also use appropriate eye contact, adequate volume, and clear pronunciation to keep audiences engaged.

Examples

- Think about the order in which you should present information. Choose the one that makes the most sense for your audience. For example, if your claim is that schools should offer healthier lunch options, make your audience aware of the problems with school lunches first. Then describe how you would solve the problem with healthier foods. Make sure your points are linked to each other logically.

- Provide a sufficient number of facts, descriptions, and details to support your claims. Look for information in reliable sources, such as news reports, news magazines, or reliable web sites. Make sure the information is pertinent, or applies directly to your topic. For example, nutritional information about school lunches would be pertinent information, while a description of what the school cafeteria looks like would not support your claim.

- Use eye contact, volume, and clear pronunciation to keep your audience engaged. Look around the room at your audience as you speak, and make sure your voice is loud enough to be heard by everyone. You can also vary your tone and volume to keep the audience interested. Be sure your delivery is not too fast or too slow and that you clearly pronounce your words. If you have trouble with certain words, practice them ahead of time.

Academic Vocabulary

accentuate to draw attention to or make more noticeable

sequence the order in which things are organized or arranged

pertinent related to the subject or idea being discussed or examined

Apply the Standard

Use the worksheets that follow to help you apply the standard. Several copies of each worksheet have been provided for you to use with different assignments.

- Summarizing and Organizing Information

- Presenting a Speech Effectively

Name _____ Date _____ Assignment _____

Summarizing and Organizing Information

Use the organizer to summarize and organize information for a presentation. State your claim in the box on the right, then list supporting details in the boxes on the left. Then, list the details in a logical sequence.

Source 1:

....

....

Summary:

....

....

Source 2:

....

....

Summary:

....

....

Source 3:

....

....

Summary:

....

....

Claim

....

....

....

....

Sequence of Findings for Presentation

Organize what you summarized into a logical sequence.

1. ....

....

....

....

2. ....

....

....

....

....

3. ....

....

....

....

....

Name _____ Date _____ Assignment _____

Summarizing and Organizing Information

Use the organizer to summarize and organize information for a presentation. State your claim in the box on the right, then list supporting details in the boxes on the left. Then, list the details in a logical sequence.

Source 1:

....

....

Summary:

....

....

Source 2:

....

....

Summary:

....

....

Source 3:

....

....

Summary:

....

....

Claim

....

....

....

....

Sequence of Findings for Presentation

Organize what you summarized into a logical sequence.

1. ....

....

....

....

2. ....

....

....

....

3. ....

....

....

....

B

Name _____ Date _____ Assignment _____

Summarizing and Organizing Information

Use the organizer to summarize and organize information for a presentation. State your claim in the box on the right, then list supporting details in the boxes on the left. Then, list the details in a logical sequence.

Source 1:

....
....

Summary:

....
....

Source 2:

....
....

Summary:

....
....

Source 3:

....
....

Summary:

....
....

Claim

....
....
....
....

Sequence of Findings for Presentation

Organize what you summarized into a logical sequence.

1. ....
....
....
....

2. ....
....
....
....

3. ....
....
....
....

For use with Speaking and Listening 4

Name _____ Date _____ Assignment _____

Presenting a Speech Effectively

Use the organizer to help you prepare your presentation and then use it to assess your delivery after you have given your speech.

	Presentation Checklist
Preparation	❏ Is my speech logically organized? ❏ Have I included pertinent descriptions, facts, and details? ❏ Have I practiced my speech enough to know it well? ❏ Have I reviewed the words I have trouble pronouncing?
Eye Contact	❏ Did I make eye contact throughout my speech? ❏ Did I look around the room at my audience? ❏ Was I able to keep my audience engaged by maintaining eye contact?
Volume	❏ Was my speaking volume loud enough for everyone in the audience to hear me? ❏ Did I vary my tone for dramatic effect at important points in my speech? ❏ Did I maintain a steady pace in my delivery?
Pronunciation	❏ Was my delivery and pronunciation of the words natural? ❏ Did I pronounce each word clearly and correctly?

A

Name _____ Date _____ Assignment _____

Presenting a Speech Effectively

Use the organizer to help you prepare your presentation and then use it to assess your delivery after you have given your speech.

	Presentation Checklist
Preparation	❑ Is my speech logically organized? ❑ Have I included pertinent descriptions, facts, and details? ❑ Have I practiced my speech enough to know it well? ❑ Have I reviewed the words I have trouble pronouncing?
Eye Contact	❑ Did I make eye contact throughout my speech? ❑ Did I look around the room at my audience? ❑ Was I able to keep my audience engaged by maintaining eye contact?
Volume	❑ Was my speaking volume loud enough for everyone in the audience to hear me? ❑ Did I vary my tone for dramatic effect at important points in my speech? ❑ Did I maintain a steady pace in my delivery?
Pronunciation	❑ Was my delivery and pronunciation of the words natural? ❑ Did I pronounce each word clearly and correctly?

Name _____ Date _____ Assignment _____

Presenting a Speech Effectively

Use the organizer to help you prepare your presentation and then use it to assess your delivery after you have given your speech.

	Presentation Checklist
Preparation	❑ Is my speech logically organized? ❑ Have I included pertinent descriptions, facts, and details? ❑ Have I practiced my speech enough to know it well? ❑ Have I reviewed the words I have trouble pronouncing?
Eye Contact	❑ Did I make eye contact throughout my speech? ❑ Did I look around the room at my audience? ❑ Was I able to keep my audience engaged by maintaining eye contact?
Volume	❑ Was my speaking volume loud enough for everyone in the audience to hear me? ❑ Did I vary my tone for dramatic effect at important points in my speech? ❑ Did I maintain a steady pace in my delivery?
Pronunciation	❑ Was my delivery and pronunciation of the words natural? ❑ Did I pronounce each word clearly and correctly?

For use with Speaking and Listening 4

Speaking and Listening 5

> **5. Include multimedia components (e.g. graphics, images, music, sound) and visual displays in presentations to clarify information.**

Explanation

When making a presentation, include visual displays and **multimedia** elements to help **clarify information** for your audience. Sometimes a photo or video clip can communicate an idea or a fact more effectively than words alone. For example, if you are presenting information about homelessness in your town, photos of families at a soup kitchen or the elderly sleeping in a park will produce a greater effect on your audience than simply telling them that this problem exists. Charts, music, graphics, photos, video, and sound can help you explain information to your listeners.

Examples

- Ask yourself which parts of your presentation would benefit most from using multimedia. For example, if you want to share statistics to make a key point, formatting them in a graph or chart will help your audience grasp them. If you plan to discuss an event that occurred in the past, showing a video clip of the event will bring it to life for your audience. Music can also be effective to set a mood or to help emphasize an important point.

- Do not include multimedia unless it will clarify information for your audience and strengthen your presentation. Images and sounds that do not specifically support what you are presenting can simply be distracting and confuse the audience. Before using multimedia in a presentation, ask yourself a few questions.

    - Does the media component help to clarify the point I am making?

    - Does the media component apply directly and clearly to the subject matter?

    - Is the media component easy to understand when one sees or hears it?

- After you have determined the multimedia components you will use, be sure to practice your presentation with the multimedia to make sure your use of the various media elements is smooth and seamless.

Academic Vocabulary

clarify information to make something clearer or more accurate

multimedia different forms of communication, such as sound, images, and video

Apply the Standard

Use the worksheet that follows to help you apply the standard.

- Using Multimedia and Visuals

Name _____ Date _____ Assignment _____

Using Multimedia and Visuals

Use the following organizer to identify multimedia components you will include in your presentation. Describe how each component will help communicate information or clarify an important point.

Multimedia or Visual Component *Brief description of what you will use*	How Media or Visual Component Will Help Clarify Presentation

Speaking and Listening 6

> 6. Adapt speech to a variety of contexts and tasks, demonstrating command of formal English when indicated or appropriate.

Explanation

When you speak in different situations and for different reasons, you need to **adapt,** or change, the way you speak. Think about your task, or the reason you are speaking. Also consider the **context** in which you will speak: Who is in the audience, and what do they know about your subject? Are you delivering a formal presentation? Are you trying to be persuasive? Are you explaining something?

When you deliver a presentation, use **formal English** to communicate your ideas. Formal English shows that you respect both your subject and your audience. Avoid using casual, everyday language or slang.

Examples

- When adapting a speech, think about your task, subject, and audience. For example, if you are giving a presentation to your entire class about Internet research, use formal English and include specific, detailed information. However, if you are speaking informally to a small group of classmates, your language may be less formal, and you may not need as much specific information.

- Effective speakers are precise and engaging while using formal English:

    Pronouns: Unclear pronoun references can easily confuse the audience. Use names and specific nouns instead of pronouns.

    Sentence Variety: Vary the length and tempo (the speed at which you speak) of your sentences. For important points, use short, simple sentences. If you use compound or complex sentences, be sure listeners can easily follow what you say.

Academic Vocabulary

adapt to change something in order to fit a specific purpose or situation

context the general situation in which a given thing happens

formal English language that strictly follows rules of grammar

Apply the Standard

Use the worksheets that follow to help you apply the standard. Several copies of each worksheet have been provided for you to use with different assignments.

- Adapting a Speech to an Audience

- Using Appropriate Language

Name _____ Date _____ Assignment _____

Adapting a Speech to an Audience

Use the following organizer to adapt your speech to different audiences. Then, answer the question at the bottom of the page.

Speaking Task: ....

<table>
<tr><td align="center">Audience</td><td></td><td align="center">Adaptations/Changes to
Your Speech</td></tr>
<tr>
<td>

Identify your audience. ....
....
....
....
....

List information about your audience.
....
....
....
....
....

</td>
<td>→</td>
<td>

List specific information you need to change or add to your speech.
....
....
....
....

Describe how you will adapt your language for your audience.
....
....
....
....

</td>
</tr>
</table>

What were the most important changes you needed to make to adapt your speech?

....
....
....
....
....

Name _____ Date _____ Assignment _____

Adapting a Speech to an Audience

Use the following organizer to adapt your speech to different audiences. Then, answer the question at the bottom of the page.

Speaking Task: ....

Audience	Adaptations/Changes to Your Speech
Identify your audience. .... *List information about your audience.*	*List specific information you need to change or add to your speech.* .... *Describe how you will adapt your language for your audience.* ....

What were the most important changes you needed to make to adapt your speech?

....

....

....

....

....

Name _____ Date _____ Assignment _____

Adapting a Speech to an Audience

Use the following organizer to adapt your speech to different audiences. Then, answer the question at the bottom of the page.

Speaking Task: ....

Audience	Adaptations/Changes to Your Speech
Identify your audience. .... *List information about your audience.*	*List specific information you need to change or add to your speech.* .... *Describe how you will adapt your language for your audience.* ....

What were the most important changes you needed to make to adapt your speech?

....

....

....

....

....

C

Name _____ Date _____ Assignment _____

Using Appropriate Language

Before you give a speech, use the following list of questions to evaluate your use of language. Then, answer the question at the bottom of the page.

	Questions to Ask Yourself
Language	Is the language in my speech formal English? Are there places where I can substitute more precise, engaging language to keep the listeners interested?
Sentences	Do I use the same sentence patterns too often? Are there places where I can vary the length of my sentences? Is the tempo of my sentences varied enough to keep the audience's attention? Do I use short sentences for dramatic effect and to emphasize key points?
Pronouns	Do I use too many pronouns? Are there places where I can substitute names and specific nouns to avoid confusion? When I use pronouns, is who or what I am referring to absolutely clear?

What changes did you make to your speech to make your language formal, precise, and engaging?

....

Name _____ Date _____ Assignment _____

Using Appropriate Language

Before you give a speech, use the following list of questions to evaluate your use of language. Then, answer the question at the bottom of the page.

	Questions to Ask Yourself
Language	Is the language in my speech formal English? Are there places where I can substitute more precise, engaging language to keep the listeners interested?
Sentences	Do I use the same sentence patterns too often? Are there places where I can vary the length of my sentences? Is the tempo of my sentences varied enough to keep the audience's attention? Do I use short sentences for dramatic effect and to emphasize key points?
Pronouns	Do I use too many pronouns? Are there places where I can substitute names and specific nouns to avoid confusion? When I use pronouns, is who or what I am referring to absolutely clear?

What changes did you make to your speech to make your language formal, precise, and engaging?

....

Name _____ Date _____ Assignment _____

Using Appropriate Language

Before you give a speech, use the following list of questions to evaluate your use of language. Then, answer the question at the bottom of the page.

	Questions to Ask Yourself
Language	Is the language in my speech formal English? Are there places where I can substitute more precise, engaging language to keep the listeners interested?
Sentences	Do I use the same sentence patterns too often? Are there places where I can vary the length of my sentences? Is the tempo of my sentences varied enough to keep the audience's attention? Do I use short sentences for dramatic effect and to emphasize key points?
Pronouns	Do I use too many pronouns? Are there places where I can substitute names and specific nouns to avoid confusion? When I use pronouns, is who or what I am referring to absolutely clear?

What changes did you make to your speech to make your language formal, precise, and engaging?

....

Language Standards

Language 1a

> **1a.** Demonstrate command of the conventions of standard English grammar and usage when writing or speaking.
> - Ensure that pronouns are in the proper case (subjective, objective, possessive).

Explanation

A **pronoun** is a word that takes the place of a noun or another pronoun. The **case** of a pronoun is the form that it takes to show its use in a sentence.

A **personal pronoun** refers to a specific noun that is named elsewhere in the sentence or paragraph. There are **two cases** of personal pronouns: **subjective pronouns** and **objective pronouns.** Their names give clues about how they are used. Use a **subjective** pronoun as the **subject** of a sentence or clause. Use an **objective** pronoun as the **object** of a verb or a preposition.

The third case of pronouns is the **possessive pronoun.** Use it to show ownership or possession.

Examples

This chart shows the three cases of pronouns.

Subjective Pronouns	Objective Pronouns	Possessive Pronouns
I, you, he, she, it, we, you, they	me, you, her, him, it, us, you, them	my, mine, your, yours, his, her, hers, its, our, ours, their, theirs

Here are examples of each case being used correctly in a sentence.

Subjective Pronouns:

Used as the **subject** of a sentence: **She** is the captain of our soccer team.

Used as the **subject** of a clause: The game that **we** played yesterday ended in a tie.

Objective Pronouns:

Used as the **direct object** of a verb: We congratulated **her** after the game.

Used as the **indirect object** of a verb: Then we gave **her** some water and orange slices.

Used as the **object of a preposition:** Because we are proud of our team, we always cheer for **them**.

Possessive Pronouns:

A different form is usually used when the possessive pronoun comes before a noun and when it stands alone.

Before a noun: Their bench is on the left side of the field.

Stands alone: The bench on the left side of the field is **theirs.**

Name _____ Date _____ Assignment _____

Apply the Standard

A. Circle the pronoun in each sentence. Then identify its case. Underline **subjective, objective,** or **possessive.**

1. Our soccer team is called The Cardinals. (subjective, objective, possessive)

2. Each season, we play fifteen games. (subjective, objective, possessive)

3. Ms. Hanes is at every practice, because she is the team coach. (subjective, objective, possessive)

4. Sometimes, Jen's older brother practices with us. (subjective, objective, possessive)

5. The team owes him a lot of thanks for giving good tips. (subjective, objective, possessive)

6. That soccer ball belongs to Jen, but this one is mine. (subjective, objective, possessive)

7. Mom gave the ball to me at the beginning of the season. (subjective, objective, possessive)

B. Choose the pronoun that completes each sentence correctly. Circle each answer.

1. In my town, children begin playing soccer when (they, them, theirs) are in kindergarten.

2. That's when Jen and (I, me, my) started playing.

3. At first, none of the kids on (we, us, our) team knew anything about field positions.

4. Often, every kid would charge after the ball whenever (it, its) seemed fun to do so.

5. Sometimes all of the players would end up inside (they, them, their) goal, kicking at the ball.

6. They didn't understand that one goal belongs to the opponents, and one goal is (they, their, theirs).

7. Mr. Sall, our first coach, tried to teach (we, us, our) the rules.

C. Use each pronoun in a sentence correctly.

1. **me** ....

2. **their** ....

3. **we** ....

4. **ours** ....

5. **she** ....

Language 1b

1b. Demonstrate command of the conventions of standard English grammar and usage when writing or speaking.

- **Use intensive pronouns (e.g., *myself, ourselves*).**

Explanation

An **intensive pronoun** is used to show strong feelings or emphasis. A **singular intensive pronoun** ends in *-self,* and a **plural intensive pronoun** ends in *-selves.*

Examples

This chart shows the intensive pronouns.

	Singular	**Plural**
First-person	myself	ourselves
Second-person	yourself	yourselves
Third-person	himself, herself, itself	themselves

Note that the third-person singular intensive pronoun for males is ***himself.*** There is no such word as ***hisself.*** Similarly, the third-person plural intensive pronoun is ***themselves.*** There is no such word as ***theirselves.***

Most often, the intensive pronoun **comes right after** the noun or pronoun that it renames. This placement serves to give added emphasis.

> It was Mary ***herself*** who suggested that she should be in charge of the search party.

> However, it was the boys ***themselves*** who discovered the hidden doorway.

Sometimes, the intensive pronoun comes a bit later in the sentence.

> I passed by the doorway ***myself*** but never noticed the big iron lock.

An intensive pronoun should **not** be used alone, without the noun or pronoun that it renames.

> **Incorrect:** ***Itself*** is a mysterious object.

> **Correct:** The door ***itself*** is a mysterious object.

Name _____ Date _____ Assignment _____

Apply the Standard

A. Circle the intensive pronoun in each sentence. Then underline the noun or pronoun it renames.

1. It was old Mr. Jameson himself who first told us about the mysterious door.

2. He wasn't sure where in the woods it was, but I myself was eager to search for it.

3. You yourselves might have some theories about who built the door and where it might lead.

4. Perhaps it was French fur trappers themselves who long ago dug a cave and closed it with that door.

5. Our search team found it ourselves and decided to solve the mystery.

B. Complete each sentence. Fill in the blank with the intensive pronoun that correctly renames the nearby noun or pronoun.

1. According to records in the library, it was animals .... who dug that old cave.

2. When the shaft was first opened, the cave .... was lined with fossils.

3. Others had seen fossils in books, but I .... had never seen one in real life.

4. Our librarian, Ms. Daniels, is .... an expert on fossils.

5. The fossils in the cave .... are probably about a thousand years old.

6. That shaft .... was built much later by the man who discovered the cave.

7. Mr. and Mrs. Jameson .... have lived nearby for years and never explored the cave.

8. I always thought that the forest trees .... were spooky and mysterious.

9. Henry, I'll bet that you .... would find the cave spooky, too.

10. By exploring the cave, we students .... now have a story to tell.

C. On the line, write a sentence using the intensive pronoun correctly.

1. myself ....

2. yourself ....

3. yourselves ....

4. herself ....

5. ourselves ....

Language 1c

> **1c. Demonstrate command of the conventions of standard English grammar and usage when writing or speaking.**
>
> • **Recognize and correct inappropriate shifts in pronoun number and person.**

Explanation

A **pronoun** takes the place of a noun. That noun is called the **antecedent.** A pronoun and its antecedent must **agree** in number. Always use a singular pronoun with a singular antecedent, and use a plural pronoun with a plural antecedent. A pronoun and its antecedent must also agree in **person.**

Examples

- *Singular Pronoun and Singular Antecedent*

  *Jane said that **she** might stay after school today.*

- *Plural Pronoun and Plural Antecedent*

  *Jane and I found out that **our** play practice starts at 3:30 p.m.*

- *Pronoun and Antecedent Agree in Person*

  *All players must bring **their** equipment to practice.*

Sometimes an **antecedent** is not a noun, but **an indefinite pronoun,** such as *all, someone, anybody, everyone, few, nothing, each,* or *many.* Errors in pronoun-antecedent agreement often happen when the antecedent is a singular indefinite pronoun.

- *Singular Indefinite Pronoun and Singular Antecedent*

  INCORRECT: ***Everyone** in the girls' chorus has practiced **their** solos.*

  CORRECT: ***Everyone** in the girls' chorus has practiced **her** solo.*

- **Plural Indefinite Pronoun and Plural Antecedent**

  ***Many** of the girls in the girls' chorus have practiced **their** solos.*

Name _____ Date _____ Assignment _____

Apply the Standard

A. Circle the pronoun that completes each sentence correctly. Underline its antecedent.

1. My friend Jane forgot (her, their) script.

2. All the students were supposed to bring (his, their) own costumes.

3. Then someone asked (her, their) mother to sew costumes for the whole cast.

4. The kind woman agreed to bring (her, their) sewing machine to the next rehearsal.

5. Jane and Helen have asked (her, their) friends to help paint the set.

B. Circle the pronoun error in each sentence, and write the correct pronoun on the line. If the sentence is correct, write "No error."

1. Jane, Helen, and I have learned all of her lines for the play. ....

2. Someone left their script in the prop room. ....

3. The girls in the dance class will practice their dance after our rehearsal is over.

   ....

4. Everybody is eager for her part in the show to run smoothly. ....

5. Each of the boys selling tickets has handed in the money they collected. ....

C. Rewrite the paragraph to include pronouns that agree with their antecedents.

   The conductor and the musicians have taken .... places in the orchestra pit. The principal will begin by sharing .... announcements. I hope the orchestra waits .... turn before beginning the first song. The cast members have found .... places and are ready to begin the show.

....

....

....

....

....

Language 1d

> **1d. Demonstrate command of the conventions of standard English grammar and usage when writing or speaking.**
>
> - **Recognize and correct vague pronouns (i.e., ones with unclear or ambiguous antecedents).**

Explanation

A **pronoun** takes the place of a noun or one or more other pronouns. For example, the pronoun *they* might take the place of the noun *students* in a sentence. The pronoun *they* might also take the place of the pronouns *he and she* in a different sentence. The noun or pronoun that is being renamed is called the **antecedent**. A pronoun and its antecedent must agree in number and person.

When you write, always check to be sure that the relationship between a pronoun and its antecedent is clear. Avoid using **vague pronouns**—those with ambiguous, missing, or unclear antecedents.

Examples

Ambiguous: When more than one word could be a pronoun's antecedent, revise the sentence to make your meaning clear:

- INCORRECT: *Mom and Ayana ate at **her** favorite restaurant. (Whose—Mom's or Ayana's?)*
  POSSIBLE CORRECTION: *Mom and Ayana ate at **Ayana's** favorite restaurant.*

Indefinite: When a pronoun's antecedent is not included in a sentence, revise the sentence to add the antecedent or rewrite the sentence without the pronoun.

- INCORRECT: *She likes to cook, and **it's** always delicious. (What is delicious?)*
  POSSIBLE CORRECTIONS: *She likes to cook **pizza**, and it's always delicious.* OR *She likes to cook, and **her meals** are always delicious.*

General: When a sentence includes a pronoun that refers to a general idea rather than a specific antecedent, revise the sentence and add a clear antecedent or rewrite the sentence without the pronoun.

- INCORRECT: *Ayana listens to music while she studies. **This** makes her distracted.* **(What makes her distracted?)**

- POSSIBLE CORRECTIONS: *Ayana listens to music while she studies. Listening to music makes her distracted.* OR *Ayana becomes distracted when she listens to music while studying.*

Name _____ Date _____ Assignment _____

Apply the Standard

Underline the vague pronouns in each sentence. On the lines, rewrite the sentences to clarify.

1. My mother, my brothers, and I took a bus to my grandparents', and they were very excited.

....

2. On most long rides, he stops the bus for snacks from time to time.

....

3. On the bus, my brothers Danny and Zach worked on puzzles in his magazine.

....

4. Toward the end of our trip, it got foggy and rainy.

....

5. Zach seemed scared, but she held his hand and got him to smile.

....

6. Grandpa met our bus. On the way to his house, it got a flat tire.

....

7. Grandma makes fantastic cookies. This is one reason why the kids love visiting.

....

8. Danny talked to Grandpa while he unloaded our bags.

....

9. Mom shared the news with Grandma as she walked in the house.

....

B. Revise the paragraph to fix the ambiguous, indefinite, and general pronoun references.

Danny, Zach, and I get to take turns bringing a friend to Grandma and Grandpa's lake house. Danny's friend Jose broke his fishing rod last year. This made him very upset. Danny and Jose played with his skateboard instead. They say that they had a great time.

....

....

....

Language 1e

1e. **Demonstrate command of the conventions of standard English grammar and usage when writing or speaking.**
  • **Recognize variations from standard English in their own and others' writing and speaking, and identify and use strategies to improve expression in conventional language.**

Explanation

The goal for writing and speaking is often to share information and feelings. Other times, it is to tell a great story. Writers and speakers must express their ideas clearly to reach these goals. Here are some basic rules for expressing your ideas clearly.

Examples

• **To improve your sentences:**

Avoid sentence fragments. The goal of a sentence is to express a complete thought. Sentence fragments don't meet that goal. Fix them by adding the words that complete your thoughts.

> **Fragment:** *On the table by my bed.*

> **Added words to form a complete sentence:** *I put the glass of water on the table by my bed.*

Avoid run-on sentences. A run-on sentence is two or more sentences stuck together without a conjunction or the right punctuation. Break run-ons apart or combine them correctly.

> **Run-on:** *My little sister loves stories I often read to her after school.*

> **As two sentences:** *My little sister loves stories. I often read to her after school.*

> **Combined correctly:** *My little sister loves stories, so I often read to her after school.*

• **To use modifiers clearly and correctly:**

To compare two things, use comparative adjectives, such as *shorter* and *more beautiful*. To compare more than two things, use superlative adjectives, such as *shortest* and *most beautiful*.

> **Two things:** *Sue is **shorter** than Ellen.*

> **More than two things:** *Sue is the **shortest** girl in my class.*

• **To use troublesome words correctly:**

Some words are often confused. *Good* is an adjective; *well* is an adverb. *Lie* means "to recline"; *lay* means "to place." *Raise* means "to lift up"; *rise* means "to get up."

> *This is a **good** dinner. You cook **well.***

> *I'll **lay** the breakfast dishes on the table before I **lie** down and go to sleep tonight.*

> *After you **rise** from bed in the morning, please **raise** the curtain and let the sunshine in.*

Name _____ Date _____ Assignment _____

Apply the Standard

Each item contains one or more errors. Rewrite each sentence correctly on the line provided.

1. We needed more storage space Dad decided to build a shed.

....

2. To store the lawn mower, the rakes, the shovels, and lots of other tools.

....

3. Because he is a carpenter, Dad builds good.

....

4. Dad drawed a diagram of the shed, and he teached me to saw boards.

....

5. When I saw the diagram, it looked like the bigger shed in the whole world.

....

6. Very cool.

....

7. "Let's lie down our tools and rest a bit," Dad said. "Come lie down on the cool grass for a while."

....

8. The next day we builded the final part of the shed we had finished our great project!

....

9. I think I am a good builder than my sister.

....

10. She loves to create things unfortunately she makes a lot of mistakes.

....

Language 2a

> **2a. Demonstrate command of the conventions of standard English capitalization, punctuation, and spelling when writing.**
>
> • **Use punctuation (commas, parentheses, dashes) to set off nonrestrictive/ parenthetical elements.**

Explanation

A **nonrestrictive** or **parenthetical** element is a word, phrase, or clause that is not essential and interrupts the flow of a sentence. **Commas, dashes,** or **parentheses** are used to set off a **nonrestrictive** or **parenthetical** element from the rest of the sentence.

Examples

- Use **commas** to set off information that is not essential but is closely related to the sentence.

  For example, the nonrestrictive clause *who is my neighbor* interrupts the following sentence but provides closely related details about Mrs. Sanchez.

  Mrs. Sanchez, **who is my neighbor,** *works for the police department.*

  Certain adverbs are typically parenthetical and should be set off with commas:

  I like listening to music. I think, **however,** *that music playing at stores is annoying.*

  Some common expressions are also parenthetical and should be set off with commas:

  He was, **in fact,** *not yet sixteen.*

- Use **dashes** to set off an abrupt change of thought or an important explanatory statement.

  For example, the dashes in this sentence signal an abrupt break in thought.

  *This restaurant—***I was here last week***—serves excellent seafood.*

  The nonrestrictive element provides important information in this sentence.

  *The two candidates—***Elmer Watts and Vivian Holmes***—will speak at our meeting tonight.*

- Use **parentheses** to set off information that is more loosely related to the sentence or that simply provides extra information. This information is helpful but not important to the overall meaning, as in this example:

  The moa **(now extinct)** *was a huge, flightless bird.*

Name _____ Date _____ Assignment _____

Apply the Standard

A. Rewrite the sentences. Use commas, dashes, or parentheses to set off the nonrestrictive elements.

1. An operetta also called "light opera" contains both songs and spoken lines.

   ....

   ....

2. Perhaps the most famous operetta writers W. S. Gilbert and Arthur Sullivan were British.

   ....

   ....

3. The well-known operetta *The Pirates of Penzance* in fact is one of their works.

   ....

   ....

4. Linda Ronstadt a great pop singer starred in a movie based on that operetta.

   ....

   ....

5. Gilbert and Sullivan's most famous operetta *H. M. S. Pinafore* takes place on a ship.

   ....

   ....

B. Each item is a nonrestrictive or parenthetical element. For each item, write a sentence using the element. Set it off with the punctuation marks appearing in parentheses.

1. who is a famous person I'd like to meet (commas) ....

   ....

2. George Washington (dashes) ....

   ....

3. my birthday (parentheses) ....

   ....

4. which is my favorite subject in school (commas) ....

   ....

Language 2b

> **2b. Demonstrate command of the conventions of standard English capitalization, punctuation, and spelling when writing.**
> - **Spell correctly.**

Explanation

Correct spelling helps readers understand what you have written. An exciting story, a strong persuasive essay, or a vivid description may become confusing if the writer fails to catch and correct spelling errors. Here are some guidelines to help you prevent—or catch—spelling errors.

Examples

Homophones are words that sound alike and have similar spellings. Homophones are commonly misspelled, and even the spell checker on a computer cannot always help you catch this type of error because the word is not being spelled incorrectly. You are using the *wrong* word! This chart shows some commonly confused homophones. Learn their definitions and their differences.

its—possessive pronoun *The dog ate all of its dinner.*	**it's**—a contraction, meaning "it is" *It's a tough hike to the top of the mountain.*
loose—"not tight" *For exercise, wear loose, comfortable clothes.*	**lose**—"to be defeated"; "to misplace something" *I hope we don't lose the game.*
passed—"to go in front of" *A speeding car passed our school bus.*	**past**—"former times" *In the past, people drove carriages.*
than—conjunction *Hal is older than his brother Tom.*	**then**—"at the time" or "next" *Pick up your pencil. Then begin to write.*
your—possessive pronoun *Is this your coat?*	**you're**—contraction meaning "you are" *You're a great dancer!*

Irregular plurals are unlike most plural nouns because they are not formed by simply adding –*s*. Here are some rules to keep in mind.

- Change a final *f* to *v* and add -*es*: *shelf/shelves; wolf/wolves; leaf/leaves*
- Add -*es* to words ending in -*sh*, -*ss*, or -*ch*: *dish/dishes; dress/dresses; bench/benches*
- Use the same form for both singular and plural: *one fish/two fish; one deer/two deer*
- Change the vowel structure: *goose/geese; mouse/mice; foot/feet*

Words with Unstressed Vowel Sounds are tricky because the unstressed sound can be spelled in different ways. These four groups show examples:

captain fiction darken   *helper sailor failure*   *trumpet benefit*   *capable sensible*

REMEMBER: Always use a dictionary if you are unsure about the spelling of a difficult or confusing word.

Name _____ Date _____ Assignment _____

Apply the Standard

A. Each sentence contains one or more misspelled or misused words. Circle them, and write the correct spellings on the line.

1. In Australia and New Zealand, your bound to find animals that are stranger then any you have seen.

    ....

2. Do you think its possable for an animel to find food when it's eyes are closed?

    ....

3. When the platypus dives into the watar to find fishes and shrimp to eat, it has both eyes firmly closed.

    ....

4. The platypus senses where they are and than uses it's beak like a shoval to scoop them up.

    ....

5. The kiwi, a strange bird that lives in New Zealand, is capible of finding food by stomping its foots.

    ....

6. It walks around the forist at night, stomping on the leafs and dirt, listening for the sound of worms.

    ....

7. The platypus and kiwi are endangered species because they are loosing their naturel habitats.

    ....

B. Use each of these pairs of easily confused words in a sentence. Make sure that your sentences clearly show the different meanings of the words.

1. loose, lose ....

    ....

2. its, it's ....

    ....

3. then, than ....

    ....

4. your, you're ....

    ....

Language 3a

> **3a. Use knowledge of language and its conventions when writing, speaking, reading, or listening.**
> • **Vary sentence patterns for meaning, reader/listener interest, and style.**

Explanation

As an established reader and writer, you know that a series of simple sentences can make a story dull. Therefore, when you write, be sure use different types of sentences. Try to include a balance of short and long sentences. Doing so will make your writing more interesting to read.

Examples

Sentence Types There are four basic types of sentences. Keep in mind their functions and the end punctuation that they require.

Sentence Type	Function	End Punctuation	Example
declarative	makes a statement	period	*The ruby is a precious gem.*
interrogative	asks a question	question mark	*Where is the road to Scottsdale?*
exclamatory	shows strong feelings	exclamation point	*What a huge spider that is!*
imperative	gives an order or direction	period or exclamation point	*Cut the bread into slices. Be careful with that sharp knife!*

Sentence Structures Sentences are classified according to the number and types of clauses they contain. A **clause** is a group of words with a subject and predicate. An **independent clause** expresses a complete thought, so it can stand alone as a sentence. A **dependent clause** cannot stand alone because it does not express a complete thought. The chart shows how clauses are used to create different sentence structures. The independent clauses are underlined, and the dependent clause is circled.

Simple Sentence	Compound Sentence	Complex Sentence
a single independent clause	two or more independent clauses	one independent clause and one or more dependent clauses
Examples: *It rained hard last night.* *Our game was cancelled.*	**Example:** *It rained hard last night, and our game was cancelled.*	**Example:** *Because it rained hard last night, our game was cancelled.*

Name _____ Date _____ Assignment _____

Combining Sentences As the chart shows, you can combine simple sentences and related thoughts to form compound or complex sentences. Follow these guidelines.

- **To form a compound sentence:** Use a coordinating conjunction and a comma to join two simple sentences. Examples of coordinating conjunctions include *and, but, or,* and *so.*
    Simple sentences: *I wanted to read a good book. I went to the library.*
    Combined: *I wanted to read a good book, so I went to the library.*

- **To form a complex sentence:** Change one of the independent clauses into a dependent clause. Set the new clause off with commas.
    Simple sentences: *I wanted to read a good book. I went to the library.*
    Combined: *Because I wanted to read a good book, I went to the library.*

Apply the Standard

A. For each sentence, write *declarative, interrogative, imperative,* or *exclamatory* on the line. Then add the correct end punctuation.

.... **1.** What a terrific camping trip it was

.... **2.** Do you need more blankets

.... **3.** Please teach me to catch a fish

.... **4.** There are trout in this stream

.... **5.** Watch out for that sharp hook

B. Combine each pair of simple sentences. Use commas and the words shown in parentheses. After your sentence, write **compound** or **complex** to identify the sentence structure of your new sentence.

1. Dad came home early. He surprised us with a great idea. **(and)**

....

2. He wanted to take us camping. We packed our clothes and gear. **(so)**

....

3. It was a chilly night. We packed warm clothes and extra blankets. **(because)**

....

4. Dad told us about our camping spot. It is a cabin in the woods. **(which)**

....

5. We arrived. We had a cookout dinner at the cabin. **(after)**

....

Language 3b

> **3b. Use knowledge of language and its conventions when writing, speaking, reading, or listening.**
> • **Maintain consistency in style and tone.**

Explanation

Voice is a writer's unique use of language that conveys his or her personality. For a story, your voice might be light and cheerful; for an essay, your voice might be serious. **Tone** is your attitude toward the topic. If you are writing about pollution, your tone might be concerned. If you are writing to an audience of children, your tone might be friendly and helpful. Together, your **voice** and **tone** create your writing **style.** Style describes *how* something is said, and the language you use contributes greatly to your style. Within a single piece of writing—a story, an essay, a report—it is important to maintain a single, consistent, and clear writing style from start to finish.

Examples

Word Choice The words that you use will play an important role in establishing and maintaining your writing style. To choose your words effectively, begin by thinking about your tone, or attitude, toward your topic and audience. If it is serious or concerned, choose formal words. If it is humorous or light, choose friendly, positive words. For example, suppose that your purpose for writing is to describe an old house. Word choice will change depending on the tone you want to express.

- **One possible tone:** concern because you want to express that the house is falling down and is a danger to neighborhood children
  Words to choose: serious words such as *dangerous, ruins, crumbling walls, sagging porch*

- **Another possible tone:** mysterious because you want to tell a spooky story
  Words to choose: spooky words, such as *dark, haunting, gray, weird cackling sounds*

Always choose vivid, specific words. Avoid such vague, bland words as *nice, bad,* and *awesome.* Instead, choose interesting words, such as *spectacular, terrifying,* and *electrifying.* A thesaurus will help you find words that will add punch to your writing.

Figurative Language Figures of speech, such as similes and metaphors, will help you create an interesting writing style. Suppose you are describing a sunny day. Study this chart to see how you can use figurative language to create tone or to support your style.

Figure of speech	Definition	Examples
simile	a comparison of two unlike ideas using *like* or *as*	a day that shimmered like gold
metaphor	a comparison of two unlike ideas in which one is described as being something else	the sand was powdered gold

Name _____ Date _____ Assignment _____

Consistency Be consistent with your tone and style throughout. Do not suddenly shift.

> **Inconsistent:** It was a cold, dreary day, and everyone seemed as silent as still water. Some people were laughing and telling jokes.

> **Consistent:** It was a cold, dreary day, and everyone seemed as silent as still water. Some people were talking quietly, but most were sitting in silence.

There are exceptions, of course. Sometimes you may want to surprise your readers with a sudden shift in tone. Use such shifts only when you want to create drama or suspense.

> **Consistent:** It was a cold, dreary day, and everyone seemed as silent as still water. Some were talking quietly, but most were sitting in silence.

> **Dramatic shift:** It was a cold, dreary day, and everyone seemed as silent as still water. Some were talking quietly, but most were sitting in silence. Suddenly Ian jumped and yelled, "Fire!"

Apply the Standard

A. Write a sentence to describe each item. Use vivid words and similes or metaphors to create the tone shown in parentheses.

1. a city park **(concerned)**

....

2. a city park **(light)**

....

3 an animal **(gentle)**

....

B. Write one or two sentences to describe the following situations. Select your own tone and writing style. Keep the tone and style consistent, or create a dramatic shift, as directed in parentheses.

1. fun on a Saturday afternoon **(consistent)** ....

....

2. what happened during a hike **(dramatic shift)** ....

....

3. an exciting show or parade **(consistent)** ....

....

Language 4a

4a. Determine or clarify the meaning of unknown and multiple-meaning words and phrases based on *grade 6 reading and content,* choosing flexibly from a range of strategies.

- **Use context (e.g., the overall meaning of a sentence or paragraph; a word's position or function in a sentence) as a clue to the meaning of a word or phrase.**

Explanation

When you come to an unfamiliar word in your reading, you can often use **context clues**—the other surrounding words, phrases, and sentences—to figure out its meaning. Most context clues are found in nearby words. You might also find clues in the general meaning of the entire sentence. Finally, you might find clues in the unknown word's position or function in the sentence.

Examples

Clues in Nearby Words Look for a word or phrase that may have a similar meaning to the unknown word or that might explain its meaning.

> **Similar meaning:** *My <u>primary</u>, or **main**, goal is to be a teacher.*
> (The clue suggests that *primary* means "main.")

> **Opposite meaning:** *It looked as though **we might lose the game, but** we were lucky to <u>prevail</u>.*
> (The clues suggest that *prevail* means "to win or succeed.")

> **Explanation of meaning:** *Because his explanation was so <u>lucid</u>, **we completely understood**.*
> (The clues suggest that *lucid* means "clear" or "easy to understand.")

Clues in the Meaning of the Sentence Look for the main idea of the sentence. Often, you can use it to figure out the meaning of an unknown word.

> *We expected Mr. Ames to be **a serious person but were surprised** that he was a <u>buffoon</u>.*
> (The general meaning of the sentence suggests that *buffoon* means "a silly or clownish person.")

Clues in the Word's Function in the Sentence. Look at where the word falls in the sentence. Think about its job, or function. Does it follow an article (*the, a*) or an adjective? If so, it is a noun. Does it express action? If so, it is a verb. Use that information, plus the first two types of clues, to figure out the unknown word's meaning.

> *The pleasant music and happy conversation <u>diverted</u> my attention from all worries and concerns.*
> (*Diverted* expresses action. Therefore, it's a verb. The general sense of the sentence suggests that *diverted* means "distracted or took one's attention away from.")

Name _____ Date _____ Assignment _____

Apply the Standard

A. Use the other words in the sentence to find the meaning of the underlined word. Write its definition on the line provided.

1. Welcome to my <u>abode</u>, a home that Grandpa built years ago. ....

2. The library subscribes to such <u>periodicals</u> as newspapers and magazines. ....

3. Cows do not eat meat, but sharks are <u>carnivores</u>. ....

4. Friendly people are more pleasant than those who are <u>aloof</u>. ....

5. I never thought of Fred as confident, but he gave that speech with great <u>aplomb</u>. ....

6. My fingers tasted salty after I swam in the <u>briny</u> sea. ....

7. At my farm, the sheep are sheltered at night in a sturdy wooden <u>cote</u>. ....

8. That was once a fine house, but lack of repairs gradually made it <u>dilapidated</u>. ....

9. I'm an <u>optimist</u>, like Mom. We both tend to look on the bright side. ....

10. Lions and dogs have teeth, but anteaters are <u>edentate</u> and must rely on their tongues. ....

B. Think about the underlined word's function and position in the sentence. Use that information, plus any other context clues, to define the underlined word. Write its meaning on the line.

1. Horses and zebras are <u>equines</u>. ....

2. When the lost children were found, everyone <u>erupted</u> with joy. ....

3. When the plumbers finish their work, they will send you an <u>invoice</u> for payment. ....

4. Sit in this comfortable chair and put your feet up on the matching <u>ottoman</u>. ....

5. Doctors <u>monitor</u> a person's illness with tests and medical tools. ....

6. Many small birds use their sharp and pointed <u>nibs</u> to pick up tiny seeds. ....

7. Please wipe your feet before entering the house to remove any <u>grime</u>. ....

8. Will the senator <u>field</u> questions from the audience after her speech? ....

9. This stone is a real ruby, but that stone is an <u>ersatz</u>. ....

10. She was tired of his <u>frivolous</u> chatter and wanted more serious talk. ....

Language 4b

> **4b.** Determine or clarify the meaning of unknown and multiple-meaning words and phrases based on *grade 6 reading and content*, choosing flexibly from a range of strategies.
>
> • Use common, grade-appropriate Greek or Latin affixes and roots as clues to the meaning of a word (e.g., *audience, auditory, audible*).

Explanation

When you come to an unfamiliar word in your reading, try breaking the word down into its parts. Look for **affixes** and **roots**. The meanings of those word parts may provide clues about the meaning of the unfamiliar word.

An **affix** is a word part that is attached to a base word in order to change the meaning of the base word. There are two kinds of affixes—**prefixes**, which are attached *before* the base word, and **suffixes**, which are attached *after* the base word. A **root** is the core of a word. Often, the root is an old word that has come into the English language from an ancient language, such as Latin or Greek.

Examples

This chart shows the meanings of some common Greek and Latin roots and affixes.

Word Part	Type	Came from...	Meaning	Example
-aqu-	root	Latin	"water"	aquarium (a water-filled tank for fish)
-cent-	root	Latin	"hundred"	cent (a coin; one hundred equal a dollar)
-bio-	root	Greek	"life"	biography (the story of someone's life)
-micr-	root	Greek	"small"	microbe (a tiny organism)
hyper-	prefix	Greek	"too much"	hypersensitive (overly sensitive)
in-, il-, ir-	prefix	Latin	"not"	irregular (not regular), illogical (not logical), irrelevant (not relevant)
pre-	prefix	Latin	"before"	preview (an introduction)
-ance	suffix	Latin	"the act of"	acceptance (the act of accepting)
-ard, -art	suffix	Greek	"one that does something too much"	dullard (someone who is often dull)
-eer	suffix	Latin	"doer or worker"	auctioneer (someone who runs an auction)

Name _____ Date _____ Assignment _____

Apply the Standard

A. On the line, write the definition of the underlined word. Use the meaning of its highlighted root or affix, as well as any context clues you discover.

1. We'll need a <u>**micro**scope</u> to see those tiny creatures.

....

2. We thought Jen was <u>**in**capable</u> of playing third base, but she did a fine job.

....

3. I was sorry to hear about the <u>discontinu**ance**</u> of half-price tickets.

....

4. This old building was built almost a <u>**cent**ury</u> ago.

....

5. This television show will be <u>**pre**recorded</u> and then shown at a later date.

....

B. Use the meanings of the highlighted affixes to answer the questions. Write your answers on the lines.

1. Would it be fun or comfortable to work for a <u>**hyper**critical</u> person? Explain why or why not.

....

2. What behavior would you expect from a <u>brag**gart**</u>? ....

3. If someone lived until her <u>**cent**ennial</u> year, how old would she be? ....

4. What examples can you give of <u>**aqua**tic</u> sports? ....

5. During what time in a concert would the <u>**pre**lude</u> take place? ....

C. Use the affixes and roots to figure out the meanings of these words. Write your answers on the lines.

1. resistance ....

2. illegal ....

3. bioscience ....

4. mountaineer ....

5. preheat ....

Language 4c

4c. Determine or clarify the meaning of unknown and multiple-meaning words and phrases based on *grade 6 reading and content*, choosing flexibly from a range of strategies.

- **Consult reference materials (e.g., dictionaries, glossaries, thesauruses), both print and digital, to find the pronunciation of a word or determine or clarify its precise meaning or its part of speech.**

Explanation

A **dictionary** provides the meanings, pronunciations, and parts of speech of words in the English language. A **thesaurus** provides **synonyms,** or words with similar meanings, for many words in the English language. You can find these books in your school or library. You can also access them online.

Examples

Notice what this **dictionary entry** reveals about the word *chapter*.

> **chapter** (chap′ tər) **n.** [L *capitulum*, head, capital, division in writing] **1** any of the main divisions of a book or other writing **2** something like a chapter; part; episode [a *chapter* of one's childhood] **3** a local branch of a club

- Following the boldface entry word are symbols that show the word's **pronunciation.** Note the stress mark that indicates which syllable is stressed (CHAP ter).

- The **n.** tells the part of speech. *Chapter* is a noun. Other abbreviations include **v.** (verb), **adj.** (adjective), and **adv.** (adverb).

- The **etymology,** or origin of the word, appears in brackets. *Chapter* comes from the Latin word *capitulum.*

- The definition follows. If there is more than one definition for the word, each is numbered. The main, or most used, definition is often placed first.

Now notice what this **thesaurus entry** for the word *smile* offers.

> **smile** (verb) look amused; beam; express friendliness; grin; look happy; laugh; simper; smirk
> *Antonyms:* frown; glower

- The part of speech follows the entry word.

- Synonyms are listed, followed by antonyms.

Name _____ Date _____ Assignment _____

Apply the Standard

Use the information in these dictionary and thesaurus entries to answer the questions.

Dictionary entry:

admit (ad mit') *v.* [L *admittere,* to send] **1** to permit to enter or use; to let in **2** to allow or entitle one to enter [this ticket *admits* one person] **3** to acknowledge or confess

Thesaurus entry:

admit (verb)
1. allow entry; give access; give the nod; okay; permit; receive; take in
Antonyms: deny access, dismiss, eject, exclude, refuse, reject, repel

2. acknowledge; bring to light; concede; confess; disclose; divulge; let on; make known; own up; reveal
Antonyms: cover up; deny; dispute; dissent; refuse

1. Which syllable in *admit* is the stressed syllable? ....

2. What part of speech is *admit*? ....

3. What language provided the origin of *admit,* and what did the original word mean?

   ....

4. According to the dictionary entry, what is the main, or most used, definition of *admit*? Explain what

   led you to your answer. ....

5. Which dictionary definition (1, 2, or 3) relates to the use of *admit* in this sentence?

   Did the man admit *that he broke the window?* ....

6. Rewrite this sentence, and use a **synonym** for *admit* found in the thesaurus.

   Did the prisoners admit *their roles in the crime?* ....

7. Write two synonyms and two antonyms for the **first** meaning of *admit* shown in the thesaurus.

   ....

8. Write a sentence using an **antonym** for the second meaning of *admit* found in the thesaurus.

   ....

Language 4d

> **4d. Determine or clarify the meaning of unknown and multiple-meaning words and phrases based on *grade 6 reading and content*, choosing flexibly from a range of strategies.**
>
> • **Verify the preliminary determination of the meaning of a word or phrase (e.g., by checking the inferred meaning in context or in a dictionary).**

Explanation

When you come to an unfamiliar word or phrase in your reading, look for **context clues** to figure out its meaning. Some clues might appear in **nearby words or phrases.** Others might be found in the **general meaning of the sentence**. If the meaning of the unknown word or phrase is still difficult to understand, **reread** the sentence or passage to look again for clues. Then **read ahead.** You may find clues in the sentences that follow the unknown word or phrase. To confirm the meaning of a word, it is sometimes necessary to look the word up in a dictionary.

Examples

Nearby Words Look for words or phrases that give clues, or help you infer word meaning.

> The horse seemed <u>frantic,</u> **or wild and nervous,** when we tried to load him into the van.

(The clues provide synonyms. They suggest that *frantic* means "wild and nervous.")

> Is this land <u>communal,</u> **or is it privately owned?**

(The clues provide an antonym. They suggest that *communal* means "public" or "shared by all.")

> **Many trees fell during** that <u>horrific</u> windstorm.

(The clues provide an explanation. They suggest that *horrific* means "terrible" or "horrible.")

Meaning of the Sentence Often the overall idea of the sentence will suggest the meaning of an unknown word or phrase.

> Some people are eager to try new methods, but Dad relies on methods that are <u>tried and true</u>.

(The general meaning of the sentence suggests that the phrase *tried and true* means "old," "established," or "proven to work.")

Sentences That Follow Read ahead. Often you can find clues in the words and phrases that appear in sentences that follow the unknown word or phrase.

> I had a <u>ghastly</u> dream last night. It was really frightening.

(The second sentence suggests that *ghastly* means "frightening.")

Dictionary If you have studied context clues, reread, and looked ahead in the text but are still unsure about the meaning of an unfamiliar word or phrase, use a dictionary to verify its meaning.

Name _____ Date _____ Assignment _____

Apply the Standard

A. Use context clues to find the meaning of the underlined word or phrase. Write its definition on the line.

1. Mr. Abel was my mother's <u>mentor</u>. He taught her to do her job. ....

2. Al was sick last week, so I was happy to see him looking so <u>hale</u> today. ....

3. Please <u>comport</u> yourself as I have taught you. Good behavior is important. ....

4. <u>Monitor</u> the drills every hour to make sure that they are working well. ....

5. He's an experienced <u>falconer</u>. In fact, he has trained at least fifty falcons. ....

6. Lilac leaves have smooth edges, but aspen leaves have <u>serrated</u> edges. ....

7. I was hoping to have a serious discussion, but this chatter is <u>inane</u>. ....

8. After they sold their house, they <u>pulled up stakes</u> and left for Houston. ....

9. We tried to <u>squelch</u> the untrue rumors by providing clear facts. ....

B. Read each group of sentences. Use context clues to find the meaning of each underlined word or phrase. Write its definition on the line. Then verify the meaning in a dictionary.

1. It was a very <u>nonproductive</u> day. We had planned to paint the den, but after an hour, Dad's back began to throb. Then the twins needed help with their homework. We'll have to paint tomorrow.

   ....

2. Although they seem like <u>puffery,</u> I really do appreciate the kind words that you used to introduce me. I will try to live up to such high praise, but please—no more exaggerations!

   ....

3. Our town wanted to <u>pay homage</u> to the men and women who served in the military, but we didn't want to build a statue. Instead, we renamed the town park "Soldiers' Field" in their honor.

   ....

4. We need to do something about the drab <u>ecru</u> walls in the kitchen. The color reminds me of sand or sawdust. We need to get a little color into that room and brighten up the walls.

   ....

5. It might seem as though I'm <u>going out on a limb</u>, but what's the worst thing that could happen? Yes, people might laugh at me, but I can take it. I just don't want to follow the crowd.

   ....

For use with Language 4d

346

Language 5a

> **5a. Demonstrate understanding of figurative language, word relationships, and nuances in word meanings.**
>   • Interpret figures of speech (e.g., personification) in context.

Explanation

Figurative language is writing or speech that is not meant to be taken literally. Based on comparisons of unlike items, it goes beyond the dictionary meaning of words. The many types of figurative language are known as **figures of speech.** Common figures of speech include **similes, metaphors, personification,** and **idioms.** Writers use these figures of speech when they want to describe things in vivid and imaginative ways. Figurative language may seem puzzling at first. However, you can use **context clues,** hints in the surrounding passage, to figure out what a figure of speech means.

Examples

- A **simile** compares two unlike things using the words *like* or *as.*
  Your dog is as big as a horse! I have to lift my hand way up to pet it.
  When I got off the carousel, *I was so dizzy my head spun like a top.*

- A **metaphor** compares two unlike things by describing one thing as if it were another.
  His mouth was on automatic pilot. He spoke many words but said nothing thoughtful.
  As the young children played, *bubbles of laughter floated out of the classroom window.*

- **Personification** gives human qualities to something that is not human.
  As he entered the ancient mansion, *the old door groaned on its hinges.*
  The angry shrieking of the wind upset him so much that he closed all the windows.

- **Idioms** are common expressions that mean something different from what they literally say.
  Don't keep hinting. Say directly what you mean. *Don't beat around the bush.*
  If you go outside, you'll get soaked. *It's raining cats and dogs.*

Name _____ Date _____ Assignment _____

Apply the Standard

A. For each item below, identify the underlined figure of speech as an idiom or an example of simile, metaphor, or personification. Then, basing your answer on the context, tell what it means.

1. The strong wind blew the rain sideways. <u>Needles of cold rain</u> pierced my cheek. ....

   ....

2. Because she used very little dough, the <u>pancakes were as light as feathers</u>. ....

   ....

3. The sprinter won the 100-yard dash in record time. <u>His legs were pistons</u>. ....

   ....

4. The <u>wind howled and moaned</u> in the forest, sending a chill through the hiker's heart. ....

   ....

5. She was an aggressive driver and <u>had a lead foot</u>. She often received tickets for speeding. ....

   ....

6. Was this the young woman he had wanted so much to meet? His <u>heart was beating like a drum</u>.

   ....

7. As we returned from our long trip, the <u>light on the front porch welcomed us</u> home. ....

   ....

8. Now, what was I going to say? I lost my <u>train of thought</u>. ....

   ....

9. The telephone rang and rang. <u>It wasn't going to take no for an answer</u>. ....

   ....

10. The blank computer screen <u>stared back at him, mocking</u>. He couldn't complete the assignment.

   ....

B. Write a paragraph that includes at least one example of each figure of speech: simile, metaphor, personification, and idiom.

   ....

   ....

Language 5b

> **5b. Demonstrate understanding of figurative language, word relationships, and nuances in word meanings.**
>
> - **Use the relationship between particular words (e.g., cause/effect, part/whole, item/category) to better understand each of the words.**

Explanation

An **analogy** compares two things that are similar in a certain way but unlike in other ways. Many tests include analogy problems. An analogy item on a test contains two pairs of words. The relationship between the first pair of words is the same as the relationship between the second pair of words. Thinking about these relationships will help you better understand the meanings of words.

Examples

Each analogy features a specific type of relationship between the words.

- **Synonyms, or Similar Meanings:** *big is* to *large* as *happy* is *to glad*

- **Antonyms, or Opposite Meanings:** *young* is to *old* as *short* is to *tall*

- **Cause/Effect:** *study* is to *learning* as *exercise* is to *fitness*

- **Part/Whole:** *flower* is to *garden* as *animal* is to *zoo*

- **Item/Category:** *dog* is to *mammal* as *apple* is to *fruit*

- **Item/Use:** *pan* is to *cooking* as *pencil* is to *writing*

To figure out an analogy problem, ask yourself how the words in the first pair are related. For example, if the words in the first pair are antonyms, then the words in the second pair should also be antonyms.

Name _____ Date _____ Assignment _____

Apply the Standard

A. Identify the relationship between the first pair of words, and write a word to complete the second pair of words. Make sure that the second pair of words has the same relationship as the first pair. Then, tell what type of analogy it is (synonyms, antonyms, cause/effect, part/whole, item/category, or item/use).

Type of Analogy

1. *squirrel* is to *mammal* as *robin* is to ....

2. *broom* is to *sweep* as *shovel* is to ....

3. *winning* is to *happiness* as *losing* is to ....

4. *letter* is to *word* as *page* is to ....

5. *up* is to *down* as *darkness* is to ....

6. *thirst* is to *drink* as *exhaustion* is to ....

7. *branch* is to *tree* as *arm* is to ....

8. *puzzling* is to *confusing* as *tiny* is to ....

9. *diamond* is to *gem* as *daisy* is to ....

10. *needle* is to *sew* as *scissors* are to ....

B. Complete the analogies by adding a second pair of words to show the relationship indicated.

1. synonyms

   Worried is to *anxious* as .... is to ....

2. antonyms

   Hot is to *cold* as .... is to ....

3. cause/effect

   Joke is to *laughter* as .... is to ....

4. part/whole

   Singer is to *choir* as .... is to ....

5. item/category

   Skirt is to *clothing* as .... is to ....

Language 5c

> **5c. Demonstrate understanding of figurative language, word relationships, and nuances in word meanings.**
> - **Distinguish among the connotations (associations) of words with similar denotations (definitions) (e.g., *stingy, scrimping, economical, unwasteful, thrifty*).**

Explanation

A word's **denotation** is its exact dictionary meaning, or definition. A word's **connotation** is the feeling that it suggests and the associations it calls up. Connotations can be negative, positive, or neutral. While they are generally agreed upon in a society, they can also be somewhat subjective and vary from person to person. They can also vary from place to place and time to time. For example, the word *slender* tends to suggest fitness to us. However, it might suggest frailty among groups that value a sturdy build.

Examples

This chart shows four words that share the same **denotation** but have different **connotations.**

Word (Noun form)	Denotation	Connotation	Example Sentence
1. *smell*	a sensation that is recognized by the nose	any sensation recognized by the nose (neutral), with the verb form sometimes connoting "having an unpleasant odor" (negative)	*Wood burning in a fireplace has a distinctive smell.*
2. *scent*		a hint of a smell, as from an animal one is tracking; the distinctive smell of a perfume (neutral to positive)	*The hunting dogs picked up the fox's scent.* *I'd know that scent anywhere—it's the perfume that Jennifer uses.*
3. *aroma*		a pleasant smell, as from spices, cooking, or baking (positive)	*The aroma of ginger cookies filled Grandma's kitchen.*
4. *odor*		a heavy smell, as from chemicals or garbage (negative)	*Open the windows to get rid of that strong odor in the kitchen.*

Name _____ Date _____ Assignment _____

Apply the Standard

A. Use context clues and what you know about the meanings of words to tell whether the underlined word has a neutral, positive, or negative connotation. Circle your answer.

neutral positive negative **1.** "Don't talk to me like that," the man <u>muttered</u>.

neutral positive negative **2.** "The coat is mine," she <u>said</u>.

neutral positive negative **3.** The fire made the room feel <u>cozy</u>.

neutral positive negative **4.** The fire made the room feel <u>stifling</u>.

neutral positive negative **5.** The fire made the room feel <u>warm</u>.

B. Use each word in a sentence. Then, tell whether the word has a neutral, positive, or negative connotation and explain your choice. Circle your answer.

1. walk: ....

....

neutral positive negative

2. stroll: ....

....

neutral positive negative

3. slender: ....

....

neutral positive negative

4. scrawny: ....

....

neutral positive negative

5. thrifty: ....

....

neutral positive negative

Language 6

> 6. Acquire and use accurately grade-appropriate general academic and domain-specific words and phrases; gather vocabulary knowledge when considering a word or phrase important to comprehension or expression.

Explanation

In your schoolwork, you will come across two main types of words that will help you achieve success:

- **Academic words** are those you use in a variety of subjects at school to solve problems, understand what you read, and express your ideas clearly and precisely. You can think of these as toolkit words, as useful in schoolwork as a hammer and saw are in carpentry. Examples of such words are *confirm, determine, fact, investigate, prove,* and *test.*

- **Domain-specific words** are words specific to a course of study. In a literature course, examples include *character, conflict, plot,* and *sonnet.* In a science course, you might encounter *cell, ecology, mammal,* and *molecule.* Examples from social studies include *climate, constitution, democracy,* and *emigrate.*

Learn and record the definitions of such words as you do your schoolwork. Gathering vocabulary knowledge will help you express yourself clearly and increase your understanding of textbooks and assignments.

Examples

In classroom assignments and on many tests, you must understand academic words and phrases to complete a task or answer a question. Here are examples:

Confirm your prediction that …	Verify that your educated guess about future events is true.
Determine the reason for …	Find out what caused something.
Identify the known *facts* of …	Point out details known to be true.
Analyze the problem to …	Break it into parts and find connections among them.

The domain-specific vocabulary that you learn in an English course helps you discuss literature more precisely. For example, you do not just "see the stuff that happens to a person in a short story." Instead, you "analyze the effect of plot events on a character." In this way, you recognize that a plot is a linked chain of events, not just a series of unrelated happenings. You also recognize that stories are about not real-life people, but characters developed by an author.

Name _____ Date _____ Assignment _____

Apply the Standard

A. Match each domain-specific word or phrase with its definition. Write the letter of the correct definition on the line provided.

.... **1.** dialogue   **a.** brief story, often with animal characters, teaching a lesson

.... **2.** denotation   **b.** clues about what may happen next in a narrative

.... **3.** persuasive essay   **c.** words that appeal to the senses

.... **4.** foreshadowing   **d.** writing that explains an idea or process

.... **5.** legend   **e.** conversation between or among characters

.... **6.** theme   **f.** struggle that propels the events of a plot

.... **7.** conflict   **g.** definition found in a dictionary

.... **8.** sensory language   **h.** writing that supports an opinion

.... **9.** expository essay   **i.** traditional, widely told story about the past

.... **10.** fable   **j.** insight into life explored by a piece of writing

B. Complete each statement with the correct definition of the italicized academic word or phrase. Write the letter of the correct answer on the line.

1. To *make a prediction* means to ....

  a. analyze a character   **c.** use clues to decide what might happen

  b. decide why an event happens   **d.** use clues to find a word's meaning

2. To *draw a conclusion* means to ....

  a. explain how things are alike   **c.** analyze an essay's organizational pattern

  b. analyze a story to find its theme   **d.** combine details to reach an understanding

3. Things that are *similar* are ....

  a. difficult   **c.** opposite

  b. alike   **d.** ideals

4. A *concept* is ....

  a. a plan   **c.** a question

  b. a puzzle   **d.** an idea

5. A *fact* is ....

  a. whatever an author believes   **c.** a statement that can be proved or disproved

  b. a scientific formula   **d.** an explanation of a series of phenomena

Performance Tasks

Name _____ Date _____ Assignment _____

Performance Task 1a

Literature 1 Cite textual evidence to support analysis of what the text says explicitly as well as inferences drawn from the text.*

Task: Support Analysis of a Short Story

Write a response to literature in which you cite textual evidence to support your analysis of a short story. Explain both what the story says explicitly and any inferences you have drawn from it.

Tips for Success

Write a response to a short story you have read. In your response, include these elements:

✓ an objective summary of the story

✓ a sentence that sums up your response to the story

✓ a detailed analysis of what the story means and why

✓ evidence from the story that explicitly supports your ideas

✓ evidence from the story that supports your inferences and conclusions

✓ language that is formal, precise, and follows the rules of standard English

Rubric for Self-Assessment

Criteria for Success	not very				very	
How objective and clear is your summary of the story?	1	2	3	4	5	6
How detailed is your analysis of the story?	1	2	3	4	5	6
How well have you supported your analysis with explicit evidence from the story?	1	2	3	4	5	6
How thoroughly have you supported your inferences and conclusions?	1	2	3	4	5	6
To what extent have you used standard English?	1	2	3	4	5	6
How successfully do you use a formal style and appropriate tone for your audience?	1	2	3	4	5	6

* Other standards covered include Writing 9a, 10; Speaking 6; Language 6.

Name _____ Date _____ Assignment _____

Performance Task 1b

> **Speaking and Listening 1** Engage effectively in a range of collaborative discussions (one-on-one, in groups, and teacher-led) with diverse partners on grade 6 topics, texts, and issues, building on others' ideas and expressing their own clearly.

Task: Discuss the Responses to a Text

Participate in a group discussion in which you explain your analysis of a short story and respond thoughtfully to others' ideas.

Tips for Success

Participate in a discussion about a literary text. As part of your participation, include these elements:

- ✓ prepare by reading the story and preparing a clear analysis of it
- ✓ work with group members on discussion guidelines and individual roles
- ✓ share with the group your ideas regarding the story and its overall meaning. Make sure you include evidence from the text to support your ideas.
- ✓ ask questions that encourage group members to elaborate on their responses to the story
- ✓ respond productively by building on others' questions and comments
- ✓ summarize different speakers' analyses of the text

Rubric for Self-Assessment

Criteria for Discussion	not very					very
How thorough was your analysis of the story?	1	2	3	4	5	6
How effective were the group's guidelines for the discussion?	1	2	3	4	5	6
How clearly and effectively did you present your ideas about the story?	1	2	3	4	5	6
How effective were your questions in helping the group explore the story and its issues?	1	2	3	4	5	6
How productive were your responses to others' questions and comments?	1	2	3	4	5	6
To what extent did group members build on the ideas of others?	1	2	3	4	5	6
How clearly did you summarize others' analyses of the text?	1	2	3	4	5	6

Name _____ Date _____ Assignment _____

Performance Task 2a

Literature 2 **Determine a theme or central idea of a text and how it is conveyed through particular details; provide a summary of the text distinct from personal opinions or judgments.***

Task: Determine the Theme of a Poem

First write an objective summary of a poem. Include the poem's key details, without providing your opinion or judgments about them. Then write a response to literature in which you draw on those key details to determine the theme of the poem.

Tips for Success

Present a response to a poem you have read. In your response, include these elements:

✓ an objective summary of the poem's key details

✓ a statement of the poem's theme (central message about life)

✓ a judgment of whether the theme is universal or specific to one time and place and why you think so

✓ an explanation of how the key details convey the theme you have identified

✓ language that is formal, precise, and follows the rules of standard English

Rubric for Self-Assessment

Criteria for Success	not very					very
How accurately have you identified and summarized key details?	1	2	3	4	5	6
How fully have you explored the poem's theme?	1	2	3	4	5	6
How well do the key details you have chosen support the theme you identified?	1	2	3	4	5	6
How clearly have you explained the connection of the key details to the theme?	1	2	3	4	5	6
To what extent have you used standard English?	1	2	3	4	5	6
How well have you succeeded in using a formal style and appropriate tone for your audience?	1	2	3	4	5	6

* Other standards covered include Writing 9a, Speaking 6, and Language 3.

Name _____ Date _____ Assignment _____

Performance Task 2b

Speaking and Listening 4 Present claims and findings, sequencing ideas logically and using pertinent descriptions, facts, and details to accentuate main ideas or themes; use appropriate eye contact, adequate volume, and clear pronunciation.

Task: Present Claims About a Poem Effectively

Give a presentation in which you describe the theme of a poem and explain what details in the poem led to your interpretation.

Tips for Success

Give a presentation on the theme of a poem. As part of your presentation, include these elements:

✓ logical sequencing of ideas, beginning with a statement of theme

✓ pertinent descriptions, facts, and details that support your ideas about theme

✓ appropriate eye contact with your audience

✓ adequate volume and clear pronunciation

Rubric for Self-Assessment

Criteria for Discussion	not very					very
How clearly did you identify the poem's theme?	1	2	3	4	5	6
How logically did you sequence your ideas in explaining the theme of the poem?	1	2	3	4	5	6
How effectively did you present descriptions, facts, and other details?	1	2	3	4	5	6
How effectively did you make eye contact with your audience?	1	2	3	4	5	6
How well did you succeed in speaking clearly and loudly enough for your listeners to hear and understand you?	1	2	3	4	5	6
How accurate was your pronunciation of words?	1	2	3	4	5	6

Name _____ Date _____ Assignment _____

Performance Task 3a

Literature 3 Describe how a particular story's or drama's plot unfolds in a series of episodes as well as how the characters respond or change as the plot moves toward a resolution.*

Task: Describe a Story's Plot and Characters

Write a description of how a short story's plot unfolds in episodes that center on a conflict or struggle to which the main character must respond. Describe how the main character responds to the conflict and grows or changes in the course of the story.

Tips for Success

Write a response to literature describing the plot and characters of a short story you have read. In your response, include these elements:

✓ a description of the major plot points (episodes), including the conflict and resolution of the story

✓ an identification and description of the story's main character

✓ an explanation of how the main character responds to the conflict

✓ an analysis of how the main character changes in response to the conflict

✓ language that is formal, precise, and follows the rules of standard English

Rubric for Self-Assessment

Criteria for Success	not very					very
How well have you described the story's major plot points?	1	2	3	4	5	6
How accurately have you identified the story's conflict and resolution?	1	2	3	4	5	6
How fully have you described the main character and how he or she responds to the story's conflict?	1	2	3	4	5	6
To what extent have you supported your ideas about ways in which the main character changed as a result of conflict?	1	2	3	4	5	6
How effective is your use of standard English?	1	2	3	4	5	6
How well have you succeeded in using a formal style and appropriate tone for your audience?	1	2	3	4	5	6

* Other standards covered include Writing 2a, 2e, 4; Speaking 4, 6; Language 3.

For use with Literature 3

Name _____ Date _____ Assignment _____

Performance Task 3b

Speaking and Listening 5 Include multimedia components (e.g., graphics, images, music, sound) and visual displays in presentations to clarify information.

Task: Use Multimedia Components in a Presentation

Use multimedia components in a presentation about a short story you have read in which you explain how the plot unfolds and how the main character changes as a result of conflict.

Tips for Success

Make a multimedia presentation about a short story. As part of your presentation, you may wish to include these elements:

✓ a graphic representation of the plot, with the major plot points labeled

✓ images (either sketches or photos) of how you imagine the characters look

✓ video or audio of someone playing the main character and describing how he or she responded to the conflict

✓ video or audio of the main character and other characters describing how the main character was changed by the conflict

✓ language that is formal, precise, and follows the rules of standard English

Rubric for Self-Assessment

Criteria for Discussion	not very				very	
How clear and effective was your overall presentation?	1	2	3	4	5	6
How effectively did you use graphics to capture the main plot events?	1	2	3	4	5	6
How convincingly did the images portray the story's characters?	1	2	3	4	5	6
How well did the main character's comments help the audience understand the conflict and what was at stake?	1	2	3	4	5	6
How well did the characters' comments deepen the audience's understanding of the main character and the ways in which the conflict changed the character?	1	2	3	4	5	6
How well did you succeed in using a formal style and appropriate tone for your audience?	1	2	3	4	5	6

Name _____ Date _____ Assignment _____

Performance Task 4a

> **Literature 4 Determine the meaning of words and phrases as they are used in a text, including figurative and connotative meanings; analyze the impact of a specific word choice on meaning and tone.***

Task: Analyze the Figurative Meanings of Words and the Impact of Word Choices

Write an essay in which you explain the figurative and connotative meanings of words and phrases and their impact on the meaning and tone of a poem.

Tips for Success

Present a response to literature in which you analyze the meanings and impact of words in a poem. In your response, include these elements:

✓ a fully developed essay that includes an introduction, body, and conclusion

✓ an explanation of the figurative meaning of at least one word or phrase in the poem

✓ a definition of the connotative meaning of at least one word or phrase, including a judgment on whether the connotation is positive or negative

✓ an analysis, using evidence from the text, of the impact these words or phrases have on the poem's meaning and tone

✓ language that is formal, precise, and follows the rules of standard English

Rubric for Self-Assessment

Criteria for Success	not very					very
How well developed are the ideas presented in the introduction, body, and conclusion of your essay?	1	2	3	4	5	6
How clearly do you define the figurative meanings of words or phrases?	1	2	3	4	5	6
How clearly do you explain the connotation of words or phrases?	1	2	3	4	5	6
How well do you explain the impact of chosen words on the poem's meaning and tone?	1	2	3	4	5	6
How well do you support your analysis with evidence from the text?	1	2	3	4	5	6
How successfully do you use standard English?	1	2	3	4	5	6
How well do you succeed in using a formal style and appropriate tone for your audience?	1	2	3	4	5	6

* Other standards covered include Writing 2e, 4; Speaking 4; Language 3, 5a, 5c.

Name _____ Date _____ Assignment _____

Performance Task 4b

> **Speaking and Listening 6** Adapt speech to a variety of contexts and tasks, demonstrating command of formal English when indicated or appropriate.

Task: Adapt Speech When Performing and Explaining a Poem

Give a presentation in which you read a poem aloud and then explain how certain word choices affect the poem's meaning and tone.

Tips for Success

Adapt the way you speak when performing and analyzing a poem. As you prepare for your presentation, follow these steps:

✓ prepare a reading copy of the poem in which you mark places to pause and words you want to emphasize

✓ read aloud the poet's exact words, no matter how informal or unusual the words are; rehearse reading so you don't stumble over any words during the performance

✓ switch to a formal tone when you present your analysis of the figurative language and connotations of words and phrases in the poem

✓ record your rehearsal and look for ways to improve your presentation

Rubric for Self-Assessment

Criteria for Discussion	not very				very	
How effectively did you mark up your reading copy of the poem?	1	2	3	4	5	6
How accurately did you speak the poet's exact words?	1	2	3	4	5	6
In general, how effectively did you perform the poem?	1	2	3	4	5	6
How well did you adapt your speech and tone during your analysis of the poem's figurative language and connotations?	1	2	3	4	5	6
To what extent did your presentation improve after repeated rehearsal?	1	2	3	4	5	6

For use with Speaking and Listening 6

Name _____ Date _____ Assignment _____

Performance Task 5a

Literature 5   Analyze how a particular sentence, chapter, scene, or stanza fits into
the overall structure of a text and contributes to the development of the theme,
setting, or plot.*

Task: Analyze How a Scene Fits into a Drama

Write an essay in which you analyze how a particular scene fits into the overall structure of a
drama. Explain how the scene contributes to the development of the theme, setting, or plot.

Tips for Success

Write an essay analyzing how a given scene fits into the structure of a drama you have read or seen
performed. In your essay, include these elements:

✓ definitions of theme, setting, and plot

✓ an objective summary of the scene you chose to analyze

✓ an analysis of how the scene fits into the drama as a whole and how it
  reinforces the play's message about life, sets the play in its place and time, or
  moves the plot forward

✓ evidence from the text that supports your analysis

✓ language that is formal, precise, and follows the rules of standard English

Rubric for Self-Assessment

Criteria for Success	not very					very
How accurately have you defined the literary terms used in your essay?	1	2	3	4	5	6
How clear and objective is your summary of the scene?	1	2	3	4	5	6
How well does your analysis explain the scene's importance to the play as a whole?	1	2	3	4	5	6
How well does your analysis explain how the scene contributes specifically to theme, setting, or plot?	1	2	3	4	5	6
How effectively have you supported your analysis with evidence from the text?	1	2	3	4	5	6
How successful is your use of standard English?	1	2	3	4	5	6
How well have you succeeded in using a formal style and appropriate tone for your audience?	1	2	3	4	5	6

* Other standards covered include Writing 1b, 2e, 4, 9; Speaking 4; Language 3.

For use with Literature 5

Name _____ Date _____ Assignment _____

Performance Task 5b

> **Speaking and Listening 1** Engage effectively in a range of collaborative discussions (one-on-one, in groups, and teacher-led) with diverse partners on grade 6 topics, texts, and issues, building on others' ideas and expressing their own clearly.

Task: Discuss How a Scene Fits into a Drama

Participate in a group discussion in which you explain how a given scene fits into a play and respond thoughtfully to others' feedback.

Tips for Success

Participate in a discussion about how a given scene fits into a play and contributes to its theme, setting, or plot. As part of your participation, include these elements:

✓ guidelines for participation, agreed upon by members of the discussion

✓ an objective summary of the scene you have chosen to analyze

✓ a clear expression of your analysis of the play

✓ evidence from the text that supports your analysis

✓ questions that will encourage other participants to share whether they agree or disagree with your analysis

✓ responses that build on other participants' feedback

Rubric for Self-Assessment

Criteria for Discussion	not very					very
How effective were the guidelines established by the group?	1	2	3	4	5	6
How complete and objective was your summary of the scene?	1	2	3	4	5	6
How clearly and effectively did you present your ideas and analysis?	1	2	3	4	5	6
To what extent did the text evidence support your analysis?	1	2	3	4	5	6
How effective were the participants at asking thoughtful questions that deepened the discussion?	1	2	3	4	5	6
How well did the discussion summarize the main perspectives of the participants?	1	2	3	4	5	6
To what extent did your responses build upon the comments of others?	1	2	3	4	5	6

Name _____ Date _____ Assignment _____

Performance Task 6a

Literature 6 Explain how an author develops the point of view of the narrator or speaker in a text.*

Task: Analyze Point of View

Write an essay in which you explain how the author of a literary text develops a character's or speaker's point of view. Cite evidence from the text to support your analysis.

Tips for Success

Present an explanation of point of view in a story or poem you have read. In your essay, include these elements:

✓ a thesis statement that explains your conclusions

✓ an identification of the point of view in the literary text you are analyzing

✓ an analysis of how the author developed that point of view and its impact on the work as a whole

✓ evidence from the text that supports the ideas you present

✓ language that is formal, precise, and follows the rules of standard English

Rubric for Self-Assessment

Criteria for Success	not very					very
How clear is your thesis statement?	1	2	3	4	5	6
How clear is your analysis of the author's development of point of view?	1	2	3	4	5	6
How well have you supported your analysis with evidence from the text?	1	2	3	4	5	6
How successful is your use of standard English?	1	2	3	4	5	6
How well do you succeed in using a formal style and appropriate tone for your audience?	1	2	3	4	5	6

* Other standards covered include: Writing 4, 9a; Speaking 4; Language 1, 2.

Name _____ Date _____ Assignment _____

Performance Task 6b

> **Speaking and Listening 6** Adapt speech to a variety of contexts and tasks, demonstrating command of formal English when indicated or appropriate.

Task: Adapt Speech When Performing and Explaining a Story

Give a presentation in which you read aloud a passage from a short story or poem. As appropriate, use different voices for the dialogue of different characters. Then, identify the narrator's or speaker's point of view and explain how the author develops it, using evidence from the text.

Tips for Success

Adapt the way you speak when reading aloud from a text and then explaining the text. Follow these tips for success:

✓ prepare a reading copy of the text passage in which you mark words you want to emphasize, places to pause, and any unusual pronunciations

✓ read aloud the author's words exactly, no matter how informal or how unusual the words are

✓ as appropriate, use different voices for the dialogue of different characters

✓ adopt a formal tone to explain your analysis of point of view and when citing text evidence

✓ avoid using incomplete sentences and filler words and phrases, such as "I mean"

Rubric for Self-Assessment

Criteria for Discussion	not very					very
How accurately and clearly did you speak the author's words?	1	2	3	4	5	6
In general, how effectively did you perform the passage?	1	2	3	4	5	6
How clearly did you explain how the author develops the point of view?	1	2	3	4	5	6
How well did you utilize text evidence to support your ideas?	1	2	3	4	5	6
How well did you adapt your speech and tone during your explanation of the story's point of view?	1	2	3	4	5	6

Name _____ Date _____ Assignment _____

Performance Task 7a

> **Literature 7** Compare and contrast the experience of reading a story, drama, or poem to listening to or viewing an audio, video, or live version of the text, including contrasting what they "see" and "hear" when reading the text to what they perceive when they listen or watch.*

Task: Compare and Contrast Reading a Play Versus Viewing It

Write an essay in which you compare and contrast the experience of reading a drama versus viewing a video (or live) version of it. Support your ideas with evidence and examples.

Tips for Success

Present a response to a drama you have both read and viewed. In your response, include these elements:

- ✓ a description of the similarities between reading the script and seeing it performed
- ✓ a description of the differences between reading the script and seeing it performed (e.g., the voices and physical appearance of characters as you pictured them versus as actors portrayed them)
- ✓ an analysis of production techniques in the film or live version, including sound, lighting, costumes, and staging
- ✓ an explanation of which version you prefer and why
- ✓ evidence from both versions that supports your opinion
- ✓ language that is formal, precise, and follows the rules of standard English

Rubric for Self-Assessment

Criteria for Success	not very					very
How clearly have you described the similarities between the two versions of the play?	1	2	3	4	5	6
How clearly have you described the differences between the two versions of the play?	1	2	3	4	5	6
How effectively have you analyzed production techniques in the film or live version?	1	2	3	4	5	6
How persuasively have you explained which version you prefer?	1	2	3	4	5	6
How convincing is the evidence you used to support your analysis?	1	2	3	4	5	6
How successful is your use of formal, standard English?	1	2	3	4	5	6

* Other standards covered include: Writing 4, 9a; Speaking 2, 4; Language 1, 3, 6.

Name _____ Date _____ Assignment _____

Performance Task 7b

Speaking and Listening 5 Include multimedia components (e.g., graphics, images, music, sound) and visual displays in presentations to clarify information.

Task: Use Multimedia Components in a Presentation

Use multimedia components in a presentation in which you compare and contrast the experiences of reading and viewing a play.

Tips for Success

Develop a multimedia presentation about reading and viewing drama. As part of your presentation, you may want to include the following elements:

✓ a powerpoint presentation or a chart comparing and contrasting your experience of the two versions

✓ sketches of how you imagined several characters (before you saw the play) next to photos of the actors portraying the characters

✓ video clips of the film version of the play that illustrate points you make about production techniques (sound effects, staging, costumes, and so on)

✓ audio or video in which you demonstrate alternate ways to interpret the play

Rubric for Self-Assessment

Criteria for Discussion	not very				very	
How effectively did your powerpoint or chart compare and contrast the two versions?	1	2	3	4	5	6
How informative was the display of your illustrated characters versus the actors' portrayals of them?	1	2	3	4	5	6
How effective was your analysis of production techniques?	1	2	3	4	5	6
How effective was your audio or video interpretation of passages from the play?	1	2	3	4	5	6
How effective was your overall use of media in your presentation?	1	2	3	4	5	6

Name _____ Date _____ Assignment _____

Performance Task 8a

> **Literature 9** Compare and contrast texts in different forms or genres (e.g., stories and poems; historical novels and fantasy stories) in terms of their approaches to similar themes and topics.*

Task: Compare and Contrast Texts in Different Forms or Genres

Write an essay in which you compare and contrast a poem and a short story. In your essay, explore their approaches to similar themes and topics. Cite text evidence to support your ideas.

Tips for Success

Develop a response to a poem and a short story you have read. In your response, include these elements:

✓ a thesis statement in which you share your conclusions about the themes and topics of the two works

✓ an analysis of the ways in which the theme and topic of the poem and the story are similar and different

✓ an analysis of symbols in the two works and their similarities of meaning

✓ evidence from the texts that supports your analysis

✓ language that is formal, precise, and follows the rules of standard English

Rubric for Self-Assessment

Criteria for Success	not very					very
How clear is your thesis statement?	1	2	3	4	5	6
How fully developed is your analysis of the two works' themes and topics?	1	2	3	4	5	6
How well have you distinguished between a theme and a topic?	1	2	3	4	5	6
How clear is your analysis of the works' symbols?	1	2	3	4	5	6
How well do you support your analysis with details from the text?	1	2	3	4	5	6
How successful is your use of formal, standard English?	1	2	3	4	5	6

* Other standards covered include: Writing 4, 9a; Speaking 5, 6; Language 1, 2, 3.

Name _____ Date _____ Assignment _____

Performance Task 8b

> **Speaking and Listening 4** Present claims and findings, sequencing ideas logically and using pertinent descriptions, facts, and details to accentuate main ideas or themes; use appropriate eye contact, adequate volume, and clear pronunciation.

Task: Comparing a Poem and a Story

Give a presentation in which you compare and contrast the theme and topic of a poem and a short story. Explain what details in the two works led to your analysis.

Tips for Success

Give a presentation about the similarities and differences between a poem and a short story. As part of your presentation, include these elements:

✓ logically sequenced ideas about the themes and topics of the two works

✓ descriptions, facts, and details that support your analysis

✓ language that is suited to your purpose and audience

✓ adequate volume and clear pronunciation; varied tone of voice and pacing

✓ appropriate eye contact and body language

Rubric for Self-Assessment

Criteria for Discussion	not very					very
How clearly and logically did you state the themes and topics of the poem and the short story?	1	2	3	4	5	6
How convincingly did you explain how those details support your analysis of topic and theme?	1	2	3	4	5	6
How well suited to your audience and purpose was your word choice?	1	2	3	4	5	6
How successful was your use of vocal technique in conveying your ideas and maintaining audience interest?	1	2	3	4	5	6
How effective was your use of eye contact and body language?	1	2	3	4	5	6

Name _____ Date _____ Assignment _____

Performance Task 9a

> **Literature 10 By the end of the year, read and comprehend literature, including stories, dramas, and poems, in the grades 6–8 text complexity band proficiently, with scaffolding as needed at the high end of the range.***

Task: Read and Comprehend Literature

Read a text of your choice, and develop an essay in response to the text. In your essay, include a summary of the main events and an analysis of the book's elements. Then, provide an evaluation of the text as a whole.

Tips for Success

Read a text of your choice and present a response to it. In your response, include these elements:

- ✓ an objective summary of the text's main events or key ideas

- ✓ an analysis of the text's elements, which may include plot, characters, theme or central idea, and author's style

- ✓ an evaluation of what you like and dislike about the text

- ✓ evidence from the text that supports your analysis

- ✓ language that is formal, precise, and follows the rules of standard English

Rubric for Self-Assessment

Criteria for Success	not very				very	
How objective and concise is your summary of the text?	1	2	3	4	5	6
How thorough is your analysis of the text's elements?	1	2	3	4	5	6
How fair and comprehensive is your evaluation of the text?	1	2	3	4	5	6
How well have you supported your analysis with evidence from the text?	1	2	3	4	5	6
How successful is your use of standard English?	1	2	3	4	5	6
How well have you succeeded in using a formal style and appropriate tone for your audience?	1	2	3	4	5	6

* Other standards covered include: Writing 4, 9a; Language 1, 2, 3.

Name _____ Date _____ Assignment _____

Performance Task 9b

Speaking and Listening 1   Engage effectively in a range of collaborative discussions (one-on-one, in groups, and teacher-led) with a partner on grade 6 topics, texts, and issues, building on others' ideas and expressing their own clearly.

Task: Literary Discussion

Participate in daily or weekly discussions in which you clearly express your response to a text and respond thoughtfully to your partner's ideas.

Tips for Success

Participate in discussions about a text of your choice. Follow these tips for success:

✓ prepare by reading several chapters of the text and taking notes

✓ with your partner, develop guidelines for equal and full participation

✓ summarize the key events or ideas presented in the text

✓ analyze the elements of the text (e.g., plot, characters, theme or central idea, author's style)

✓ evaluate what you like and dislike about the text

✓ use evidence from the text that supports your analysis

✓ ask questions that propel the discussion forward in order to explore the work fully

Rubric for Self-Assessment

Criteria for Discussion	not very					very
How clear and concise was your summary?	1	2	3	4	5	6
How effective were the discussion guidelines?	1	2	3	4	5	6
How clearly have you presented an evaluation of the text?	1	2	3	4	5	6
How effectively did you cite evidence from the text to support your analysis?	1	2	3	4	5	6
How well did you build on the ideas of your partner during your discussions?	1	2	3	4	5	6
How polite and respectful of your partner's ideas were you?	1	2	3	4	5	6

For use with Speaking and Listening 1

Name _____ Date _____ Assignment _____

Performance Task 10a

Informational Text 1 Cite textual evidence to support analysis of what the text says explicitly as well as inferences drawn from the text.*

Task: Support Analysis of a Narrative Essay

Write an essay in which you cite textual evidence to support your analysis of a narrative essay. Explain both what the essay says explicitly (directly) and any inferences you have made.

Tips for Success

Present a written response to a narrative essay. In your response, include these elements:

✓ an objective summary of the essay

✓ a thesis statement that sums up your response to the essay

✓ a detailed analysis of the essay

✓ evidence from the essay that supports your analysis

✓ evidence from the essay that supports your inferences

✓ language that is formal, precise, and follows the rules of standard English

Rubric for Self-Assessment

Criteria for Success	not very					very
How objective and concise is your summary of the essay?	1	2	3	4	5	6
How clear is your thesis statement?	1	2	3	4	5	6
How detailed is your analysis of the essay?	1	2	3	4	5	6
How well have you supported your analysis with explicit evidence from the essay?	1	2	3	4	5	6
How clearly have you explained the inferences you drew from reading the essay?	1	2	3	4	5	6
How well have you supported your inferences with evidence from the essay?	1	2	3	4	5	6
How successful is your use of standard English?	1	2	3	4	5	6
How well have you succeeded in using a formal style and appropriate tone for your audience?	1	2	3	4	5	6

* Other standards covered include: Writing 4, 9a; Speaking 5, 6; Language 1, 2, 3.

For use with Informational Text 1

Name _____ Date _____ Assignment _____

Performance Task 10b

Speaking and Listening 4 Present claims and findings, sequencing ideas logically and using pertinent descriptions, facts, and details to accentuate main ideas or themes; use appropriate eye contact, adequate volume, and clear pronunciation.

Task: Present Your Response to a Narrative Essay

Give a presentation in which you deliver an analysis of a narrative essay, citing both explicit evidence and inferences to support your ideas. Invite questions from the audience at the conclusion of your presentation.

Tips for Success

Give a presentation in which you share your analysis of a narrative essay. Follow these tips for success:

- ✓ present your claims and findings in a logical way
- ✓ include descriptions, facts, and details from the essay that explicitly support your ideas
- ✓ cite evidence from the essay that supports your inferences and conclusions
- ✓ use adequate volume, varied tones of voice, and clear pronunciation
- ✓ make appropriate eye contact
- ✓ give thorough, informative responses to questions from your listeners

Rubric for Self-Assessment

Criteria for Discussion	not very					very
How clearly have you presented your claims and findings?	1	2	3	4	5	6
How thoroughly did you support your ideas with details from the text?	1	2	3	4	5	6
How well did you succeed in speaking clearly and loudly enough for your listeners to hear and understand you?	1	2	3	4	5	6
How effectively did you use and maintain eye contact?	1	2	3	4	5	6
How thorough and informed were your responses to audience questions?	1	2	3	4	5	6

Name _____ Date _____ Assignment _____

Performance Task 11a

Informational Text 2 Determine a central idea of a text and how it is conveyed through particular details; provide a summary of the text distinct from personal opinions or judgments.*

Task: Determine the Central Idea of a Scientific Article

Write an essay in which you first summarize a scientific article's important details without providing your opinion or judgments about them. Be sure to include any important information from graphs, charts, photo captions, or other non-text parts of the article. Then state the central idea of the article and explain how you used those key details to determine the central idea.

Tips for Success

Present an essay about a scientific article you have read. In your essay, include these elements:

✓ a statement of the article's central idea

✓ a summary, without opinions or judgments, of the article's important details

✓ an explanation of how the key details convey the central idea you have identified

✓ language that is formal, precise, and follows the rules of standard English

Rubric for Self-Assessment

Criteria for Success	not very				very	
How accurately have you identified the article's central idea?	1	2	3	4	5	6
How thoroughly have you looked for key details in charts, graphs, and other non-text parts of the article?	1	2	3	4	5	6
How accurately have you identified important details?	1	2	3	4	5	6
How well have you summarized those details?	1	2	3	4	5	6
How well have you succeeded in using a formal style and appropriate tone for your audience?	1	2	3	4	5	6
How successfully have you used standard English?	1	2	3	4	5	6

* Other standards covered include Writing 9b, Speaking 4, Language 3.

Name _____ Date _____ Assignment _____

Performance Task 11b

> **Speaking and Listening 2** Analyze the main ideas and supporting details presented in diverse media and formats (e.g., visually, quantitatively, orally) and explain how the ideas clarify a topic, text, or issue under study.

Task: Present Claims About a Scientific Article

Give a presentation in which you describe the central idea of a scientific article and explain what details in the article led you to your interpretation.

Tips for Success

Give a presentation on the central idea of a scientific article. As part of your presentation, include these elements:

- ✓ a statement of the article's central idea
- ✓ a chart that lists the main details of the article and shows which ones are important
- ✓ a clear explanation of how the important details support the central idea
- ✓ appropriate eye contact and body language
- ✓ adequate volume and clear pronunciation
- ✓ an opportunity for your audience to ask questions

Rubric for Self-Assessment

Criteria for Discussion	not very				very	
How well did you state the central idea of the article?	1	2	3	4	5	6
How effectively did you present the key details of the article?	1	2	3	4	5	6
How accurately did the chart identify which details are important?	1	2	3	4	5	6
How clear was your explanation of how the details support the central idea?	1	2	3	4	5	6
How effective were your eye contact and body language?	1	2	3	4	5	6
How well did you succeed in speaking clearly and loudly enough for your listeners to follow you?	1	2	3	4	5	6
How well was time managed? Was the audience given time to ask questions?	1	2	3	4	5	6

Name _____ Date _____ Assignment _____

Performance Task 12a

> **Informational Text 3** Analyze in detail how a key individual, event, or idea is introduced, illustrated, and elaborated in a text (e.g., through examples or anecdotes).*

Task: Analyze a Persuasive Speech or Essay

Write an analysis of how the ideas in a persuasive speech or essay are introduced, illustrated, and elaborated. Discuss which ideas are backed up by examples, which by anecdotes, which by statistics, which by quotations, and so on. Evaluate whether these methods of presenting a claim and point of view succeed in persuading you to agree with the author's conclusions.

Tips for Success

Write an analysis of the arguments in a persuasive speech or essay you have read and evaluate their effectiveness. In your response, include these elements:

✓ an identification of the key ideas in the speech or essay

✓ an analysis of how those ideas are introduced, illustrated, and elaborated

✓ an analysis of how the clarity of the writing is improved by the ways that key ideas are developed

✓ an evaluation of whether the author's conclusions are persuasive

✓ language that is formal, precise, and follows the rules of standard English

Rubric for Self-Assessment

Criteria for Success	not very					very
How accurately have you identified the key ideas?	1	2	3	4	5	6
How thoroughly have you analyzed how ideas are introduced?	1	2	3	4	5	6
How thoroughly have you analyzed how ideas are illustrated and elaborated?	1	2	3	4	5	6
How clearly have you analyzed how the text's clarity is improved by the ways key ideas are developed?	1	2	3	4	5	6
How thoughtfully have you evaluated whether the author's conclusions are persuasive?	1	2	3	4	5	6
How accurate is your analysis of the degree to which the development of key ideas made the conclusions persuasive?	1	2	3	4	5	6
How well have you succeeded in using a formal style, appropriate tone for your audience, and standard English?	1	2	3	4	5	6

* Other standards covered include: Writing 4, 9b; Speaking 4; Language 1, 2, 3.

For use with Informational Text 3

Name _____ Date _____ Assignment _____

Performance Task 12b

Speaking and Listening 3 Delineate a speaker's argument and specific claims, distinguishing claims that are supported by reasons and evidence from claims that are not.

Task: Present an Analysis of a Persuasive Argument

In an oral presentation about a televised opinion piece or editorial, describe the speaker's argument and analyze specific claims. Explain which claims are supported by evidence and which are not.

Tips for Success

Give a talk analyzing an opinion piece or editorial on television. As part of your presentation, include these elements:

✓ a description of the claim and main parts of the argument

✓ an explanation of the difference between fact and opinion

✓ an analysis of which claims are supported by reasons and evidence and which are not

✓ an analysis of the quality of the reasons and evidence supporting various claims

✓ an evaluation of whether the speaker's argument is persuasive or not

Rubric for Self-Assessment

Criteria for Discussion	not very				very	
How accurately did you identify the claim and main parts of the argument?	1	2	3	4	5	6
How clearly did you explain the difference between fact and opinion?	1	2	3	4	5	6
How effectively did you analyze which claims are supported and which are not?	1	2	3	4	5	6
How effectively did you analyze the quality of the support for claims?	1	2	3	4	5	6
How clearly did you evaluate the persuasiveness of the speaker's argument?	1	2	3	4	5	6
How well did you succeed in using a formal style, appropriate tone for your audience, and standard English?	1	2	3	4	5	6

Name _____ Date _____ Assignment _____

Performance Task 13a

Informational Text 4   Determine the meanings of words and phrases as they are used in a text, including figurative, connotative, and technical meanings.*

Task: Analyze the Figurative and Technical Meanings of Words and Phrases

Write an essay in which you explain the figurative and technical meanings of several words and phrases in a memoir and how they contribute to the author's style.

Tips for Success

Write an essay in which you analyze the meanings of figurative and technical words in a memoir you have read. In your essay, include these elements:

- ✓ definitions of the figurative meanings of at least two words or phrases in the memoir

- ✓ definitions of the technical or specialized meanings of at least two terms in the memoir

- ✓ an analysis, using evidence from the text, of how these word choices contribute to the author's style

- ✓ language that is formal, precise, and follows the rules of standard English

Rubric for Self-Assessment

Criteria for Success	not very					very
How clearly have you defined the figurative meanings of the terms?	1	2	3	4	5	6
How well have the figurative words or phrases you chose lent themselves to analysis?	1	2	3	4	5	6
How clearly have you defined the technical meanings of the terms?	1	2	3	4	5	6
How well have the technical terms you chose lent themselves to analysis?	1	2	3	4	5	6
How thoroughly have you explained how the author's word choice contributed to his or her style?	1	2	3	4	5	6
How thoroughly have you supported your analysis with evidence from the memoir?	1	2	3	4	5	6
To what extent have you used standard English?	1	2	3	4	5	6
How well have you succeeded in using a formal style and appropriate tone for your audience?	1	2	3	4	5	6

* Other standards covered include: Writing 4, 9b; Language 3, 5a, 5c.   **For use with Informational Text 4**

Name _____ Date _____ Assignment _____

Performance Task 13b

> **Speaking and Listening 1 Engage effectively in a range of collaborative group discussions (one-on-one, in groups, and teacher-led) with diverse partners on *grade 6 topics, texts, and issues*, building on others' ideas and expressing their own clearly.**

Task: Discuss How Figurative and Technical Terms Contribute to an Author's Style

Participate in a discussion in which you and classmates define figurative and technical meanings of several words and phrases in a memoir and discuss how they help create the author's style.

Tips for Success

- ✓ prepare by reading the memoir and identifying figurative language and technical terms
- ✓ agree with all members of the group on guidelines for goals and roles
- ✓ pose questions that encourage group members to elaborate on their opinions
- ✓ respond to questions and comments with relevant observations and ideas

Rubric for Self-Assessment

Criteria for Discussion	not very					very
How successful were you at identifying figurative language and technical terms in the memoir?	1	2	3	4	5	6
How thoroughly had you thought through your responses to the text before the discussion?	1	2	3	4	5	6
How effective were the group's discussion guidelines?	1	2	3	4	5	6
How clearly and accurately did you define figurative and technical terms in the memoir?	1	2	3	4	5	6
How effectively did you present your analysis of how the author's word choices contributed to his or her style?	1	2	3	4	5	6
How convincing was your evidence for your analysis?	1	2	3	4	5	6
How effective were your questions in helping the group explore the memoir and the author's style?	1	2	3	4	5	6
How relevant were your responses to others' questions and comments and how respectful of other points of view?	1	2	3	4	5	6

Name _____ Date _____ Assignment _____

Performance Task 14a

> **Informational Text 5** Analyze how a particular sentence, paragraph, chapter, or section fits into the overall structure of a text and contributes to the development of the ideas.*

Task: Analyze a Part of an Article

Write an essay in which you analyze how a particular section fits into the overall structure of a historical article and contributes to the development of the ideas in the article.

Tips for Success

In the essay, include these elements:

✓ an outline of the article showing all the heads and subheads

✓ an overview of how the heads and subheads relate to the overall subject of the article

✓ an analysis of how the information in the section contributes to the development of the ideas in the article

✓ evidence from the text that supports your analysis

✓ language that is formal, precise, and follows the rules of standard English

Rubric for Self-Assessment

Criteria for Success	not very					very
How accurately have you outlined the article?	1	2	3	4	5	6
How clear is your overview of how the section head and subheads relate to the subject?	1	2	3	4	5	6
How well does your analysis explain how that part or section contributes to the development of ideas in the article as a whole?	1	2	3	4	5	6
How effectively have you supported your analysis with evidence from the article?	1	2	3	4	5	6
How successfully have you used standard English?	1	2	3	4	5	6
How well have you succeeded in using a formal style and appropriate tone for your audience?	1	2	3	4	5	6

* Other standards covered include: Writing 4, 9b; Speaking 4; Language 3.

Name _____ Date _____ Assignment _____

Performance Task 14b

Speaking and Listening 5 Include multimedia components (e.g., graphics, images, music, sound) and visual displays in a presentation to clarify information.

Task: Use Visual or Multimedia Components in a Presentation

Use multimedia components in a presentation about an informational article you have read in which you analyze how a particular section fits into the overall article and contributes to the development of its ideas.

Tips for Success

Make a visual or multimedia presentation about an informational article. As part of your presentation, include these elements:

✓ a large chart presenting the outline of the article

✓ visuals related to the content of the article to accompany the chart

✓ music or sound related to the content of the article to accompany the chart

✓ a talk in which you analyze how the section contributes to the development of the article's ideas and provide evidence from the article to support your analysis

✓ use effective body language, voice, volume, and eye contact

✓ a question-and-answer session

Rubric for Self-Assessment

Criteria for Discussion	not very					very
How effective was the visual or multimedia in helping the entire audience understand your presentation?	1	2	3	4	5	6
How well did the music or sound relate to the chart?	1	2	3	4	5	6
How well did your analysis explain how the section contributes to the development of the overall article?	1	2	3	4	5	6
How convincing was the evidence from the article to support your analysis?	1	2	3	4	5	6
How effective were you as a speaker in the way you used voice, eye contact, and body language?	1	2	3	4	5	6
How effective were your responses to questions?	1	2	3	4	5	6

Name _____ Date _____ Assignment _____

Performance Task 15a

Informational Text 6   Determine an author's point of view or purpose in a text and explain how it is conveyed in the text.*

Task: Determine an Author's Point of View

Write an essay in which you identify the point of view of the author of a reflective essay you have read and explain how that viewpoint is conveyed. Cite evidence in the essay to support your explanation. Also, research the author's background and beliefs and explain how they influenced his or her point of view.

Tips for Success

In your essay, include the following elements.

- ✓ A brief definition of what forms an author's point of view
- ✓ An identification of the author's point of view in his or her reflective essay
- ✓ An explanation of how the essay shows the author's point of view
- ✓ Evidence from the text that supports your opinions
- ✓ Research showing how the author's background and beliefs influenced his or her point of view
- ✓ Formal, precise language and adherence to the rules of standard English

Rubric for Self-Assessment

Criteria for Success	not very					very
How well do you define what forms an author's viewpoint?	1	2	3	4	5	6
How accurately do you identify the author's viewpoint?	1	2	3	4	5	6
How clear is your explanation of how the essay shows the author's viewpoint?	1	2	3	4	5	6
How well do you support your opinions with evidence from the text?	1	2	3	4	5	6
How well have you researched the author's background and beliefs?	1	2	3	4	5	6
How successfully do you use formal, precise language and follow the rules of standard English?	1	2	3	4	5	6

* Other standards covered include Writing 4, 9b; Speaking 4; Language 1, 2.

Name _____ Date _____ Assignment _____

Performance Task 15b

> **Speaking and Listening 6** Adapt speech to a variety of contexts and tasks, demonstrating command of formal English when indicated or appropriate.

Task: Adapt Speech When Explaining Author's Viewpoint

Give a presentation in which you play the author of a reflective essay you have read. First, identify a passage from the essay that shows the author's point of view. You will read this passage in the voice of the author as a brief formal speech. Next, research the author's background and beliefs to determine how they influenced his or her viewpoint.

Then, deliver your speech to a classmate. Have your partner interview you (as the author) about what your viewpoint is, how your background and beliefs shaped your viewpoint, and how you conveyed this information in the essay.

Tips for Success

When presenting your speech, adapt the way you speak by using a formal (serious and professional) tone. Use the following checklist.

- ✓ Prepare a reading copy of the passage in which you mark words you want to emphasize.

- ✓ Read aloud the author's words exactly, and rehearse several times first so you don't stumble over any words.

- ✓ Speak in a formal tone (as the author) when you deliver your speech and answer the interviewer's (your partner's) questions.

- ✓ Avoid using partial sentences and filler words and phrases, such as "you know" and "I mean."

Rubric for Self-Assessment

Criteria for Discussion	not very					very
How effectively did you mark up your reading copy of the passage?	1	2	3	4	5	6
How accurately did you speak the author's words?	1	2	3	4	5	6
How well did you adapt your speech and tone so that they appeared formal?	1	2	3	4	5	6
How successfully did you avoid using incomplete sentences and filler words?	1	2	3	4	5	6
How clear was your explanation of the author's viewpoint and what life experiences formed it?	1	2	3	4	5	6

Name _____ Date _____ Assignment _____

Performance Task 16a

Informational Text 7 Integrate information presented in different media or formats (e.g., visually, quantitatively) as well as in words to develop a coherent understanding of a topic or issue.*

Task: Integrate Information in Different Formats

Write an informational essay in which you describe a country or region based on facts you gather from texts and atlases.

Tips for Success

In your essay, include these elements:

✓ A description of where the place is, based on both maps and text

✓ Descriptions of the people and ways of life

✓ An analysis of how the maps and text work together to provide a complete picture of the place

✓ Evidence from both maps and text that supports your analysis

✓ Language that is formal, precise, and follows the rules of standard English

Rubric for Self-Assessment

Criteria for Success	not very					very
How well do you integrate text and maps to describe the place?	1	2	3	4	5	6
How well do you integrate text and maps to describe the people and ways of life?	1	2	3	4	5	6
How effective is your analysis of how maps and text work together to provide a complete picture of the place?	1	2	3	4	5	6
How convincing is the evidence you used from maps and text to support your analysis?	1	2	3	4	5	6
How well do you use a formal style, an appropriate tone for your audience, and standard English?	1	2	3	4	5	6

* Other standards covered include Writing 4, 9b; Speaking 4, 5; Language 1, 3, 6.

Name _____ Date _____ Assignment _____

Performance Task 16b

Speaking and Listening 2 Interpret information presented in diverse media and
formats (e.g., visually, quantitatively, orally) and explain how it contributes to a
topic, text, or issue under study.

Task: Present and Interpret Maps, Graphs, and Text

Present maps and graphs in a talk about a country or region. Ask your audience how the combined
formats contribute to their understanding of the place.

Tips for Success

Include these elements in your presentation:

✓ At least two maps of the place: one close-up and one that shows it in relation
to other countries

✓ At least one graph about the place (for example, it might show temperatures,
education levels, median incomes, or revenues from exports)

✓ A five-minute talk about the place, drawing on material you learned from
visuals and texts

✓ A request for classmates to evaluate how the combined visual, quantitative,
and oral elements contribute to their understanding of the place

Rubric for Self-Assessment

Criteria for Discussion	not very					very
How visible and effective were the maps and graphs for the audience, especially for people at the back of the room?	1	2	3	4	5	6
How useful were the maps and graphs in adding information about how the place compares to other countries?	1	2	3	4	5	6
How useful were the graphs in showing additional information, such as temperatures, incomes, and exports?	1	2	3	4	5	6
How effectively did you present your talk (eye contact, volume, pauses, emphasis, and so on)?	1	2	3	4	5	6
How helpful was your audience in evaluating how the combined elements contributed to their understanding?	1	2	3	4	5	6

Name _____ Date _____ Assignment _____

Performance Task 17a

Informational Text 8 Trace and evaluate the argument and specific claims in a text, distinguishing claims that are supported by reasons and evidence from claims that are not.*

Task: Evaluate the Argument in an Editorial

Write an essay in which you trace and evaluate the argument and claims in a newspaper editorial.

Tips for Success

Write an essay in which you trace and evaluate the argument and claims in a newspaper editorial you have read. In your essay, include these elements:

✓ a description of the editorial's argument and claims

✓ an analysis of which claims are supported by reasons and evidence and which are not

✓ an evaluation of the quality of the evidence used (the truth of facts stated and the reasons behind value judgments)

✓ an explanation of whether or not you agree with the editorial's conclusions and why

✓ language that is formal, precise, and follows the rules of standard English

Rubric for Self-Assessment

Criteria for Success	not very					very
How well do you describe the editorial's argument and claims?	1	2	3	4	5	6
How effectively do you analyze which claims are supported by reasons and evidence and which are not?	1	2	3	4	5	6
How thoroughly do you evaluate the quality of the evidence and reasons behind the claims in the editorial?	1	2	3	4	5	6
How clearly do you explain whether or not you agree with the conclusion and why?	1	2	3	4	5	6
How successfully do you use standard English?	1	2	3	4	5	6
How well do you succeed in using a formal style, appropriate tone for your audience, and standard English?	1	2	3	4	5	6

* Other standards covered include Writing 4, 9b; Speaking 1, 4, 5; Language 1, 3.

Performance Task 17b

Speaking and Listening 3 Delineate a speaker's argument and specific claims, distinguishing claims that are supported by reasons and evidence from claims that are not.

Task: Evaluate the Claims of a TV Editorial

With your class, view a television editorial and take notes on it. Then discuss which of its claims are supported by reasons and evidence and which are not.

Tips for Success

View a television editorial and discuss it with your class. As part of your participation in the discussion, include these elements:

✓ take notes on the editorial's argument and specific claims

✓ discuss the claims, distinguishing between facts and opinions

✓ discuss which claims are supported by reasons and evidence and which are not

✓ state whether or not you agree with the editorial's conclusions and why

✓ respond to others' questions and comments with relevant points

Rubric for Self-Assessment

Criteria for Discussion	not very					very
How prepared were you and how useful were your notes from viewing the editorial?	1	2	3	4	5	6
How helpful was the discussion of facts versus opinions in the claims?	1	2	3	4	5	6
How helpful was the group's analysis of which facts are supported by reasons and evidence?	1	2	3	4	5	6
How insightful was the group's evaluation of the quality of the evidence and logic?	1	2	3	4	5	6
How compelling was your explanation of why you agree or disagree with the editorial's conclusions?	1	2	3	4	5	6
How relevant were your responses to others' questions?	1	2	3	4	5	6

Name _____ Date _____ Assignment _____

Performance Task 18a

Informational Text 9 Compare and contrast one author's presentation of events with that of another (e.g., a memoir written by and a biography on the same person).*

Task: Compare Two Authors' Presentations of Events

Write an essay in which you compare and contrast a memoir and a biography of the same person.

Tips for Success

Write an essay comparing and contrasting a memoir and a biography about the same person. In your essay, include these elements:

- ✓ descriptions of both authors' perspectives (the beliefs, backgrounds, and feelings that shape their writing)

- ✓ an analysis of the similarities and differences between the two authors' versions of one specific event

- ✓ an analysis of how the details the two authors choose to emphasize differ and how those choices reflect their perspectives

- ✓ evidence from both texts that supports your findings

- ✓ language that is formal, precise, and follows the rules of standard English

Rubric for Self-Assessment

Criteria for Success	not very					very
How clearly do you describe the two authors' perspectives?	1	2	3	4	5	6
How insightful is your analysis of the similarities and differences between the two authors' versions of one event?	1	2	3	4	5	6
How comprehensive is your analysis of the details the two authors emphasized and how they reflect the authors' perspectives?	1	2	3	4	5	6
How well do you support your analysis with details from both texts?	1	2	3	4	5	6
How successfully do you use standard English?	1	2	3	4	5	6
How well do you succeed in using a formal style and appropriate tone for your audience?	1	2	3	4	5	6

* Other standards covered include Writing 4, 9b; Language 1, 2, 3.

Performance Task 18b

Speaking and Listening 6 **Adapt speech to a variety of contexts and tasks, demonstrating command of formal English when indicated or appropriate.**

Task: Adapt Speech When Comparing Memoir and Biography

With two classmates, give an interview in which you play the author of a memoir, one classmate plays your biographer, and the other plays the interviewer. First, you and your biographer will each read aloud a passage from your books about the same event. Then the interviewer will ask you both what your perspective is, how and why the two versions vary, and how you both differ in your attitudes and purposes. Research the author to answer some of the interviewer's questions.

Tips for Success

Adapt the way you speak when role-playing the author of a memoir being interviewed with your biographer. As part of your performance, include these elements:

✓ prepare a reading copy of the passage in which you mark words to emphasize and places to pause

✓ research the author, especially the event you are reading about in the passage

✓ read aloud the author's exact words; rehearse before your presentation

✓ speak in a formal tone (as the author) when you answer the interviewer's questions

✓ avoid using incomplete sentences and filler words and phrases

✓ use a more informal tone when you respond to questions from the audience

Rubric for Self-Assessment

Criteria for Discussion	not very					very
How effectively did you mark up your reading copy of the passage?	1	2	3	4	5	6
How accurately did you speak the author's words?	1	2	3	4	5	6
How well did your research prepare you to answer the interviewer's questions?	1	2	3	4	5	6
How well did you adapt your speech and tone to being interviewed formally?	1	2	3	4	5	6
How well did you avoid using incomplete sentences and filler words?	1	2	3	4	5	6
How well did you adapt your speech and tone when responding to questions and comments from the audience?	1	2	3	4	5	6

Name _____ Date _____ Assignment _____

Performance Task 19a

Informational Text 10 By the end of the year, read and comprehend literary nonfiction in the grades 6-8 text complexity band proficiently, with scaffolding as needed at the high end of the range.*

Task: Read and Comprehend Essays

Read an essay collection of your choice. Write an analysis of the essayist's style and choices of topic and theme and how they reveal his or her perspective.

Tips for Success

Read an essay collection and present a response to it. In your response, include these elements:

✓ a summary of the topics and themes the author revisits most often in different essays

✓ an analysis of the author's style

✓ an analysis of how the author's style and choices of topics and themes reveal his or her perspective

✓ evidence from the essays that supports your analysis

✓ language that is formal, precise, and follows the rules of standard English

Rubric for Self-Assessment

Criteria for Success	not very					very
How satisfactorily do you choose a collection of essays to read?	1	2	3	4	5	6
How helpful is your summary of the essay topics and themes?	1	2	3	4	5	6
How thorough is your analysis of the author's style?	1	2	3	4	5	6
How thorough is your analysis of how the author's style, topics, and themes reveal his or her perspective?	1	2	3	4	5	6
How well do you support your analysis with evidence from the essays?	1	2	3	4	5	6
How successfully do you use standard English?	1	2	3	4	5	6
How well do you succeed in using a formal style and appropriate tone for your audience?	1	2	3	4	5	6

* Other standards covered include Writing 4, 9b; Speaking 4; Language 1, 2, 3.

Name _____ Date _____ Assignment _____

Performance Task 19b

> **Speaking and Listening 1 Engage effectively in a range of collaborative group discussions with diverse partners on *grade 6 topics, texts, and issues,* building on others' ideas and expressing their own clearly.**

Task: Discuss the Author's Perspective in Essays

Participate in a group discussion in which you and several classmates discuss how the writing style and choices of topic and theme in an essay collection reveal the author's perspective.

Tips for Success

Participate in a series of discussions about an essay collection. As part of your participation in the discussions, include these elements:

- ✓ prepare by reading the collection and studying the author's style, topics, and themes

- ✓ agree with all of the group on goals and individual roles in the discussion

- ✓ analyze how the author's style reveals his or her perspective

- ✓ find evidence in the essays that supports your analysis

- ✓ pose questions that encourage group members to elaborate on their opinions

- ✓ respond to others' questions and comments with relevant observations

Rubric for Self-Assessment

Criteria for Discussion	not very					very
How completely had you thought through your responses to the text before the discussion?	1	2	3	4	5	6
How successful were you at analyzing the author's style and choices of topic and theme?	1	2	3	4	5	6
How useful were the group's guidelines for the discussion?	1	2	3	4	5	6
How effectively did you present your analysis of how the style, topic, and theme reveal the author's perspective?	1	2	3	4	5	6
How convincing was your evidence from the essays for your analysis?	1	2	3	4	5	6
How effective were your questions in helping the group explore the essays and the author's style and perspective?	1	2	3	4	5	6
How relevant were your responses to others' questions and comments?	1	2	3	4	5	6
How polite and respectful of other viewpoints were you?	1	2	3	4	5	6

For use with Speaking and Listening 1